# Mercy Under Fire

Larry Minear
and Thomas G. Weiss

# Mercy Under Fire

War and the Global
Humanitarian Community

WESTVIEW PRESS
Boulder • San Francisco • Oxford

Copyright © 1995 by Westview Press, Inc.

Published in 1995 in the United States of America by Westview Press, Inc., 5500 Central Avenue, Boulder, Colorado 80301-2877, and in the United Kingdom by Westview Press, 12 Hid's Copse Road, Cumnor Hill, Oxford OX2 9JJ

Library of Congress Cataloging-in-Publication Data
Minear, Larry, 1936–
    Mercy under fire : war and the global humanitarian community /
Larry Minear and Thomas G. Weiss.
        p.  cm.
    Includes bibliographical references and index.
    ISBN 0-8133-2566-8 (hard). — ISBN 0-8133-2567-6 (pbk.)
    1. War relief.   2. International relief.   3. Humanitarianism.
I. Weiss, Thomas George.   II. Title.
HV639.M56  1995
363.3'4988—dc20
                                                            94-46568
                                                                CIP

Printed and bound in the United States of America

The paper used in this publication meets the requirements
of the American National Standard for Permanence of Paper
for Printed Library Materials Z39.48-1984.

10    9    8    7    6    5    4    3    2    1

*For Beth and Priscilla*

# Contents

# Illustrations

# Preface

This book describes the experience of the international community in responding to the increased violence against humanity of the early post–Cold War era. It reviews international efforts to provide assistance and protection to civilian populations caught in situations of armed strife. Conflicts in the Persian Gulf, the Horn of Africa, Central America, Cambodia, and the former Yugoslavia are featured. Other struggles are mentioned as well.

The volume is written for the concerned international public, upon whom sustained and effective humanitarian action depends. We believe that if the public understands better the awesome dilemmas faced by humanitarian organizations, it will support continued and even expanded efforts—and hold humanitarian practitioners to higher standards of accountability. However, a more informed public requires a broader sense of the major humanitarian actors, a deeper understanding of their principles, and a fuller appreciation of their challenges.

The illustrative material used in this book draws on more than a thousand interviews conducted over the past five years with individuals involved in humanitarian activities. The research has formed the core of the Humanitarianism and War Project, an independent research initiative launched in 1991 to reflect upon recent experience and to make recommendations to strengthen future activities. The project built upon an earlier case study of Operation Lifeline Sudan conducted in 1990.

The project was cosponsored initially by the Thomas J. Watson Jr. Institute for International Studies at Brown University and the Refugee Policy Group in Washington, D.C., and, more recently, by the Watson Institute alone. To date it has published a wide array of articles and books, many of them listed in the suggested readings and some of them in use for training humanitarian practitioners. In addition to studies of conflicts in particular countries and regions, the project has

Rwandan refugees set up camps outside Goma because of a cholera epidemic in the city. (UN Photo 186811/J. Isaac)

produced *Humanitarian Action in Times of War: Handbook for Practitioners,* now available in Spanish and French as well as in English, and an edited volume of essays on critical issues of humanitarian theory and practice, *Humanitarianism Across Borders: Sustaining Civilians in Times of War.* We are grateful to Lynne Rienner Publishers for permission to draw on these earlier works.

Unlike earlier publications, the current volume provides nonspecialists with a close-up picture of the challenges faced by humanitarian professionals. Although we quote extensively from project interviews, we have tried to limit the number of references to other scholarly works. These are found in the endnotes at the back of the book and in the suggested readings. Practitioners themselves may find this book of interest; many acknowledge that they have a better sense of individual "trees"—a region, program specialty, or aid organization—than of the humanitarian "forest" as a whole.

The Humanitarianism and War Project has been underwritten by funds from the several dozen United Nations, governmental, and private aid organizations and foundations listed at the end of this volume. We express gratitude to them for making our work possible and for their continuing interest in our findings and recommendations. We are especially indebted to the Rockefeller Foundation, whose study and conference center in Bellagio, Italy, provided the setting in July 1993 for the initial work on our manuscript. We also wish to acknowledge support from The Pew Charitable Trusts and the United States Institute of Peace, which enabled us to update and polish the text in 1994.

We also express special appreciation to a wide range of agencies and colleagues who have assisted us in our research and have helped shape our own perceptions of the issues. Among the institutions involved in our work are the Arias Foundation of San José, Costa Rica, and the InterAfrica Group of Addis Ababa, Ethiopia.

Initial research on major conflicts was done in 1991 by Laura Holgate, Eugenia Jenkins, Arthur Keys, Hazel McPherson, Cheryl Morden, Joy Olson, and Bill Rau. Serving on various country and regional studies have been U.B.P. Chelliah, Jarat Chopra, Jeffrey Clark, Roberta Cohen, Jeff Crisp, Cristina Eguizábal, Iaian Guest, David Lewis, John Mackinlay, and Peter Sollis. An earlier draft of our manuscript was read by three colleagues, Mary B. Anderson, Juergen Dedring, and Giles Whitecomb, whose candid reactions figured prominently in substantial revisions.

Administrative support to the project has been provided by a number of persons. In Washington, Judy Ombura has been tireless in addressing day-to-day needs as they have arisen. In Providence, Alexander Thier, Sarah Lum, David Lewis, and Suzanne Miller have also been helpful. Invaluable editorial assistance at the Watson Institute came from Fred Fullerton and Mary Lhowe, and production help was provided by Susan Costa, Amy Langlais, and Jennifer Patrick.

We are also extremely grateful to Dennis Gallagher, executive director of the Refugee Policy Group of Washington, D.C., who provided a home for the project in its early years, contributed substantively to our approach to the issues, and served on the team that reviewed the UN's response to the crisis in the former Yugoslavia.

We would be remiss if we failed to express gratitude to those around the globe, too numerous to list individually, who took time to share with us their insights, experience, and recommendations. Their reflections have enriched and shaped our work. We view this as their book, too.

The illustrative woodcuts in Chapters 1, 2, and 5 were originally published in "Humanitarian Principles and Operational Dilemmas in War Zones." They are reprinted with permission from the Disaster Management Training Programme (DMTP).

Notwithstanding the many institutions and individuals who helped to make this book possible, we are fully responsible for any errors and shortcomings.

*Larry Minear*
*Thomas G. Weiss*
May 1994

# Acronyms

| | |
|---|---|
| ACROSS | Association of Christian Resource Organizations Serving Sudan |
| ACUNS | Academic Council on the United Nations System |
| AID | Agency for International Development [United States] |
| ASEAN | Association of Southeast Asian Nations |
| BBC | British Broadcasting Corporation |
| CERF | Central Emergency Revolving Fund [United Nations] |
| CIDA | Canadian International Development Agency |
| CIREFCA | International Conference on Refugees in Central America |
| CIS | Commonwealth of Independent States |
| CNN | Cable News Network |
| CONADES | National Commission for the Displaced [El Salvador] |
| CONGO | Conference of Nongovernmental Organizations in Consultative Status with ECOSOC |
| CPR | Communities of People in Resistance |
| CRS | Catholic Relief Services |
| CSCE | Conference on Security and Cooperation in Europe |
| DAC | Development Assistance Committee |
| DHA | Department of Humanitarian Affairs [United Nations] |
| EC | European Community |
| ECA | Economic Commission for Africa |
| ECAFE | Economic Commission for Asia and the Far East |
| ECE | Economic Commission for Europe |
| ECHO | European Community Humanitarian Office |
| ECLAC | Economic Commission for Latin America and the Caribbean |
| ECOMOG | Economic Community of West African States Monitoring Group |
| ECOSOC | Economic and Social Council [United Nations] |
| ECOWAS | Economic Community of West African States |

| | |
|---|---|
| ECWA | Economic Commission for Western Asia |
| EEC | European Economic Community |
| EPLF | Eritrean People's Liberation Front |
| ERA | Eritrean Relief Association |
| ESCAP | Economic and Social Commission for Asia and the Pacific |
| ESCWA | Economic and Social Commission for Western Asia |
| EU | European Union |
| FAO | Food and Agriculture Organization [United Nations] |
| FMLN | Farabundo Martí National Liberation Front |
| G-77 | Group of 77 developing countries |
| GONGO | Government-organized nongovernmental organization |
| IADB | Inter-American Development Bank |
| IBRD | International Bank for Reconstruction and Development [World Bank] |
| ICJ | International Court of Justice |
| ICRC | International Committee of the Red Cross |
| ICVA | International Council of Voluntary Agencies |
| IGADD | Intergovernmental Authority on Drought and Development |
| IGO | Intergovernmental organization |
| ILO | International Labour Organisation |
| IMF | International Monetary Fund |
| INSSBI | Nicaraguan Social Security and Welfare Institute |
| IOM | International Organization for Migration |
| JRP | Joint Relief Partnership [Ethiopia] |
| LWF | Lutheran World Federation |
| MPLA | Popular Movement for the Liberation of Angola |
| MSC | Military Staff Committee [United Nations] |
| MSF | Doctors Without Borders |
| NAM | Non-Aligned Movement |
| NATO | North Atlantic Treaty Organization |
| NGO | Nongovernmental organization |
| NIEO | New International Economic Order |
| NPA | Norwegian People's Aid |
| OAS | Organization of American States |
| OAU | Organization of African Unity |
| ODA | Overseas Development Administration |

| | |
|---|---|
| OECD | Organization for Economic Cooperation and Development |
| OEOA | Office of Emergency Operations in Africa [United Nations] |
| OLS | Operation Lifeline Sudan |
| ONUC | United Nations Operation in the Congo |
| ONUCA | United Nations Observer Group in Central America |
| ONUMOZ | United Nations Observer Mission in Mozambique |
| ONUSAL | United Nations Observer Mission in El Salvador |
| ONUVEH | United Nations Observer Group to Verify the Electoral Process in Haiti |
| ONUVEN | United Nations Observer Group to Verify the Electoral Process in Nicaragua |
| OPEC | Organization of Petroleum Exporting Countries |
| PAHO | Pan-American Health Organization |
| PRODERE | Development Program for Displaced Persons, Refugees, and Repatriates |
| PVO | Private Voluntary Organization |
| QUANGO | Quasi-nongovernmental organization |
| RASS | Relief Association of the Southern Sudan |
| RENAMO | Mozambique National Resistance |
| REST | Relief Society of Tigray |
| SPLA | Sudanese People's Liberation Army |
| SPLM | Sudanese People's Liberation Movement |
| SRRA | Sudan Relief and Rehabilitation Association |
| SWAPO | South-West Africa People's Organization |
| TPLF | Tigrayan People's Liberation Front |
| UDI | Unilateral Declaration of Independence |
| UNAVEM | United Nations Angola Verification Mission |
| UNCTAD | United Nations Conference on Trade and Development |
| UNDOF | United Nations Disengagement Observer Force |
| UNDP | United Nations Development Program |
| UNDRO | United Nations Disaster Relief Organization |
| UNEF | United Nations Emergency Force |
| UNESCO | United Nations Educational, Scientific and Cultural Organization |
| UNFICYP | United Nations Peacekeeping Force in Cyprus |

| UNGOMAP | United Nations Good Offices Mission in Afghanistan and Pakistan |
| UNHCR | United Nations High Commissioner for Refugees |
| UNICEF | United Nations Children's Fund |
| UNIFIL | United Nations Interim Force in Lebanon |
| UNIIMOG | United Nations Iran-Iraq Military Observer Group |
| UNIKOM | United Nations Iraq-Kuwait Observation Mission |
| UNITA | National Union for the Total Independence of Angola |
| UNITAF | Unified Task Force [Somalia] |
| UNMOGIP | United Nations Military Observer Group in India and Pakistan |
| UNOMIL | United Nations Observer Mission in Liberia |
| UNOMUR | United Nations Observer Mission in Uganda and Rwanda |
| UNOSOM | United Nations Operation in Somalia |
| UNPA | United Nations Protected Area |
| UNPROFOR | United Nations Protection Force [in the former Yugoslavia] |
| UNSEPHA | United Nations Special Emergency Programme for the Horn of Africa |
| UNTAC | United Nations Transitional Authority in Cambodia |
| UNTAG | United Nations Transition Assistance Group [in Namibia] |
| USC | United Somali Congress |
| VOLAG | Voluntary Agency |
| WEU | Western European Union |
| WFP | World Food Programme |
| WHO | World Health Organization |

# Introduction

Events in the late 1980s that signaled an end to the Cold War—the top-pling of the Berlin Wall, the revolutions in Eastern Europe, the disinte-gration of the Soviet Union—were accompanied by widespread eupho-ria. After more than forty years of East-West struggle during which geopolitical considerations had dominated the international agenda, the human needs of civilians would at long last receive overdue atten-tion—or so the reasoning went. Even developed countries, it was hoped, might finally address their own deferred social agendas.

Years later, early optimism about the prospects for reconstruction, democratization, and peace have given way to a more sober assess-ment of the likelihood of continuing and rising levels of armed con-flict.[1] Moreover, as the dust of the Cold War has settled, the wide gash left in the fabric of the world's economic and social life has become more apparent.[2] The nature and cost of rehabilitation needs, to say nothing of longer-term development challenges, is staggering. Prog-ress on unfinished business in major industrial nations such as the United States and a united Germany also has languished.

The various regional and national conflicts that raged during the Cold War have responded differently to its passing. Attempts to reach political solutions to the struggles in Central America, Cambodia, and the Middle East have benefited from the easing of superpower ten-sions, which has made political resolution of their conflicts more pos-sible. Yet in Afghanistan, Angola, and Mozambique, conflicts fueled largely by superpower rivalry have taken on lives of their own. More-over, strife dampened for decades by the Cold War is being rekindled in the Balkans and various republics of the former Soviet Union. In set-tings with no direct links to East-West rivalry such as the Sudan, Libe-ria, and Sri Lanka, seething ethnic and religious tensions have contin-ued unabated.

Refugees wait near the northern border of Kuwait in March 1991, during the Iraqi occupation. (UN Photo 158237/J. Isaac)

In the early post–Cold War years, local factors have assumed greater importance in their own right. Civil wars are no longer as easily internationalized as when rival factions served as pawns in a big-power chess game. In some instances, fragmentation has led to the virtual absence of law and order and the deterioration or disappearance of civil society, as reflected in the concept of "failed states."[3] In armed conflicts in places such as Liberia, Somalia, Rwanda, and perhaps soon Zaire, the lack of accountable authorities has created a precarious situation for civilians and humanitarian workers alike. Both are denied the necessary recourse to the structures that facilitate their normal functioning. Civil wars, as someone has pointed out, are anything but civil.

The waning of superpower engagement in developing countries also has been accompanied by an increased level of international humanitarian involvement in what were once considered the internal affairs of states. The centuries-old notion that sovereign states are beyond challenge in treatment of their own citizens has given way to a new sense that sovereignty must be used responsibly if it is to be respected internationally. Challenges have come not only from insurgent forces whose own exercise of authority often has left much to be desired but also from the emerging global humanitarian community, which has become more prepared to insist that reprobate regimes act responsibly in matters of humanitarian access and human rights.

In another striking irony, civil wars have increased the need for humanitarian assistance and protection, but at the same time have made such succor more difficult to provide effectively. As those under fire have found themselves in more desperate need of mercy from the outside world, those seeking to provide assistance have more frequently come under fire themselves.

In fact, humanitarians have come to resemble the objects of their labors. Those who work for the Red Cross or the United Nations often are denied their right of access, harassed and held hostage, injured, and killed. Long-established symbols no longer command automatic respect or assure implicit protection. In many conflicts, relief convoys have been hijacked or blocked, drivers wounded or killed, and emergency assistance activities commandeered or shut down. International humanitarian actors suffer indignities differing only in degree from those experienced by distressed civilian populations.

In earlier wars, civilian populations were from time to time caught in the crossfire or displaced by the fighting. (A frequently cited statistic places civilian casualties at about 5 percent of the total casualties in World War I.) The peril of civilians, and occasionally as well of those who came to their aid, was incidental to the warfare. By contrast, civilians are often now the explicit objects of military operations. Humanitarian organizations and activities are equally vulnerable. Civilians now constitute about 95 percent of the casualties in places such as Somalia and Bosnia. Food and medicine are often withheld from civilian populations. They are the ready weapons in the arsenals of governments and insurgents who manipulate them in ways that violate basic provisions of international law as well as the fundamental tenets of civilized societies.

Why is the present historical moment such a watershed? Massive alterations have taken place in the geography of the former Soviet Union and Eastern Europe, including some twenty new states born from the former Soviet Union and Yugoslavia. In a development once unthinkable, there is now only a single superpower on the world stage.

The ripple effects, not only on the societies and peoples involved but also on international political, economic, and military institutions, have been far-reaching.

The United Nations, which had been largely paralyzed by East-West conflict, has assumed a more central place on the world stage.[4] After a decade during which "UN bashing" was a favorite sport along the Potomac and in a number of other Western capitals, the world organization went through a renaissance of sorts, beginning in the late 1980s. Although its operational and political warts have not disappeared, the UN nonetheless occupies a prominent place on the front pages of newspapers and in the policy calculations of major and lesser powers. The revitalization of multilateralism is a major contemporary leitmotif.[5]

Changes in the international geopolitical climate also have had an important bearing on the humanitarian arena, affecting the perception of fundamental values and the possibilities for concerted action. During the Cold War, geopolitics infiltrated such cardinal principles as the sanctity of life. In the frenzied competition between communism and anticommunism, a premium was placed on scoring ideological points rather than on protecting human lives. The right to food or to freedom from persecution was treated in many quarters as anything but absolute or universal, upstaged by considerations of whether a given regime using food as a weapon or violating the human rights of its citizenry was deemed "friendly" or "unfriendly."

East-West rivalries spurred action—or deterred it, as the case might be. Washington, Moscow, and their respective allies judged a Nicaraguan life as more—or less—important than a Salvadoran, the welfare of a Cambodian refugee as more—or less—valuable than that of an Angolan. National and international responses to human rights violations in East Timor were calibrated according to the perceived importance of the Indonesian government, not according to the nature and pervasiveness of the abuses.

Foreign ministries evaluated entire regions and populations according to their strategic significance. Flip-flops in the Horn of Africa dramatized the primacy of ideology over humanity. The face-off between the United States and the Soviet Union initially was reflected in support for Washington's principal regional client, Ethiopian Emperor Haïle Selassie, or for Moscow's favorite, Somalian strongman Siad Barre. Shortly after the coup d'état against Selassie in 1974, the superpowers, in an ideological do-si-do, exchanged partners and adjusted flows of military and economic aid accordingly. The ripples have contributed to the instability that is part of the current legacy of Ethiopia and Somalia.

Geopolitical instincts politicized humanitarian impulses. Initially, the Reagan administration treated the massive suffering in the Ethiopian famine of 1983–1985 as the responsibility of the Soviet Union, which proffered only limited assistance. Pressed by the American public and humanitarian groups to view U.S. values and interests as better served by helping rather than hindering aid delivery, Washington eventually was embarrassed into becoming the main provider of relief assistance to the Ethiopian people.

The affiliation of a government or insurgent group in the global struggle affected the international attention paid to the emergency needs of people within its jurisdiction. Even the work of the humanitarian agencies of the United Nations system was politicized, reflecting pressure from the United States, the UN's principal financial backer. The UN Security Council, the international community's most influential and powerful organ, never vigorously addressed humanitarian issues during the Cold War.

Geopolitical fault lines notwithstanding, East-West tensions did not divide the world neatly into two camps. Some governments and private relief organizations sought to remain steadfastly above the fray and to give unswerving priority to the sanctity of human life. However, so thorough was the prevailing politicization that few humanitarian organizations effectively challenged the constraints on their freedom of action imposed by the Cold War psychosis. The prevailing bipolar divisions cut surprisingly wide and deep. "People second, ideology first" might stand as an appropriate humanitarian epitaph for this period.[6] In retrospect, the perversion of principle seems as questionable and as calamitous as does the construction of nuclear weaponry without proper attention to the disposal of radioactive ingredients or the conduct of Cold War medical experiments on unwitting subjects.

Things are different now. The transformation in world politics has illuminated the extent of human need and elevated the relative importance of humanitarian considerations. Humanitarian values are coming to be viewed as important in their own right, not as a means to the attainment of political objectives. As a corollary, the need to build or

6

# Wars Between 1945 and 1993

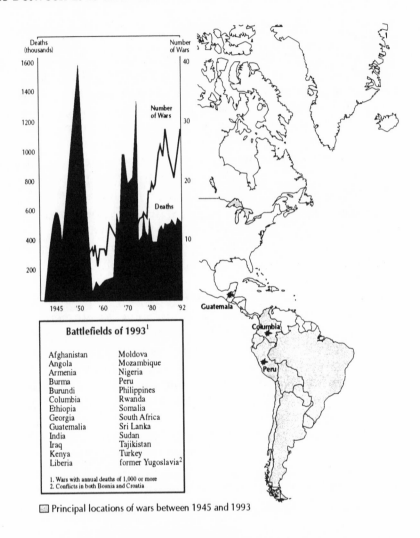

Source: Adapted from Ruth Leger Sivard, *World Military and Social Expenditures 1993* (Washington, D.C.: World Priorities, 1993), p. xxv

rebuild institutions that can effectively assist and protect people has taken on new urgency.

There are, to be sure, major obstacles to more effective humanitarian action during the remainder of the century and beyond. First, some basic humanitarian instincts and the humanitarian apparatus that exists to put flesh on them have atrophied during the Cold War interregnum. Like a patient released from the hospital after an extensive stay, the world must relearn the use of long-dormant capacities and limbs. In particular, the humanitarian organizations of the United Nations system, itself enjoying a renaissance, are now faced with higher expectations and new demands. They have yet to fill the bill.

Second, there is something of a failure of worldwide humanitarian fortitude in the face of the apparently intractable situations in which human suffering is set. When centuries-old animosities erupt in the "formers" of this world—the former Yugoslavia, the former Soviet Union—many people of goodwill sense the limits of intervention. Like governments that are willing to commit troops to the United Nations only for duty when "hot war" has cooled, some favor dispatching humanitarian resources only when the situation has stabilized. Logical at face value, such an approach makes succor least available when it is most needed.

Third, the resources at the disposal of the international community are limited. Having skewed their budgets and deepened their levels of national indebtedness to wage the Cold War, the United States and other major donors are now confronted with the bill for domestic spending on overdue economic and social priorities. On the international front, in a combination of rationalization and reason, they now plead "donor fatigue." The resources that they do provide tend to be earmarked for particular crises, or particular countries and activities in a given crisis, and tied to the procurement of goods and services that will benefit their own suppliers.

Fourth, a new paradigm has yet to be developed to replace the Cold War rationale for involvement in international affairs. The East-West fight offered an all-purpose rubric under which appropriations for aid—military, economic, and humanitarian—could be justified. Absent the need to do global battle with the forces of communism, what is the energizing rationale for helping to prevent starvation in Somalia or rape in Bosnia, to say nothing of carnage in Rwanda or human rights abuses in Tibet?

Figure I.1
Source: *Baltimore Sun*, August 29–30, 1992. KAL/Baltimore USA Cartoonists &
Writers Syndicate

Such clouds on the humanitarian horizon do not alter the fact that
internationally the moment is propitious for directing overdue attention to assist and protect those affected by wars. Within that context,
this volume seeks to review the humanitarian system—some professionals use the term "regime" for the emerging network of principles,
rules, and procedures—as it has developed to date. This book also
identifies the major humanitarian challenges the world faces and pro-
poses a number of improvements for the current system.

Chapter 1 examines the setting within which humanitarian action
takes place. Elaborating on the current historical moment, it introduces a set of basic concepts, examines what is understood by the term

"humanitarian," and reviews the basic premises and provisions of humanitarian law. The chapter also analyzes the concepts of humanitarian space and humanitarian intervention and introduces the major humanitarian actors, governmental and private.

Chapter 2 presents eight fundamental humanitarian principles that have evolved over time and illustrates each by reference to recent armed conflicts. Different organizations attach different weight to the various individual principles, making for significant differences in approach, which are also reviewed. Noting that some actors downplay the importance of principles altogether and favor a more pragmatic approach, this chapter raises the question of whether fidelity to principles contributes to more—or less—effective action.

Chapter 3 identifies certain fundamental challenges that humanitarian organizations confront in every war. These include assessing the nature and severity of a particular crisis, negotiating access to the affected populations, mobilizing resources to assist and protect them, delivering services, ensuring coordination, pursuing education and advocacy tasks in the countries that are providing resources, and looking beyond the emergency itself. Each of these tasks may be more or less arduous in a given situation, but each requires attention.

Chapter 4 depicts interactions among major humanitarian actors as they respond to the various challenges in war zones. There are eight sets of such actors. Five are external to the geography of the conflicts: the United Nations and other intergovernmental organizations, donor governments and their bilateral aid agencies, nongovernmental organizations (NGOs), the International Committee of the Red Cross (ICRC), and outside military forces. Three sets of humanitarian actors are located in the conflict areas themselves: host governments, armed opposition groups, and local NGOs. This chapter reviews the interactions among the eight with a particular eye toward which actors do particular tasks the best.

Chapter 5 offers recommendations to improve the responses of the global humanitarian community to the challenges it faces. It details a set of necessary changes in current institutions and activities and urges more attention to preventing major humanitarian crises and, when intervention is necessary, to intervening more effectively and quickly. It also examines the ominous resurgent interest in triage, a concept that, although morally repugnant in its attempt to determine who will and

The UN Security Council votes in November 1990 to use all necessary means to uphold its previous resolutions if Iraq fails to withdraw from Kuwait. (UN Photo 177766/M. Grant)

will not receive aid, is receiving renewed attention because of the precariously overstretched global humanitarian safety net.

The overall goal of this volume is to examine the experiences of the international community in dealing with the humanitarian consequences of armed conflicts. With past conflicts in mind, with ongoing wars presenting continuing challenges, and with a conflict-laden future on the horizon, we proceed inductively rather than deductively, moving from practice to theory rather than imposing conceptual constructs onto the real world. In the process, we highlight creative tactics and little-known success stories to help combat the cynicism that naturally emanates from the proliferation of horrors that seemingly overwhelm the world's resources and resourcefulness. Learning the lessons from wars around the world also should help dissipate the notion that hardheadedness is incompatible with an active conscience. The essence of humanitarianism is hopefulness, born not of the naïveté of do-gooders but of the seasoned experience of creative professionals.

In highlighting successes and failures, there is no intent to elevate or denigrate particular agencies or individuals. Experiences are cited for their expository merit, not with congratulatory or invidious intent. The focus on necessary improvements is not intended to minimize the creative and selfless contributions made by persons of goodwill in the face of enormous tragedies.

It also needs to be understood at the outset that there are no simple pat answers to thorny humanitarian challenges. Lessons are not universal in their application and always require customizing to local circumstances. Humanitarian tools require adaptation with each new war.

The title of this volume, *Mercy Under Fire,* reflects both painful realities and aspirations for the future. The humanitarian system labors under many strains. It is under fire from many directions, not just from the pressures of armed conflicts. Its creaks and groans are institutional and financial, political and moral. Strained or not, the system has abundant empathy, energy, and experience, qualities that need to be reinforced and used effectively.

*Mercy* is a concept that is at once both appropriate and misleading. The essence of humanitarian action reflects kindness and compassion toward those who suffer. Yet those who suffer also have rights that are affirmed in international charters and that impose clear international obligations.

In this sense, what is under fire is not simply mercy but justice.

# 1
# The Setting

An examination of the challenges to effective humanitarian action necessarily begins with a word about the current historical and political moment. Early in the post–Cold War era, pivotal changes have occurred both in political and humanitarian institutions and in the concept of humanitarian action itself. Situating the major humanitarian actors within the contemporary landscape, this chapter reviews such fundamental concepts as the nature of humanitarianism, the dimensions of humanitarian responses, international humanitarian law and intervention, and the notion of humanitarian space. Chapter 2 will build upon these fundamentals to explore the key principles of humanitarian action.

## The Changing Scene

The nature and extent of the violence now confronting the world was hardly imagined by the framers of the United Nations Charter when they met in San Francisco as the bloodshed of World War II abated.[1] At that time, the major actors in the world were composed of about fifty sovereign states. Most problems of international importance were perceived to concern interrelationships among those states. Insurgent political movements were rare, and the roles of other nonstate actors such as private organizations and the media were narrowly circumscribed.

The UN itself was originally envisioned as a modest institution of a diplomatic rather than programmatic nature. The idea that the new world body might be involved in feeding refugees and sheltering the internally displaced, protecting human rights and promoting economic development, or pressing for better stewardship of the global environment was not contemplated at the time.

As the United Nations prepares to celebrate its fiftieth anniversary in 1995, the organization and the world it serves have undergone enormous changes. Some 185 accredited governments now participate in General Assembly debates and, to one degree or another, provide resources for its work. The breakup of the former Soviet Union and the former Yugoslavia recently spawned almost 20 states, augmenting the 125 created from decolonization in earlier decades. According to Brian Urquhart, the world organization "is now increasingly perceived by the press and the public to be, or to have the potential of being, the world's police force and humanitarian rescue service."[2]

The Security Council, whose numbers increased in 1965 from the original eleven to the current fifteen, has retained its original constellation of permanent members in spite of growing pressures to change its composition and procedures. Yet the council now addresses a wider array of issues. Rarely seized with quality-of-life concerns during the Cold War, it now categorizes humanitarian crises in places such as northern Iraq and Somalia among the recognized threats to international peace and security and takes assertive action accordingly.

A host of UN organizations now carries out activities for particular population groups such as refugees or women and children and in specialized sectors such as food, health, family planning, development, meteorology, and nuclear nonproliferation. Staffed by more than 50,000 international civil servants, the world organization has headquarters on Turtle Bay in New York and major offices in Geneva, "the humanitarian capital of the world," and in Vienna, Paris, Rome, Nairobi, and Vancouver. UN staff are stationed in virtually all nations, with significant numbers in developing countries, the scene of most of the UN's operational activities. In early 1994, there were about 80,000 soldiers wearing UN blue berets in conflict zones,[3] an eightfold increase from only three years earlier. More operations have been initiated in that time than in the previous four decades.

The world's humanitarian apparatus now also includes thousands of NGOs,[4] some enjoying formal consultative status with the UN and others operating completely on their own. They bring to the scene their own specialized expertise and constituencies, including an increasingly knowledgeable and engaged public. They also benefit from and help nurture a media more actively engaged in humanitarian affairs. Some NGOs concentrate on activities to educate their publics and influence government and UN policies; many have their own humanitarian and development programs, some rivaling in scale and impact those of their governmental and intergovernmental counterparts.

If there are more numerous and diverse international actors today than fifty years ago, the humanitarian crises to which they respond are also more complex. Our understanding of the nature of those crises has itself evolved. Not long ago, such cataclysms were divided neatly into natural disasters, also known as acts of God, and man-made emergencies. It is now realized that "natural" disasters such as droughts and floods often reflect human decisions, such as the policies of governments and the practices of peoples.

Even the "relief-to-development continuum"—once applauded as a novel insight—is now viewed as simplistic and misleading. Taking exception with the idea that there is a straight-line progression between meeting a society's emergency needs and addressing its longer-term development agenda, experts now warn that the concept of a continuum plays down real-world discontinuities. Many societies that are making impressive strides toward development find their progress interrupted by emergencies, whereas their prevention had been a major priority in the past. For others preoccupied with the crises of the day, development is not a realistic expectation, yet it remains key to averting future disasters that require emergency relief. Development itself is now widely understood to range well beyond increases in gross national product to involve difficult issues of equity, empowerment, and sustainability.

Despite theoretical and practical differences, there is widespread agreement that more must be done to pick up the early warning signs of impending crises and to address underlying problems before they escalate. There is also growing consensus that international humanitarian action needs to be taken in ways that strengthen indigenous capacities, thus reducing vulnerability to future difficulties.

The humanitarian crises discussed in this book do not represent the entire range of disasters. Nor is the full spectrum of responses charted. The focus is more narrowly on wars. War encompasses clashes both between and within territorial states. Some wars have elements of both internal or civil conflict and international or interstate strife. The crisis in the former Yugoslavia involved war between the Federal Republic of Yugoslavia and the newly independent Republic of Croatia. Within newly independent Bosnia and Herzegovina, there was warfare between the Bosnian government and an insurgent Bosnian Serb faction.

Figure 1.1
Source: Danziger in *The Christian Science Monitor*, 1992 TCSPS

In focusing on significant armed conflicts, this volume acknowledges the existence of violence that has not reached the threshold of what could be called war. There is, in fact, a continuum that encompasses isolated incidents of violence (for example, the abuse of an individual's human rights) and systematic patterns of abuse (for example, gross violations of the human rights of an entire ethnic group or population).

From a humanitarian viewpoint, the significant indicators are not whether a certain level of violence exists or whether an interstate or internal war has been formally declared but rather the magnitude of civilian deaths due to conflict or famine, the numbers of displaced persons within a country or fleeing its borders, and the extent of deprivation of shelter, health, and other vital social services. Substantial human need often exists as a result of institutional or structural violence in settings where war has not erupted. While acknowledging that all violence harms people, we focus on war as the principal humanitarian challenge.

In this perspective, this book focuses on the major conflicts in places such as the Horn of Africa, Bosnia, Central America, the Persian Gulf, and Cambodia, where the formal or implicit thresholds that might be devised have been crossed and where we have done fieldwork and significant research. In contrast, the situations in Haiti and Liberia receive less attention in this volume, although the impacts of international economic sanctions on the Haitian poor are reviewed. Similarly, the situations in South Africa and in the West Bank and Gaza are not addressed.

In the post–World War II era there has been a general, if somewhat jagged, increase in the number of wars and war-related deaths. The rule of thumb defines a major war as one with at least an estimated 1,000 deaths per year; in 1992 and 1993 there was a historical high of twenty-nine such wars.

"Aside from the upward trend in both the frequency and destructiveness of wars," according to the fifteenth edition of the now classic *World Military and Social Expenditures,* "this half-century has been marked by a concentration of hostilities in the developing regions of the world," where more than 90 percent of all such conflicts in the post–World War II period have taken place. "Only in the latest years— beginning in 1989 in the former Soviet Union and in 1991 in the former Yugoslavia—have the developed countries suffered a serious escalation of violence on a national scale."[5]

Whether within or among nations, wars frequently create what have come to be called complex emergencies. The term refers to situations that may be triggered by natural disasters such as droughts or floods, by intercommunal violence with roots in ethnic or religious tensions or exclusionary politics, by economic or environmental stress, or by some combination of these factors. Whatever the specific cause, complex emergencies are characterized by a high degree of political or military conflict, which complicate efforts to provide humanitarian assistance and protection.

Today's wars and complex emergencies make new and unprecedented demands on those who seek to provide humanitarian aid. Not only are relationships among a bewildering array of actors and institutions more multifaceted and interactive, the problems themselves are also more complex and highly charged. Practitioners frequently confront situations in which there are no easy answers, in which solving one problem creates others, and in which well-intended assistance is misunderstood, rebuffed, or manipulated.

Understanding the challenges of mounting effective humanitarian action requires clarity in the language used to describe humanitarian activities. Although the ideas seem straightforward, the basic term "humanitarian" and the associated concepts of humanitarian law, humanitarian intervention, and humanitarian space require careful definition and precise usage.

## The Humanitarian

The core meaning of "humanitarian" has to do with activities undertaken to improve the human condition. As a noun, the term "humanitarian" describes "a person promoting human welfare and social reform," states *Webster's New Collegiate Dictionary*. As an adjective, "humanitarian" denotes being "concerned with the needs of mankind and the alleviation of human suffering," according to the *American Heritage Dictionary of the English Language*. "Humanitarianism," adds *Webster's*, is a concept used to describe "the ideas, principles, or methods of humanitarians; charity; philanthropy."

In legal and colloquial usage, the concept is maddeningly imprecise. In international law, the term "humanitarian" has never been defined with the precision accorded such concepts as human rights and refugee. The four Geneva Conventions of 1949 and the two Additional Protocols of 1977,[6] which comprise the heart of international humanitarian law, spell out in detail the obligations of warring parties and of the international community. What emerges from the applicable references, however, tends to be less definitional than illustrative.

Even the accepted arbiter of such matters, the International Court of Justice, has stopped short of providing a definition that would lay to rest all confusion. It had an excellent opportunity to do so several years ago in a case brought by Nicaragua against the United States. The Nicaraguan government claimed that covert U.S. government assistance to the Nicaraguan Contras represented a violation of international law. Washington countered that the food, tents, and telecommunications equipment it had supplied the insurgents were entirely humanitarian and, as such, did not represent a violation of Nicaraguan sovereignty. Although the court ruled in favor of Nicaragua, it studiously avoided defining humanitarian aid. The aid was not humanitarian, the court found, but what was humanitarian? The humanitarian *is* simply what the International Committee of the Red Cross *does*.

The United Nations also has steered clear of a definition. When the Security Council imposes economic embargoes on countries, it normally exempts "humanitarian" items. The determination of what qualifies as humanitarian, however, is entrusted to a UN Sanctions Committee, which must review specific applications for exemptions to each embargo and make case-by-case, shipment-by-shipment determinations. Committee staffers vigorously deny that there could or should be a list of items that in every instance would qualify as humanitarian and be allowed entry where nonhumanitarian commerce is banned. A shipment of bananas to Port-au-Prince would provide part of the essential diet of Haitians, staffers point out, whereas the same shipment, a luxury item in Belgrade, would help unscrupulous entrepreneurs subvert the global economic embargo against the Federal Republic of Yugoslavia.

In the absence of a checklist for all countries and seasons, the United Nations proceeds with a laborious, case-by-case review of individual items. Should health kits, dialysis units, kerosene, gasoline, and children's toys be considered humanitarian aid for Haiti? Should spare parts for water purification plants, detonator caps for coal mining, and tubing for residential gas pipelines for Serbia qualify as humanitarian? What about infant formula for Libya, vegetable seeds and fertilizer for Iraq? The review process is cumbersome at best and, most recently in the case of Serbia, resulted in two-month delays that undercut the emergency nature of the international humanitarian response.

The process is further complicated when powerful governments inject political judgments into the approval process. Could not scissors from health kits be melted down into weapons and swords transformed into pruning hooks? The very fact that determinations are made in sessions behind closed doors from which the public, nongovernmental organizations, and the media are barred does violence to the necessary transparency of humanitarian aid.

Individual governments have had their own histories of problems with defining "humanitarian." The U.S. Congress and a succession of U.S. administrations have struggled with adjudicating which items should be exempted from the prohibitions of its Trading with the Enemy Act to reach suffering people in places like Vietnam, Cambodia, and Cuba. The same private relief groups that urged that humanitarian aid be defined narrowly to disallow army boots for the Nicaraguan insurgents had appealed for a broad definition so that pencils and fishing nets could be included, along with food and medicine, for needy civilians in otherwise unreachable Indochina.

Other meanings of the term exist as well. The *Oxford English Dictionary* of 1993 defines humanitarianism in the first instance as "having regard to the interests of humanity or mankind at large; relating to, or advocating, or practicing humanity or humane action." It then offers a second meaning: "often contemptuous or hostile." Other dictionaries speak of humanitarians as meddlers and busybodies.

Today the concept evokes multiple associations, ranging from the unabashedly positive to the strongly pejorative. In some quarters, calling a person or institution humanitarian suggests high praise and deep respect. In others, humanitarians are viewed as do-gooders whose rosy view of human nature leads to meddlesome activities that at their worst draw in governments and entire nations.

Those who stayed the course in Somalia in the abject days of deepening famine in 1991 to 1992 and eventually mobilized the world were deemed heroic. Equally courageous action in the former Yugoslavia, however, got mixed reviews. Those who tried to rescue people in the Balkans from "ethnic cleansing" are criticized for their naïveté in the face of centuries-old animosities. They are said to have thwarted more decisive and indispensable political and military action to halt the bloodshed.

The association of humanitarian activities with the specific act of distributing relief gives such action a negative ring in cultures in which "welfare," "charity," and "doing good" are loaded terms. Alternatively, the identification of humanitarian instincts with organized traditions of philanthropy perturbs some anthropologists, who see traits such as generosity and altruism as universal and human rather than as the product of organized institutional structures. Languages other than English also use the term in a variety of ways; some languages such as Spanish have no specific equivalent.

At the end of the day, the term "humanitarian" needs to be understood both as delimited and expansive. The meaning articulated by the International Court of Justice is clearly the bedrock. Humanitarian action resembles the undertakings of the ICRC: emergency assistance and protection activities carried out devoid of extraneous agendas—political, religious, or otherwise.

At the same time, humanitarian action encompasses a broader range of longer-term activities that affirm the essential humanity and dignity of humankind. In this larger context, such action includes not only the provision of food and medicine but also the reconstruction of war-torn infrastructure and psychological counseling for rape victims. It includes elements indispensable to keeping life human: for the population of Sarajevo, newsprint and ink for the daily newspaper; for the uprooted people of Afghanistan, assistance in contacting relatives; for people in the southern Sudan, support of confidence-building measures between the warring parties to hasten a negotiated end to the conflict.

In its more focused sense, humanitarian action has two major elements: the provision of emergency assistance and the protection of fundamental human rights. Assistance encompasses a wide range of activities, from the supplemental feeding of infants during famines to measures designed to strengthen indigenous social and institutional coping mechanisms for avoiding future crises. In fact, providing emergency assistance with an eye to empowering populations at risk is particularly valuable and humane. Protection encompasses such measures as interposing one's self as a physical barrier to deter abuses of a person's human rights, providing an accompanying presence for a threatened community in grave jeopardy, arranging the evacuation of at-risk people, and interceding diplomatically on behalf of an individual or group.

Connecting and animating all such actions is the essence of humanitarianism: relieving life-threatening suffering and ensuring respect for human rights. Commenting on the twin aspects of humanitarian action in the former Yugoslavia, the UN's High Commissioner for Refugees (UNHCR), Sadako Ogata, noted, "Humanitarian assistance is much more than relief and logistics. It is essentially and above all about protection—protection of victims of human rights and humanitarian violations."[7]

To what extent is humanitarianism universal in this broad sense? Is humanitarianism a feature of all societies, corresponding perhaps to certain humane instincts inherent in the human species? The concept of humanitarianism is most fully developed in the cultures and jurisprudence of Judeo-Christian nations. Reflecting those roots, the origin and constituencies of many of the better-known humanitarian organizations are Western—occasionally, as subsequent chapters will demonstrate, to a fault.

The dominant ideologies and styles of such agencies sometimes alienate non-Western countries and populations in which major disasters have occurred. This was the case with the response to the plight of persons who had fled into Jordan and Iran during the upheaval following Iraq's invasion of Kuwait in 1990. This was also the case in Cambodia in 1991, when many international organizations made little effort to connect with indigenous traditions and resources. Some observers have noted that Islamic fundamentalist politicians in the northern Sudan have capitalized ten years later on a residual backlash against the marginalization of the Sudanese government and private institutions by Western relief agencies that responded to the 1984–1986 famine.

At the same time, recent research and reflection confirm that the concept of humanitarianism resonates across the globe with elements of religion, law, and ethics in traditions other than the Judeo-Christian.[8] A variety of books and journal articles lays to rest the presumption that all humanitarian institutions, wherever they exist, are creations, extensions, or subsidiaries of the Judeo-Christian West. Likewise, humane instincts and their institutional expression are not limited to persons or societies who have reached a certain stage of economic development.

### The Dimensions of Humanitarian Responses

Humanitarian institutions are called upon to function in a wide range of conflicts. Some armed conflicts are international, such as the Ogaden War between Ethiopia and Somalia or the Gulf War. Others are internal, for example, the conflict between Indonesia and secessionists on the island of East Timor or within the island nation of Sri Lanka.

The logic and provisions of the UN Charter were designed to counter clear-cut aggression across state boundaries, but the growth industry for conflict managers in recent years has been internal wars such as between the Iraqi authorities in Baghdad and Iraqi Kurds in the north and Shiites in the south. Some conflicts involve disputed legalities, exemplified by the self-declared Bosnian Serb republic or by Palestinians in the Israeli-occupied territories.

Weapons surrendered to ONUCA soldiers by Nicaraguan resistance forces as part of the Central America peace process. (UN Photo 157592/S. Johansen)

Conflicts also differ in scope. Some are localized in one part of a country, such as the activities of isolated guerrilla groups in the Philippines or in Guatemala. Others are country-wide, such as in recent years the Sudan's civil war. Still others are more regional in their implications and involvement. Civil strife in Liberia has generated substantial refugee migrations into neighboring countries, whose soldiers have joined a regional effort to keep the peace and stem the flow of refugees.

Some conflicts involve isolated incidents against individual members of minority groups that may not have reached the stage of outright intergroup warfare or are at such low levels of violence as not yet to have generated significant numbers of refugees. Others may have deteriorated to a point that ethnic rivalries have convulsed entire nations.

Some wars have sputtered on again, off again, as in Rwanda and Burundi at regular intervals since their independence from Belgium in the early 1960s. Others have burned steadily for decades. The Sudan has experienced ongoing civil war since its independence from Great Britain in 1954, with the exception of the brief period from 1972 to 1983. Some wars erupt almost overnight—as in the case of Croatia in 1991. Others are long-festering, the subject of academic treatises and desultory discussions, such as in Guatemala and Myanmar.

As noted earlier, the end of East-West rivalry clearly has not meant unemployment among humanitarian workers. In conflicts like those in Afghanistan, Angola, Mozambique, Somalia, and North and South Yemen that were fueled by superpower support for their Third World proxies, violence has taken on a life of its own. At the same time, caldrons that were kept from boiling over during a forty-year period have now done so in the Balkans and various republics of the former Soviet Union. Local ethnic and religious upheaval seethes in other areas, such as the Sudan, Liberia, and Sri Lanka, with only the most tenuous relationship to Cold War politics.[9]

With the demise of the Cold War, local conflicts are no longer kept in check by the need to avoid flash points for big-power involvement that could lead to a possible, and wider, nuclear conflagration. Belligerents can no longer jockey for international attention or catapult their causes into international forums because of their perceived importance to world politics.

Within this vastly altered geopolitical context, domestic strife sometimes leads to virtual chaos. Anarchy also provides a treacherous new obstacle course for outside actors, as the tragic deaths of so many humanitarian personnel and journalists attest. The breakdown of civil society can become a source of regional instability, as illustrated by the Horn of Africa and the surrounding area. The Sudan, Ethiopia, Eritrea, Djibouti, Somalia, Uganda, and Kenya all provide temporary homes for large numbers of refugees from local conflicts.[10] In fact, faced with proliferating drought and civil unrest across a broad area, the Agency for International Development (AID) began applying in 1994 the term "the wider Horn of Africa" to include Rwanda, Uganda, and Tanzania, as well as the traditional Horn countries of Somalia, Ethiopia, Eritrea, Djibouti, Kenya, and the Sudan.

How a conflict is viewed has a direct bearing on the response mounted. In politicized settings, perceptions about a conflict often differ significantly and influence decisions by humanitarian organizations accordingly. What international observers view as a multi-decade war by authorities against the indigenous Indian population in Guatemala the government describes as a police action against terrorists. Identifying a famine as a product of war rather than drought also affects the resource mobilization, publicity, and involvement of the international community.

Moreover, the timing and choice of humanitarian responses are critical. There are normally several phases within a conflict, some of them more favorable than others for humanitarian action. Each phase requires different kinds of involvement. In recent armed conflicts, the aid organizations that have assisted civilians while the fighting raged have been fairly few. Many groups have assisted as the fighting has subsided and the prospects for reconstruction have improved.

In civil wars, governments and armed insurgents may resort to different tactics. These include periods of intense fighting, pitched battles, hit-and-run attacks, strafing, mining, and lulls in the action. Depending upon the military situation—which may reflect such seasonal variables as the weather and the availability of troops and weapons—humanitarian delivery may be more or less feasible. The ups and downs experienced by Operation Lifeline Sudan from 1989 to 1993 provide ample illustration of variety in the phases within a conflict.

A cease-fire or peace agreement often does not mean the end of a conflict but rather the beginning of a new phase. Following Eritrea's thirty-year struggle for independence, both this new state and neighboring Ethiopia faced enormous challenges from the detritus of war:

demining, demobilization, and the reintegration of soldiers into civilian society. Even though the curtain on the conflict has now descended, many tasks—ethnic, social, economic, and political—remain that were unaddressed by and in many instances exacerbated by the war.

For many Westerners, war was treated in schoolbooks as a phenomenon of the past. Apart from the nuclear sword of Damocles, the war faded into historic memory or at most was considered a Third World problem that began with decolonization and received scant attention. In the past decade or so, war has become the subject of daily media reports. With the eruption of war in the former Soviet Union and the former Yugoslavia, developing countries no longer have a demonstrable monopoly on armed conflicts.

Some civil wars have ended, the warring factions having taken crucial steps to put armed conflict behind them. After a bitter ten-year struggle, Zimbabwe has assumed a formal place in the world community, having established a new national army composed of soldiers from both the former regular Rhodesian army and the guerrilla forces who wrested the new nation's independence. A similar experiment is under way in El Salvador, where demobilization is being accompanied by efforts to resettle former Farabundo Martí National Liberation Front (FMLN) fighters on the land. Insurgents will account for 20 percent of a new national police force, and former members of the Salvadoran Armed Forces will compose another 20 percent. The remaining 60 percent will be new recruits.

Strategists of humanitarian action need to consider not only the evolution of a given conflict but also the geography of the fighting. Unlike the wars of yesteryear, today's conflicts are rarely characterized by clear-cut battle fronts with demarcated trenches. Sometimes even contiguous areas are not controlled by the same belligerent. In some conflicts, there even may be more than two warring factions.

In some countries still at war, zones therefore may include areas in which rehabilitation and development rather than only emergency relief may proceed. During the worst of the famine and bloodshed in Somalia in 1992 to 1993, there remained pockets of tranquility where tribal elders addressed tensions and development activities were able to proceed. In fact, the highly visible international intervention was criticized for riveting attention to the areas of clan warfare, to the detriment of those where the situation was more promising.

Iraqi forces set oil wells near Rumaila ablaze in March 1991 during their retreat from Kuwait. (UN Photo 158131/J. Isaac)

Analyzing the dynamics of an armed conflict assists outside organizations in charting their own involvement. In active war zones, the negotiation and maintenance of access to populations at risk may be arduous and security for agency personnel and operations problematic. Once a conflict winds down, physical security is less critical, but establishing trust among suspicious former enemies may remain a challenge.

The state of an armed conflict also has a direct bearing on the financial costs of mounting humanitarian action. Activities undertaken where fighting is raging are considerably more expensive than those elsewhere. Programs in civil wars, in which air transport is often necessary when overland routes are unavailable, are more expensive than programs that deal with famines caused by natural disasters. Higher costs reduce resources available both for the country in conflict as well as for other needy countries, creating an obvious dilemma for agencies with limited resources.

The costs of picking up the pieces from armed conflicts should not be underestimated. Expenditures to counteract decades of arms sales and violence may need to be commensurate with those that went into fighting the wars and may need to be sustained for at least as long as the wars themselves. It is easier and cheaper to destroy than to rebuild.

The nature of humanitarian responses may range from short-term emergency relief through reconstruction of essential infrastructure to medium- and longer-term development. Examples are providing food and medicine by land convoys and airdrops to the people of eastern Bosnia and equipping and training civil service and municipal workers in Somalia.

In terms of protection, efforts are undertaken to safeguard the lives of threatened individuals or of entire populations. Examples include international pressure on Myanmar authorities in support of 1991 Nobel laureate Daw Aung San Suu Kyi and the initiative of international personnel to station themselves in the homes of minority families threatened with ethnic cleansing in Bosnia-Herzegovina.

There is now general agreement that emergency relief and protection affect the longer-run prospects of communities and societies. There is also consensus that relief should be provided in ways that reduce dependence on outside assistance and vulnerability to future emergencies.

The normal impulse earlier had been to approach relief as a separate activity designed to alleviate the specific emergency needs arising from a disaster. In this sense, the quick relief of suffering was valued in its own right, regardless of the consequences. Societies with recurrent wars and other disasters were seen to have underlying problems: endemic poverty; tribal, religious, or ethnic tensions; and the lack of basic human rights and representative political structures. Yet these deeper problems traditionally were viewed as distinct from the emergency at hand and, within the domain of development, as distinct from relief, institutions, and personnel.

More recently, relief and development have come to be viewed as ends of a continuum, interacting rather than existing in static isolation. Relief can be carried out in ways that increase a society's vulnerability to recurring crises—or it can enhance the indigenous coping mechanisms of communities and empower local leadership and institutions.

Although relief and development are compatible activities, there are sometimes significant tensions and trade-offs. Alleviating life-threatening suffering does not automatically ensure that responses to disasters will strengthen local capacities to ward off future emergencies. Working through local institutions may, in fact, delay effective action. Whatever the short-run benefits of proceeding as quickly as possible, the medium- to longer-run costs of a narrow-gauged approach to emergencies can be profoundly negative.

In the northern Sudan in 1984 to 1986, outside aid officials brushed aside local authorities in their rush to save lives. Not only were the resulting activities ill considered but the backlash against the massive expatriate presence and programs also led Khartoum authorities to resist outside aid when a more severe famine recurred later in the decade.[11] There are also lessons about the relief-to-development continuum to be gleaned from the crises in the former Yugoslavia and Somalia in 1992 and 1993. In each, the failure to resolve longstanding tribal and ethnic tensions erupted in bloody warfare, dramatizing the costs of ignoring the interactions along the emergency-to-development continuum.

Mary Anderson and Peter Woodrow[12] hold that humanitarian action should be judged not only according to its cost-effective relief of life-threatening suffering. It also should be expected to reduce local vulnerability to disasters and improve prospects for equitable economic development and peace. Emergency aid must be provided in ways that help societies prevent future emergencies or, if they recur, to draw more fully on locally available resources.

The now hackneyed Chinese proverb summarizes the point: Give a starving man a fish, and he will need more fish; give him a pole and he will provide for himself. Such an approach requires resisting the visceral reaction to do something quickly in the face of human tragedy. Relief workers now try to provide tools and seeds to displaced populations well before planting time and rely upon village elders to organize medical facilities within refugee camps. These approaches have developed after years of providing foodstuffs and medical help through expatriates, which have relieved suffering in the short term but have done little to forestall future disasters. Although the approach seems axiomatic, it must be tailored to a specific crisis. Knowledge of local conditions and constraints is crucial. Providing a fishing pole to people in war zones with no access to water is hardly sensible.

The continuum between relief and development makes theoretical sense, but many practitioners—and their constituencies—are impatient when confronted by desperate situations. Yet using local resources can have economic as well as institution-building benefits. After the Gulf War, for example, the international community ignored underemployed Jordanian physicians and instead flew in European doctors at ten times the cost. Likewise, expensive expatriate drivers with no skills in Arabic were hired instead of local Iraqis.[13]

Resisting the quick fix also can be difficult for reasons other than organizational routine. Publics, parliaments, and politicians are more likely to respond to appeals for assistance in complex emergencies than to attack longer-term problems. The United Nations Children's Fund (UNICEF) distinguishes between the attention-grabbing *loud* emergencies of dramatic wars and the *silent* emergencies of poor families who suffer from malnutrition and preventable diseases. In 1993, UNICEF Executive Director James P. Grant rejoiced that the world had reacted vigorously to the deaths the previous year of about half a million children under the age of five in war-ravaged Somalia. Yet it had done little, he noted, to prevent the deaths of 13 million other children around the world—about 35,000 per day—who had died during the same period from poverty.[14] In August 1993, the British and Swedish governments mounted an expensive and attention-getting evacuation of fifty children from Sarajevo's pathetic hospitals, a small number indeed contrasted to the daily decimation of preventable infant mortality.

Using local talent and avoiding recurrent disasters have a particular urgency in view of limited resources and the marked proliferation of emergencies. Every dollar expended in silent emergencies is an estimated ten to twenty times more cost-effective than the dollar spent in loud ones. Attention to the relief-to-development continuum is a necessary correction to narrow-gauge humanitarian action.

### International Humanitarian Law and Intervention

Discussions of humanitarian action need to be situated within the context of international law. A baseline is provided by the Geneva Conventions of 1949 and the Additional Protocols of 1977. Monitored and promoted by the Geneva-based International Committee of the Red Cross, this legal framework recognizes the right of civilians to have access to humanitarian assistance and of impartial aid organizations to provide assistance to them. It also distinguishes between what lawyers call *jus in bello,* or the conduct of armed conflicts, and *jus ad bellum,* or the resort to force.[15]

Strictly speaking, the conventions and protocols impose legal obligations only on those governments that have ratified them. About 175 governments have ratified the conventions, and 120 of these have acceded as well to one or both protocols. Yet the texts, which reflect a carefully calibrated balance between the needs of civilians and the military and security requirements of political authorities, enjoy an authority exceeding the number of formal signatories. Some major powers that have chosen not to ratify the protocols have nevertheless incorporated key provisions into their military manuals and practice. Some insurgent groups also have pledged to abide by the letter and spirit of these provisions.

At work is what international lawyers describe as the power of custom. That is, international norms influence views and behavior even in quarters where they have not been formally endorsed. Governments are anxious to exhibit what American revolutionary Thomas Paine called "a decent respect for the opinion of mankind."

At the same time, international law is not as binding or as hard as its domestic equivalent in its enforceability by national police and judicial processes. Although international norms matter and political authorities wish to be seen as complying with them, they represent a softer form of law as it affects the behavior of soldiers and government officials.

However useful legal constraints may be in moderating inhumane behavior, warring parties and the international community often honor them only in the breach. Reviewing the rampant disrespect for international law that characterized the 1980s, the Independent Commission on International Humanitarian Issues, chaired by former UN High Commissioner for Refugees Prince Sadruddin Aga Khan, euphemistically described government attitudes toward humanitarian norms as often "relaxed."

That is to say, international norms are treated as axiomatic and self-evident—until such times as fidelity to them would constrain behavior. The commission noted that in situations in which national security is perceived to be at stake—at precisely those times when the authorities are most tempted to cut humanitarian corners—political considerations often prevail over humanitarian requirements, and these requirements then are used to promote political aims.[16]

Humanitarian rationales are also frequently given as rationalizations for the behavior of states that is driven by other considerations. Political wolves frequently masquerade as humanitarian sheep. Japan voiced humanitarian concerns in invading Manchuria in 1931 to "protect its people," as did Hitler when he marched into Czechoslovakia in 1938 to "protect" ethnic Germans from mistreatment. More recently, the Soviet Union cloaked its intervention in Afghanistan in 1979 in terms of protecting the people of that nation; India covered its invasion of Sri Lanka as an effort on behalf of Tamils; and the United States justified its invasion of Grenada as intended to rescue U.S. nationals in 1983.

Despite the traditional invocation of humanitarian concerns to justify a multitude of sins and the indisputably political impacts of humanitarian action, international humanitarian law takes care to insulate bona fide action from infiltration by extraneous political and other considerations. As the global political context more strongly supports intervention to assist and protect civilian populations, the legal constraints against the use of force in support of humane values need to be better understood.

As noted in the Introduction, sovereign states in recent years have ceded prerogatives that touch upon matters once considered the essence of domestic jurisdiction. They have come to attach greater importance to humanitarian issues and have agreed to enhanced protection for human rights. The process of devolving some authority over human rights from states is not just a recent phenomenon. Although reinforced by dramatic events since the end of the Cold War, promoting and protecting human rights across borders has paralleled progress in international humanitarian law over the last century.

The evolution has been particularly dramatic since the founding of the United Nations in 1945.[17] The Covenant of the League of Nations, adopted in the wake of World War I, was notably silent about obligations in the humanitarian sphere. Prior to World War II, the treatment of a nation's civilian population was rarely considered a legitimate matter for international attention. War crimes trials against Japanese and German officials were a critical turning point, as was the formulation in 1948 of the Universal Declaration of Human Rights. These events redefined traditional ideas of what was permissible for governments in relation to their own citizens.

Domestic jurisdiction of nation states, or *sovereignty*, has always existed in a certain tension with the needs of civilians. Even the UN Charter, the quintessential document ratified by states to regulate their relations, does not support the conventional view that state sovereignty is absolute and uncontested. The Security Council has always been able to decide for itself what type of crisis represents threats to international peace and security. Long before the council decided that

Admiral Jonathan T. Howe (third from right), special representative of the secretary-general for Somalia, meets with village elders in Baar, Somalia. (UN Photo 159780/ M. Grant)

northern Iraq and Somalia presented such threats, a central tension was already evident in the charter.

Governments that flaunt international standards frequently justify their freedom to act totally as they see fit by referring to Article 2 of the charter. Its seventh paragraph shelters from international scrutiny "matters which are essentially within the domestic jurisdiction of any state." The same governments, however, also have agreed to respect several other provisions in the charter that challenge the common notion that state sovereignty remains absolute.

The United Nations Charter is replete with references to specific rights "without distinction as to race, sex, language, or religion" and to the UN's responsibility to promote fundamental human rights. States have agreed that major areas of national policy that they otherwise might seek to protect by appeals to state sovereignty and exclusive domestic jurisdiction fall within international purview.

A principal beneficiary of the erosion of state sovereignty therefore has been the "other" side of the UN Charter and those institutions of the United Nations system with mandates in the humanitarian, human rights, social, and economic spheres. As the treatment of civilian populations by political authorities has become a more established international concern, efforts to improve the international mechanisms for dealing with humanitarian assistance and human rights protection have gained new urgency. The ferment has been particularly apparent regarding those displaced within national borders.

Since World War II, the international legal status of refugees has been perhaps the most clearly delineated of any single group. Their rights have steadily become better protected. The 1951 convention relating to the Status of Refugees has provided a text as well as a large body of practice surrounding the work of the UN High Commissioner for Refugees. The original protections were confined to people who had become refugees as a result of events that took place before January 1951. The convention's applicability was generally limited to Europe.

In 1967, a protocol was introduced that abolished the dateline and made the coverage universal. The term "refugee" was defined as a person who had fled his or her country of origin because of a well-founded fear of persecution due to race, religion, nationality, or membership in a particular social or political group. The application was widened further to include victims of external violence, public disorder, and massive violations of human rights in the 1969 Convention Governing the Specific Aspects of Refugee Problems in Africa, promoted by the Organization of African Unity, and by its Latin American counterpart, the 1984 Cartagena Declaration on Refugees.

Although refugee protection now enjoys firm standing in international humanitarian law, no clear-cut legal protections are available to internally displaced persons.[18] Currently more numerous than refugees, who themselves number at least 20 million, displaced persons do not normally qualify for comparable legal protection or United Nations help because they have not crossed an international border. Although many find themselves in refugee-like situations within their countries of origin, they fall outside the mandate of the UN's refugee agency and are not the specific charge of any other international organization.

This anomaly results in serious practical problems. Iraqi Kurds who fled into Iran in April 1991 qualified for UN aid, whereas those who remained within Iraq at the closed Turkish border a few miles away did not, although they eventually received assistance. The needs of people trapped in such situations can be attended by UNHCR or other UN agencies if authorized by the secretary-general or others in authority, as has been done in the cases of the Kurds imperiled on the Turkish border and persons in Central America, the former Yugoslavia, and Somalia.

New attention to the appropriateness and utility of intervention as a means of reaching these persons has come with the evolution of international humanitarian law on the one hand and the growing attention to the needs of civilian populations on the other. The subject is complex, involving an array of legal, institutional, and practical problems. It is one on which experts are deeply divided, particularly on the point of associating humanitarian action with military force.[19]

The present will no doubt come to be seen as a watershed comparable to the turning points after each of the world wars in this century. A cornerstone of the Cold War era was the notion of sovereignty. In one sense, the concept of sovereignty has been evolving steadily since the founding of the modern state system in 1648, when the Peace of Westphalia ended the religious madness of the Thirty Years' War. But it is a sign of the times that even the secretary-general of the United Nations could write in the prestigious U.S. periodical *Foreign Affairs* in late 1992 that "the centuries-old doctrine of absolute and exclusive sovereignty no longer stands, and was in fact never so absolute as it was conceived to be in theory."[20]

The international community is groping toward arrangements by which egregious aggression, life-threatening suffering, and human rights abuses are universally acknowledged to be subjects of legitimate international concern. The world view in which state sovereignty served as an all-purpose rationalization for narrowly defined *raisons d'état* (or national interests) has become less acceptable to more people. States and armed opposition groups, along with newer breeds of actors such as nongovernmental organizations and the media, now insist that conventional notions of territorial sovereignty, if retained at all, be infused with a greater sense of responsibility.[21]

As generally used, *intervention* includes a broad spectrum of actions. These range from telephone calls by a foreign ministry official expressing concern about a particular policy, practice, or endangered person to the actual dispatch of foreign troops on a military mission. International relations themselves are made up of myriad actions by one or more states to influence the behavior of other states.

Moreover, intergovernmental organizations can function as agents of intervention. For example, the World Bank and the International Monetary Fund (IMF) set certain preconditions for structural adjustment loans that limit the options of governments borrowing resources from these institutions. NGOs also seek to influence the domestic affairs of states. For example, Human Rights Watch urges that economic aid be conditioned on greater respect for human rights by a recipient government. Even outside humanitarian aid is an intrusive act, but in most cases it is not coercive. In a broad sense, all such actions constitute interventions and represent the day-to-day stuff of world politics.

In this book, intervention has a far narrower focus and refers to coercive actions, including economic and military sanctions taken to alter the domestic affairs, behavior, or policies of a government or insurgency that has chosen to resist the expressed will of the international community. Our focus is on punitive international intervention sanctioned by Chapter 7 of the United Nations Charter, a provision in the world organization's constitution authorizing enforcement—by military force in extreme situations—of international decisions. This reflects not only normative preferences but also the present reality, in which major governments, including the United States, look increasingly to the UN to legitimize and on occasion undertake intervention.

But controversy remains. Some specialists view the concept of "humanitarian intervention" as a contradiction in terms. They note that the Geneva Conventions treat humanitarian access as a right that governments have freely acknowledged. That being the case, efforts must be made to persuade the authorities to meet their expressed obligation to allow access by recognized international humanitarian agencies to civilian populations.

Since it is difficult—some would say, impossible—to sustain humanitarian action in the absence of the consent of the authorities, force is likely to be counterproductive. Although governments separately or together have the right to apply economic or military coercion, this is "humanitarian intervention" and should not be portrayed as such. The ICRC has traditionally championed this approach.

Other experts view humanitarian intervention as a right and, in the view of some who cite the UN Charter and other affirmations of human rights, even a duty of states. The French government has advanced this viewpoint over the years.[22] When obstinate regimes are involved, that right may need to be backed by military force. To be unprepared to intervene on behalf of abused populations is to strengthen the hand of those who blatantly flout international norms. The application of economic or military force may be the only means to protect human rights and dignity.

The disagreement about how much implementing the humanitarian imperative requires the consent of the relevant political authorities divides not only scholars but also practitioners. Humanitarian actors have different views, not about the importance of reaching vulnerable populations but about the respective roles of consent and coercion in gaining access.

UN organizations, which are accountable to governing boards composed of constituent governments, tend to work firmly within prevailing legal strictures. At the same time, some UN agencies—UNICEF is the most notable example—have a tradition of working on all sides of a given conflict, whatever their reservations about the seated government. The ICRC, as a matter of principle, avoids engaging in extralegal activities such as cross-border operations without the consent of the seated political authorities. Some NGOs are less hesitant to violate the law in the interest of reaching needy civilians than most UN organizations and the ICRC.[23]

The United Nations, meanwhile, is showing a new level of assertiveness by backing up humanitarian concerns with military resolve. In two of its most significant recent decisions in this regard (Resolutions 688 of April 1991 and 794 of December 1992), the Security Council authorized the use of military force on behalf of civilian populations in northern Iraq and Somalia. The protection of humanitarian operations in Bosnia by "all measures necessary" was the stated rationale for the deployment of UN soldiers in Bosnia (Resolution 770 of August 1992), although the level of force actually provided was less than in northern Iraq and Somalia.[24]

Half a century of tension between the principle of sovereignty and growing concerns with humanitarian access has also been reflected in debates in the UN General Assembly and in international governmental conferences. The dynamics in the General Assembly, the globe's quintessential political forum, reflect the prevailing views of governments more accurately than do the assessments of legal scholars and humanitarian officials. Breaking new conceptual and political ground, Resolution 46/182, adopted in December 1991, allows the United Nations to mount humanitarian activities in exceptional circumstances in which neither the express request nor formal consent of the political authorities is forthcoming.

Recent UN discussions of humanitarian access suggest a continuing, but not unilinear, evolution toward more progressive norms. At the World Assembly on Human Rights in Vienna in June 1993, some retrenchment was evident as primarily Asian and Middle Eastern governments questioned the universality of human rights and reasserted a more traditional view of the prerogatives of sovereign governments. Nevertheless, although the United Nations remains an organization of governments, the human rights of civilians receive greater weight.

The overall direction of the evolution in international norms and its practical implications are clear. They echo a social and moral sense widely shared across cultures that human beings should not be denied assistance and that food or other relief should not be provided, or denied, to serve military and political objectives. The fact that governments are now debating these issues is positive, even though the legal formulation and the operational mechanisms for a more assertive approach are still being crafted. International humanitarian law is gaining in importance, but its relation to humanitarian intervention remains contentious and unresolved.[25]

## Humanitarian Space

The difficulties experienced by the international community during the past decade in providing assistance and protection to distressed populations have contributed to the evolution of the concept of humanitarian space. Although the particulars vary from conflict to conflict, the concept refers to the access that must be secured and maintained if humanitarian activities are to have integrity and effectiveness.

Humanitarian space is a dynamic concept with multiple dimensions. The spatial metaphor suggests not a walled room with fixed dimensions but something more akin to an accordion. That is, available access to vulnerable populations may shrink or expand in accordance with the policies or actions of local political and military authorities. Rather than simply filling existing space, outside humanitarian institutions may expand this space through their presence and the international attention that they attract. When they leave, however, the space does not automatically transfer to other groups.

Soldiers in Cacaopera, El Salvador, in November 1986. (ICRC Photo SALV 86-48/0 Ph. Merchez)

Experience in Central America over the last decade and a half illustrates this concept.[26] The wars in Nicaragua, El Salvador, and Guatemala, their effects spilling over into Honduras and Costa Rica, divided the three principal countries and the region as a whole. A common thread throughout was that regardless of the government and the insurgency, involvement by humanitarian agencies with civilian populations was highly suspect.

Belligerents sought to reduce humanitarian space as part of their overall strategy of control. Some external governments, NGOs, and media succeeded in preserving and enlarging space; others accepted the constraints provided and even contributed to the prevailing politicization. The Central American experience illustrates five separate but related aspects of humanitarian space and five sets of companion constraints on humanitarian access.

The first was geographical. The wars were fought in some of the most remote parts of the isthmus, inhabited largely by subsistence peasants and ethnic minorities. These areas invariably had poor transportation and communications networks. Their isolation was compounded by the warfare itself.

Much of Nicaragua's Atlantic coast and the northern parts of Guatemala are inhabited by indigenous peoples. These regions are generally without all-weather roads and national communications systems. Limited access to civilians was disrupted further by the conflicts. Military action frequently severed cross-border arteries. Poor infrastructure deteriorated or was altogether destroyed. The ensuing economic collapse exacerbated the isolation of remote populations and their overall plight.

The geographical implications of the conflicts for humanitarian agencies were formidable. War-affected populations could not be reached through the kinds of cross-border operations from neighboring countries that were mounted in other parts of the world such as the Sudan, Tigray, and Eritrea. Many of those at risk were also cut off from the capital cities, where most aid agencies based their operations. The greater difficulty of reaching remote areas was a major factor that contributed to the escalation of costs for providing assistance in nonwar situations by a factor of ten to twenty.

Humanitarian space also had a social dimension. The degrees of access enjoyed by humanitarian actors depended also upon the extent of their previous involvement with the affected population groups. Knowledge of communities and mutual trust, usually established through earlier development-related activities, facilitated access. Conversely, lack of prior contact made the prevailing suspicion difficult to overcome.

Existing governmental administrative structures were hardly prepared to cope with the plethora of humanitarian tasks resulting from conflict. Many of their own development programs of the 1970s had been designed to thwart effective participation by the groups most affected by the wars of the 1980s. Since an underlying cause of the conflict in El Salvador was government neglect of the rural areas associated with FMLN insurgents, it was no surprise that Salvadoran governmental agencies and their associated indigenous and expatriate humanitarian organizations would not be particularly welcome.

The extremely limited prior contact that most organizations of the United Nations system had cultivated with the distressed populations, particularly those in insurgent-controlled areas, became a major handicap when humanitarian relief was needed. UNHCR, which became the lead UN agency for what High Commissioner Sadako Ogata called "mopping up" after the wars, had been largely absent in Central America before the crises erupted. The United Nations Development Programme (UNDP) was present as the system's principal coordinating body, but its own preoccupation had naturally been with its development mandate, again mediated through government ministries. As a result, little expertise and few relationships attuned to emergency needs were nurtured. Among the UN agencies, only UNICEF had a few programs in the poorest and most remote areas.

The ability of UN organizations in many settings around the world to develop and maintain access reflects the quality, experience, and outreach of local counterparts. In Central America, however, the international NGOs to which UN agencies frequently turned had themselves not been particularly active among rural peasants affected by the war, having given priority instead to agricultural laborers and the urban poor. Meanwhile, the region's own NGOs were not organized at the national level in ways that made them easy or natural interlocutors.

Best equipped by prior association to deal with rural populations and others most severely hurt by the conflicts were church-based organizations. Building on trust established over years of pastoral activities and development work, Catholic and Protestant churches—the Archbishopric of San Salvador was a prime example—mobilized aid to the displaced, many of whom at the time distrusted well-established political and humanitarian institutions. The conflicts also sharpened the traditional struggle within ecclesiastical hierarchies over the proper role of churches in promoting social change. The murder and harassment of archbishops, parish priests, nuns, and lay workers reflected the costs of their efforts.

A third dimension of humanitarian space concerned politics. In the highly politicized atmosphere of the 1980s, this space contracted or expanded as a reflection of the attitude of the host authorities, the perceived political affiliation of humanitarian organizations seeking access, and the state of the political-military struggle at any given time.

In the case of Nicaragua, the Reagan administration's view of the Sandinista revolution as Communist-inspired and expansionist led to attempts to overthrow it. U.S. support of the Contras, whose activities increased the number of civilian casualties in the war, reflected an ideological approach to assistance. Aid was channeled through U.S. NGOs to communities within Nicaragua and in neighboring countries presumed loyal to the Contras. At the same time, aid was denied to NGOs whose programs included victims of Contra violence or involved Nicaraguan government ministries and facilities (for example, public health centers) as implementing partners.

European governments compensated by channeling assistance to and through the Nicaraguan government. International and local NGOs that used European resources often became Contra targets. Food convoys were attacked and destroyed; aid workers from grass-roots groups, Nicaraguan government ministries, and expatriate volunteers were ambushed, kidnapped, and killed. Thoroughly politicized by the conflict, humanitarian space was conspicuous by its scarcity.

In El Salvador, the expansion and contraction of humanitarian space reflected the dynamic interplay between the Reagan administration and the U.S. Congress. Although successive Salvadoran governments had a staunch ally in the former, continued humanitarian, economic, and military aid depended on the latter. Widespread outrage among the American public over thousands of death-squad killings and other human rights abuses, channeled to the Congress with the encouragement of humanitarian and solidarity groups, provided a counterweight to executive branch requests for assistance to a succession of Salvadoran regimes.

Civilian regimes that are elected and accountable are generally more susceptible to international public opinion and more sensitive to the impact of their policies on civilians. The emergence of electoral politics in El Salvador during the 1980s also made the plight of internally displaced persons a more public issue. The UN-brokered peace talks in 1991 provided space for augmented activities by nongovernmental groups.

The Guatemalan government was never as dependent upon outside support as were its counterparts in Nicaragua and El Salvador. As a result, humanitarian space was less susceptible to outside influence. The armed forces viewed displaced persons as a subversive threat rather than a humanitarian challenge. Guatemala's low levels of outside military aid reinforced the disposition of its armed forces to ignore international criticism and silence the opposition. Elected Guatemalan regimes also were less subject to outside pressures to gain access to isolated indigenous communities.

In addition to its geographical, social, and political dimensions, humanitarian space has a security aspect. The counterinsurgency strategies followed by each country's armed forces and the responses of each armed opposition movement circumscribed access to civilians at risk throughout the region. The authorities in Managua, San Salvador, and Guatemala City, like counterparts elsewhere around the world facing insurgent challenges, sought to divide civilian populations from their would-be insurgent protectors—that is, to drain the sea in order to catch the fish.

Humanitarian organizations were associated through political rhetoric with threats to security and subjected to constant surveillance, persistent harassment, and periodic repression throughout the region. Firsthand collection of data and monitoring of abuses became more difficult as international personnel often were confined to capital cities. Information filtering out of the more remote regions arrived mainly through back channels provided by religious groups.

Military authorities viewed the report of human rights violations to the outside world as a direct security threat. Functioning as the eyes and ears of the international community, humanitarian aid and human rights personnel were in particular jeopardy. Dozens of international and local human rights workers were abducted and murdered by security forces and death squads in Central America during the 1980s. In a dramatic illustration of the contraction of humanitarian space in the face of heightened security concerns, only one in five of the expatriates present in San Salvador before the insurgent offensive in November 1989 was present at the end of that year. Many had been expelled and circumstances forced others to leave.

Intimidating humanitarian assistance and human rights officials was a tactic employed with particular success in Guatemala. Although such organizations exist there today, monitoring of government policies—much less criticism of them—remains risky. Human rights work is fraught with special danger, particularly for local staff. The continued residence in Mexico of a highly visible activist such as 1992 Nobel laureate Rigoberta Menchú suggests the persistent absence of humanitarian space in her native Guatemala. At the same time, she expressed solidarity through her personal presence at the time of the self-organized repatriation by refugees in Mexico to rural Guatemala in early 1994.

Humanitarian space is also a function of specific administrative controls, a dimension perhaps less obvious to outside observers but no less debilitating to practitioners on the scene. Particularly vulnerable are international agencies and their personnel, whose ability to operate depends on agreements negotiated with national authorities. Inside organizations as well as nationals employed by outside organizations and their dependents are also susceptible.

Even in peacetime, when officials are generally more committed to facilitating humanitarian work, bureaucratic requirements, customs, and foreign exchange controls can keep outsiders on a short leash. These difficulties are compounded when war rages and well-meaning initiatives attract additional scrutiny. Conflicts make civilian and military authorities more nervous about their ability to control volatile situations. Administrative procedures are tailor-made to constrict humanitarian space.

Outside organizations—UN, government, and NGO alike—operate on the basis of negotiated protocols with the national authorities and with the consent, or acquiescence, of their local counterparts. The desire of these organizations to continue their presence and programs may discourage a willingness to challenge decisions by the authorities not to extend work permits or to deny visas to new staff, devices that keep expatriate workers on their best behavior. Currency exchange, banking procedures, and import restrictions provide additional methods for control.

A tactic used by military leaders in El Salvador—as effective from their standpoint as it was frustrating to those against whom it was applied—was the requirement of safe conduct passes for travel outside the capital city. The passes were granted when the high command wished to appear cooperative and withheld when it did not. A safe conduct pass was often valid only for a single day, when a given trip would require an overnight stay, or was refused by local military commanders who claimed to know of local extenuating circumstances of which their commanding officers, who had granted the permission, were of course unaware.

The geographical, social, political, security, and administrative elements in the preservation of humanitarian space in Central America during the 1980s have their counterparts in other armed conflicts around the world. The constraints may be idiosyncratic, but the need for space and the difficulties of maintaining it are generic, as subsequent chapters will demonstrate.

The remoteness of civilians in Central America recalls the difficulties of reaching those within Afghanistan and the relative ease of helping those who had fled to Pakistan. The strategic view of civilians in insurgent-controlled territory and the suspicions directed against those seeking to assist them have hobbled humanitarian efforts throughout the southern Sudan. Access granted by authorities in national capitals and denied at the local level recalls obstacles faced in eastern Bosnia. Those who seek to constrict humanitarian space learn from each other, as the Guatemalan did from the Salvadoran armed forces. Conversely, humanitarian interests also can learn from past successes and failures to achieve greater space in the future.

## Humanitarian Actors

Within the historical context described above and the basic framework provided by the concepts of humanitarian action, international humanitarian law and intervention, and humanitarian space, the contemporary cast of humanitarian actors carries out various assistance and protection activities.

Eight major institutional actors make up the existing system of international assistance and protection. Five are based outside the areas in conflict: United Nations and other international agencies, donor governments, nongovernmental organizations, the International Committee of the Red Cross, and outside military forces. The remaining three sets of actors are situated within the conflict areas: host governments and military forces, insurgent political and military authorities, and national and local private agencies. Introduced here, the eight will receive more detailed review in subsequent chapters, where their respective strengths and weaknesses will be analyzed.

The actors are grouped according to outside (or external) actors and internal (or local) ones. The former are often described as international, but the term is not altogether accurate. External agencies often are based in a single country and internal actors maintain a variety of international relationships.[27]

Prominent among outside actors are intergovernmental organizations. These are composed of agencies of the United Nations system, such as the United Nations Children's Fund (UNICEF), the World Food Programme (WFP), the UN High Commissioner for Refugees (UNHCR), the UN Development Program (UNDP), and the World Health Organization (WHO). Also included are regional organizations such as the European Union (EU), the Organization of American States (OAS), the

Organization of African Unity (OAU), the Economic Community of West African States (ECOWAS), and the Horn of Africa's Intergovernmental Authority on Drought and Development (IGADD).

These organizations are a diverse lot. The terms "family" and "system" are something of a misnomer when applied, as they often are, to the organs of the United Nations. The secretary-general is not really the chief executive of anything except the UN Secretariat itself. The executive heads of UN agencies are responsible for their own programs, including raising resources and reporting to autonomous governing bodies composed of member governments. Coordination is the overall responsibility of the UN under secretary-general for humanitarian affairs, but it is difficult, despite efforts in New York and Geneva and, through UNDP, in countries experiencing emergencies.

There are also major differences among the operating styles of various UN organizations. Some, with no resident staff within affected countries, are perceived as aloof and top-down in their approach (for example, the Washington-based World Bank and International Monetary Fund). Others, with staff in the capital cities and outlying areas, are more closely tied to grass-roots activity (for example, UNICEF).

In addition to serious problems of coordination among the UN's humanitarian organizations, there also are difficulties between them as a group and the political and military arms of the world body. The Security Council's decisions to employ economic and military sanctions complicate and sometimes politicize the work of humanitarian agencies. The assignment of UN troops, particularly in cases such as Bosnia, where the consent of the warring parties is not obtained, may create a certain tension between UN humanitarian and political agendas. Nevertheless, the universality of the UN system, and in recent years its growing visibility and serviceability, make it more central to international responses in war-induced emergencies.

In principle, the presence of states as members of UN governing bodies means that initiatives by or through intergovernmental organizations tend to be more acceptable when undertaken on a government-to-government, or bilateral, basis. In practice, however, there may be difficulties with multilateral initiatives. Complicating factors may include the presence of a regional hegemon, a general paucity of expertise and resources, and potential foreign policy gains and losses for neighboring states.[28]

The extent to which intergovernmental organizations outside the United Nations family become players in humanitarian emergencies varies greatly. Initially, the role of the European Union was relatively minor, serving as a channel for contributions to other organizations by member states. In recent years, however, with the formation of the European Community Humanitarian Office (ECHO) in April 1992, the EU has developed its own programs, posted its own staff in conflict areas, and asserted a significant financial and institutional interest in the issues.

Other regional intergovernmental organizations have been much less active in general. The Organization of African Unity has been conspicuous for its lack of direct involvement in either conflict resolution or humanitarian action in most of the continent's many conflicts. By contrast, the Economic Community of West African States has played a pivotal role in responding to the political, military, and humanitarian dimensions of the Liberian civil war, although that response has been uneven in its effects.

In addition to their support of international organizations, governments are major actors in their own right. As the second set of humanitarian actors, their involvement takes two forms. First, their foreign policies address matters such as trade and commerce with countries experiencing conflict and sometimes the conflicts themselves. In this way, the governments of the United States and the United Kingdom, through their foreign ministries and ambassadors in Khartoum, have sought to deal with the political causes of the Sudan's long-running civil war.

Second, governments are providers on a government-to-government, or bilateral, basis of humanitarian assistance to countries experiencing conflict. For example, the United States and the United Kingdom have had their own aid personnel from the Agency for International Development and the Overseas Development Administration in the Sudan, managing their nation's humanitarian interests.

Governments have multiple relationships with the governments of countries in conflict. A European government such as the Netherlands may be involved in a place like El Salvador, for example, both through its foreign ministry on the political side and, on the humanitarian, through funds provided by its own Netherlands International Development Agency, the European Union, and several UN agencies.

The political relationships of a government and its history of involvement in a region may make it more or less welcome as a humanitarian resource when disaster strikes. Because of its resources, traditions, and influence, the United States normally plays a major contributing role—with food, funds, experts, and logistic support. Yet the United States is often more suspect than countries such as the Nordics or Austria, whose power and leverage are considerably less. Former colonial powers have historical and cultural links to many areas, and this affects their acceptability. Although bilateral assistance agencies have their own limitations reflecting political perceptions of their governments, they also control more resources than many other actors do.

A third major category of external actors involves not governments but nongovernmental organizations. These include such familiar names as CARE, Catholic Relief Services (CRS), Doctors Without Borders (MSF), World Vision, Save the Children, Oxfam, Amnesty International, and the International Rescue Committee. There are also scores of organizations that have yet to reach the status of household words beyond their loyal contributors: Partners of the Americas, the U.S. Committee for Refugees, and the International Medical Committee, for example.

Once again, heterogeneity makes across-the-board generalizations difficult. Some outside NGOs carry out major operational activities themselves; others channel their resources through counterparts within countries in crisis. Some outside NGOs accept no funds from governments to underscore their nongovernmental status; other private groups are prepared to accept half or more of their total budgets from governments, extending what they accomplish with funds from private contributors.

The hallmark of NGOs is their activity at the grass-roots level. In the case of conflicts, this often means working on the front lines to provide humanitarian assistance and protection. NGOs as a group tend to be more action-oriented and more closely linked to the grass roots than UN or bilateral aid agency personnel, more flexible and creative, and less constrained by the formalities of law. Yet they often tend to be uncoordinated, sometimes uncollegial in their approach, and more seized with the necessity of mounting immediate humanitarian action than with fitting their own activities into a broader framework.

NGOs sometimes work together in national and international professional associations to exchange information and orchestrate dealings with the United Nations and donor governments, the public, and the media. For example, InterAction is the focal point for interagency discussions among some 140 private U.S. agencies. At the international level, the Geneva-based International Council of Voluntary Agencies (ICVA) has more than 100 member organizations, one of which is InterAction. A third entity, also based in Geneva, is a consortium entitled the Steering Committee for Humanitarian Response, which draws together seven of the major international NGOs that respond operationally to complex emergencies.

NGOs have become more important actors during the past several decades and are likely to continue growing in influence and operations. Their current status contrasts markedly to that of a decade or two ago, when they were largely dismissed by the other major actors as well-meaning do-gooders. Today, they receive substantial resources for their work from the UN and governments and have more active and energized constituencies than many multilateral and bilateral agencies.

A fourth category of external actor consists of a single organization, the International Committee of the Red Cross. A private organization with a board of governors of eminent Swiss citizens, the ICRC, like NGOs, receives substantial contributions from governments. However, it is separate and distinct from those categories of actors because of its specific recognition in international humanitarian law, of which it is also the designated custodian.

Unlike most other humanitarian actors, the ICRC has a clear and carefully elaborated body of doctrine that provides consistency to its operations in armed conflicts. Unlike many NGOs that mount a range of activities in a wide variety of relief, reconstruction, and development settings, the ICRC works only in international and internal armed conflicts, and then only to monitor compliance with humanitarian law, provide urgent humanitarian aid, visit prisoners, and exchange letters among persons cut off from each other.

The ICRC, together with the International Federation of Red Cross and Red Crescent Societies and their national chapters in individual countries, constitute the International Red Cross Movement. Founded in 1864 by Henri Dunant in response to the carnage at the Battle of Solferino in northern Italy five years earlier, the ICRC has its headquarters in Geneva, Switzerland, and is staffed in key international posts largely by Swiss nationals. For specific assignments, it accepts the services of persons provided by national chapters such as the American Red Cross and the Sudanese Red Crescent Society. Its location in a neutral country and its staffing policy underscore its belief, reinforced by its mandate in the Geneva Conventions and Protocols, that effective humanitarian action must remain strictly neutral and impartial.

The fifth category of external humanitarian actor is composed of outside military forces. Strictly speaking a subcategory of intergovernmental organizations or governments, military actors constitute a category of their own by virtue of cultures, operating styles, hierarchical structures, and accountabilities that distinguish them from their civilian counterparts.

Recent humanitarian crises have attracted military personnel in three basic forms. First have been the troops wearing the blue beret of the United Nations and reporting to UN commanders. Based on earlier procedures developed for peacekeeping in Lebanon and Cyprus, the activities in Croatia of the United Nations Protection Force (UNPROFOR) for the former Yugoslavia and of the second phase of United Nations Operations in Somalia (UNOSOM II) have represented such experiments.

A second variety has been composed of national government contingents functioning with UN blessing but under non-UN command. In the case of the military operation against Iraq, a United Nations Security Council resolution authorized all necessary means, which resulted in a coalition with troops from about thirty nations orchestrated

Military observers with the UN Transitional Authority in Cambodia distribute radios in October 1992 to convey information on elections for a constituent assembly. (UN Photo 186079/P. S. Sudhakaran)

by the United States and employing North Atlantic Treaty Organization (NATO) procedures. Subsequent efforts to ensure access to Kurds in northern Iraq were authorized by the Security Council but carried out by a Western coalition. Similarly, the U.S.-led coalition of Operation Restore Hope in Somalia, from December 1992 to May 1993, operated under the auspices of Chapter 7 of the UN Charter.

Finally, in several recent theaters, military actors have operated under the authority of their own capitals in initiatives that have not required or received the explicit blessing of the United Nations. Responding to a major natural disaster, U.S. troops in Operation Sea Angel helped rescue people from the devastating Bangladesh cyclone of 1991. In a highly charged conflict setting, Indian troops airlifted supplies to Tamil populations caught in the Sri Lankan civil war in 1987.

Soldiers now play an increasing and varied set of roles in humanitarian emergencies. These include advising aid officials on security and logistics matters, providing physical escorts for relief shipments, protecting humanitarian operations and personnel, delivering supplies through airdrops or overland convoys, and occasionally distributing relief items themselves. Each role, and often a combination of roles, has been played in the past several years by troops in northern Iraq, Somalia, Cambodia, and the former Yugoslavia.

For example, in northern Iraq, after a dramatic troop rescue of Kurdish civilians from along the Turkish border, U.S. and coalition planes provided air cover from bases in Turkey for aid operations carried out largely by UN agencies and NGOs. Lightly armed UN guards lent a largely symbolic international security presence in and around UN humanitarian operations. In the former Yugoslavia, in addition to UNPROFOR troops, unarmed military observers under the European Union Monitoring Mission, military personnel provided by governments as advisors on security and logistics to the UN's humanitarian organizations, and retired military officials who played similar advisory roles to aid agencies were present.

A current policy issue reviewed in later chapters concerns how much of an expanded humanitarian role for military establishments should be created in the post–Cold War era. Although there is no doubt about the greater availability of military personnel and infrastructure thanks to the winding down of East-West tensions, serious questions exist as noted about the appropriateness and utility of the use of force to serve humanitarian objectives, particularly in complex emergencies in which a high degree of politicization and volatility is already present.

In addition to these five sets of external actors, the current international system involves three categories of internal institutional actors, that is, institutions located within a given area at war. The fact that they are outnumbered by external counterparts should not obscure their importance. Local actors play the pivotal role in setting the terms within which external actors function and humanitarian activities are conducted.

This is obviously the case with host governments and their military authorities. In some countries, an existing governmental ministry or ministries serves as the point of contact for outside organizations; in others, an interministerial committee is set up during a given crisis or an existing national NGO is designated as the focal point. Military as well as civilian authorities may be involved at the regional, local, and national levels.

The 1933 Montevideo Convention on the Rights and Duties of States lists sovereignty, permanent population, defined territory, and government as the essential attributes of states. These may be accurate for host governments dealing with natural disasters, but they are more problematic for those engaged in armed conflicts.

Within boundaries inherited from colonial days, many host governments do not represent in a meaningful way the multiplicity of ethnic, religious, and cultural groups. Their effective control may be limited to the capital city and the main export sector, as in the active war theaters of Sri Lanka, Liberia, Afghanistan, and Angola and in wartime Ethiopia and El Salvador as well.

However tenuous or unrepresentative, most host governments must be taken seriously by humanitarian organizations. As in the earlier discussions of humanitarian space, their consent—or at a minimum their acquiescence—is needed for most externally supported humanitarian activities to be sustained.

The roles of insurgent political and military forces are roughly analogous, even if they enjoy less international political and legal standing. These inside actors are the functional equivalent of host governments within the zones under their jurisdiction and play a determining role in establishing the framework within which humanitarian actors operate in areas outside of government control. In some conflicts, insurgent political authorities create special structures to meet the needs of civil populations in the areas they control. Such structures may enjoy greater or lesser independence, depending on the circumstances.

In the case of the insurgents struggling against the government of Ethiopia, the Eritrean People's Liberation Front (EPLF) created the Eritrean Relief Association (ERA) and the Tigrayan People's Liberation Front (TPLF) the Relief Society of Tigray (REST) as points of contact for interested external humanitarian actors. Both aid agencies were central elements in the overall political-military strategy of the parent insurgent groups, but ERA and REST both enjoyed considerable day-to-day independence in carrying out their activities. By contrast, the insurgent Sudanese People's Liberation Movement (SPLM) created the Sudan Relief and Rehabilitation Association (SRRA), which remained on a short leash from the Sudanese People's Liberation Army (SPLA) and its leaders.

Differences in the relative autonomy of agencies in these two sets of circumstances were accentuated by variations in the seriousness and competence with which the respective humanitarian officials approached their tasks. The bona fides of the SRRA, already in question

A briefing for medical volunteers is held in Monrovia, Liberia, in June 1990.
(ICRC Photo/LIBE 90-2/4/R. Sidler)

by virtue of its close relationship to the SPLA, were further impaired by
the caliber and performance of its leaders. However, by 1994 there
were indications that the SRRA leadership was seeking greater independence from its political and military masters.

In other conflicts, insurgent political authorities themselves were
the point of contact with whom external actors dealt on humanitarian
concerns. The Farabundo Martí National Liberation Front played this
role during the civil war in El Salvador. In Bosnia, humanitarian issues
had to be taken up with not only the Bosnian government ministries
but also with Bosnian Serb political and military officials. Many external political and humanitarian actors had difficulties relating to insurgencies, even on humanitarian issues.

The final category of internal actors is composed of national and local NGOs. Nongovernmental groups exist in virtually every conflict
area, although there is variation in how much necessary humanitarian
space they have. They vary in number and vitality, in degree of independence from political authorities, and in technical capacity for comprehensive and autonomous activities.

In El Salvador, for example, there was a plethora of such organizations during the civil war of the 1980s. In stark contrast, the devastation of the Pol Pot years was such that few indigenous Cambodian institutions survived and represented ready points of contact for external humanitarian actors. Reviewing the situation in 1991 as it prepared to launch a major reconstruction effort, the United Nations concluded that there were no Cambodians at all in the country with the requisite skills in macroeconomic planning. By contrast, at the time of the major international humanitarian initiative in 1992, Somalia's civil institutions had been seriously ravaged by famine and warfare. Yet local leadership and structures existed in the form of religious elders and subclan figures who could have been more fully enlisted.

Indigenous NGOs often include religious, civic, and philanthropic organizations and national Red Cross and Red Crescent societies. In many countries, they exist at the regional, local, and national levels. Like their external counterparts, internal NGOs have grown more important in recent years, both as actors in their own right and as channels through which outside humanitarian institutions may reach affected populations.

This presentation of definitions, legal context, and analytical categories establishes the basis for the chapters that follow. Chapter 2 will outline fundamental values that underpin humanitarian action and help clarify the fit between existing organizations and challenges.

# 2
# Guiding Principles

The uncertain political moment, the various understandings of what constitutes the humanitarian, and the plethora of humanitarian actors raise the question of whether there are indeed principles common to humanitarian action in all forms and circumstances. Do centrifugal pressures overpower those centripetal tendencies that might hold humanitarian action together and provide some coherence throughout this diverse community of organizations?

The factors that work against there being any common set of guiding principles are formidable. The diversity of humanitarian actors is mind-boggling. On the one hand are organizations with virtually universal presence. UNICEF has programs, personnel, and national support committees to assist women and children in well over 100 countries, touching the lives of more than 12 million persons a year. The activities of the UN High Commissioner for Refugees, which in 1993 involved more than 3,700 staff in Geneva and 177 field offices in 106 countries, affect some 20 million people a year. On the other hand are agencies with very focused mandates, such as the relief of vitamin A deficiency and river blindness, or very localized activities, such as the Wisconsin Partners for Nicaragua and the Convoy of Mercy in the former Yugoslavia.

The scale of such programs also varies greatly. At the global level, UN organizations tend to command the most resources, followed by bilateral aid organizations such as the U.S. Agency for International Development and the Canadian International Development Agency (CIDA). But UN and bilateral resources in a given country may be exceeded by the operating budgets of NGOs such as Oxfam or Save the Children, and the levels of activity of the government's own social welfare ministries may pale by comparison. In the former Yugoslavia, a single $50

Kuwaitis supply information about missing relatives at a registration center in Kuwait City. (UN Photo 158120/J. Isaac)

million contribution from financier George Soros dwarfed the resources available to most agencies.

Some organizations carry out humanitarian activities in virtually every emergency, be it in UNITA-controlled Angola, northern Iraq, Haiti under international sanctions, or sanction-free Croatia. Others are more selective in their involvement, picking and choosing their conflicts. Rather than mounting their own programs, some agencies provide resources in the form of funds, personnel, or materiel to front-line agencies that do the job themselves. Some do not operate indirectly or directly but publicize emergencies and press governments and aid organizations to respond.

Some organizations have programs that are managed by the latest technology and by senior executives on salaries comparable to their counterparts' in business and industry. Others are no-frills agencies with anything but up-to-date communications systems and with staff who volunteer or work for subsistence wages. Some organizations have been around for more than a century; others come and go in response to specific needs, whether in Biafra, Bosnia, Vietnam, or Guatemala. Some aid personnel move comfortably in government circles; others eschew contact with the political sphere and are more comfortable working on the front lines and in the trenches.

Organizations also differ in their approach to prevailing law and custom. The International Committee of the Red Cross is recognized by name in international humanitarian law; in fact, humanitarian action is defined by the kinds of activities the ICRC carries out. Other institutions function without reference to that law and are prepared to violate statutes or understandings of sovereignty in order to assist across recognized international boundaries.

Viewed from outside of the conflicts, the major actors are the *external* humanitarian organizations, based primarily in industrialized countries. They tend to reflect the interests and concerns of governments, their parliaments and constituencies, and people voluntarily banding together for religious or moral reasons. Countries that are the scenes of tragedies have their own humanitarian institutions that mirror local religious traditions and patterns of social organization and play a major role in addressing human suffering.

Most of the organizations that make up this diverse universe share a commitment to the relief of suffering and the protection of human life. They have a common set of overarching principles that guide their disparate and far-flung activities. For some, the principles are carefully articulated and observed; for others, they are at best implicit and provide only the most general guidance. Most agencies approach principles not so much as moral absolutes but as norms toward which they strive. Nevertheless, general adherence to basic principles broadly defines membership in the humanitarian community.

Eight guiding principles have emerged from analyses of recent and current wars and from interviews with humanitarian practitioners around the world. They have been dubbed the Providence Principles because they first took shape at a meeting in 1991 at Brown University.[1] This chapter elaborates these eight principles, using illustrations from recent experiences in a range of settings.

## Relieving Life-Threatening Suffering

At the heart of the humanitarian impulse is the desire to relieve immediate life-threatening suffering. Springing from that impulse is the international humanitarian enterprise, the organized global effort to meet the needs of the world's people at risk. Humanitarian action seeks to decrease the numbers of those in need and ameliorate their suffering.

Today's news abounds in human misery. More than thirty-five major armed conflicts are raging. According to such expert chroniclers as Ruth Sivard,[2] who annually compiles comparative data on such matters, "major" means conflicts in which one or more governments are involved and at least a thousand people lose their lives each year. Most people are doubtless familiar with the mayhem in Bosnia and the massive distress in Somalia, but the extent of civil strife in Liberia and the Philippines may not have come to their attention.

Major humanitarian crises have other indicators beyond the tally of deaths in active warfare. The number of refugees and asylum seekers at the end of 1993 stood at about 20 million, a figure that has grown by a factor of more than six in twenty years. Still another group of 4 million to 5 million persons, unable to return home for fear of persecution or harm, lack formal refugee or asylum-seeker status. Another 25 million persons have not crossed an international border but have nonetheless been uprooted by violence within their own countries.[3]

The figures on the number of people facing life-threatening suffering change from year to year. In 1992, about 2 million refugees re-

turned to their homes in Afghanistan and Cambodia. At the same time, 3 million others fled ethnic conflagration in the former Yugoslavia and Soviet republics, the long-running war in Mozambique, human rights violations by the military government in Burma, and the chaos in Somalia.

As of 1993, the combined tally of the uprooted stood at about 45 million. This total is roughly the population of France or twice that of Central America. It is also as changeable as the people themselves. For example, 700,000 refugees appeared on the international scene in late 1993 as the result of the failed coup d'état in Burundi. In April 1994, amid resurgent tribal warfare between majority Hutus and minority Tutsis in Rwanda following the deaths of the presidents of Rwanda and Burundi in a plane crash, some 200,000 people were killed and a new wave of close to half a million refugees fled the country. Unfortunately, the global trend of displacement is upward. It is charted in a new series of annual reviews published for the first time in 1993 by the United Nations Office of the High Commissioner for Refugees.[4]

Migration, involuntary or voluntary, has been described as the preeminent human crisis of the day. A 1993 UN report described migration as "the visible face of social change," noting that it is "a barometer of changing social, economic and political circumstances, at the national and international level." Sounding a cautionary note, the UN observed that "the growth of a global economy has emphasized rather than reduced inequality between nations." At the end of the 1980s, 1 person in every 100 lived outside the country in which he was born.[5]

Fortunately, not all of the world's uprooted people are in life-threatening situations. Some are economic migrants who have found greener pastures abroad or more remunerative jobs in urban areas within their own countries. Many, however, have traded domestic poverty for international vulnerability, or rural misery in familiar surroundings for urban distress in strange metropolises. Whether they have sought refuge abroad or make up part of the population of the internally displaced in what are called refugee-like situations, the uprooted make up the primary group in need of urgent humanitarian attention. Resourcefulness and resilience may come to their aid, but the uprooting can do violence to their ability to provide for themselves.

As noted earlier, like the familiar "loud emergencies" in Yugoslavia and Somalia, Liberia and the West Bank and Gaza Strip, "silent emergencies" affect large population groups in so-called developed and developing countries throughout the world. Current data indicate that 1 billion of the world's citizens live in conditions of absolute poverty, unable to meet minimum requirements for food, clothing, and shelter. Many others are precariously close to such poverty. In recent years, persons on the margin have come to be called the two-thirds world, a term that underscores both their sheer numbers and their location in rich and poor countries alike.[6]

Although persons suffering in silent emergencies are not the specific focus of this study, they constitute a major element in the broader challenge to the global humanitarian community, especially when war breaks out, because they have so little margin for maneuver and so few reserves. Moreover, international objectives for those who suffer grinding poverty and underdevelopment and for those pinned down by gunfire or victimized by human rights abuses are the same: to make it possible for people to live in dignity in their own countries or, if that is not possible, then elsewhere.

The daily challenge confronting the international community is expressed by the familiar images of stick-like children in Baidoa in 1992 and the grimacing faces of the old and the young crammed into trucks leaving Srebrenica in 1993. Although it is a basic principle that life-threatening suffering merits and requires relief, much such human need goes unattended. Current humanitarian activities are frequently scattershot and fragmentary, stop-gap and ineffective. Instead of acting with dispatch on humanitarian concerns, the international community frequently settles for a lethargic or otherwise ineffective response.

In today's global village, people who would have suffered in anonymity a generation or two ago are now visible, assaulting the world's conscience. "If you watch TV and then go to bed," observed an Italian woman in mid-1993, troubled by events in the former Yugoslavia, "what you have seen unconsciously works in your head. You cannot forget the families, the children, the animals, the towns, the soldiers, the hospital where the staff locked the children in and left." Struggling to put her thoughts into words, she concluded, "We know there's a war and in wars bad things happen, but it is hard to accept these kinds of things. I myself cannot accept the fact that the war is killing people in this way."[7]

Translating widely shared revulsion into effective programs to relieve suffering and to protect human rights, however, is not easy. Yet there is no place to hide from the need for prompt and sustained humanitarian action. The ties that bind the human family together to relieve life-threatening suffering also enmesh it in patterns of commerce and consumption, consumer imports and arms exports, politics and tourism, and in the conflict and poverty that require response.[8]

**Proportionality**

Confronted by human suffering and misery, how does the global humanitarian community decide where to respond and what action to take? The second principle is that humanitarian action should correspond to the degree of suffering, wherever it occurs.

From a humanitarian standpoint, the idea that human life is equally precious everywhere in the world seems self-evident. In practice, however, the world's humanitarian system has great difficulty putting flesh on that proposition.

When a tragedy of major proportions was brewing in Liberia in 1990, some humanitarian groups and diplomats sought to turn the UN Security Council's attention to the bloody civil war between the forces of President Samuel Doe and those of Charles Taylor, who were eventually joined in the mayhem by Prince Johnson. By early August, 1.5 million Liberians had been displaced, some within their own country, others fleeing abroad.

In spite of this cataclysm, the world's highest political body was pre-occupied with the August 1990 invasion of Kuwait that prompted the flight of 850,000 third-country nationals and 300,000 Palestinians. In an effort to force Iraq's withdrawal from Kuwait, the council imposed first economic and then military sanctions against the Baghdad authorities. In the wake of the upheaval in northern Iraq following the end of the war against Iraq, the Security Council addressed the plight of 1.5 million Iraqis who fled to the Turkish border and into Iran.

Although the Security Council did not err in addressing the problems of the Persian Gulf, other major crises were shortchanged as a result. The contrast is particularly striking in that for several months in 1990 the numbers of persons affected and the degree of their distress were greater in Liberia than in the Persian Gulf. The disparate responses to the two simultaneous upheavals offered dramatic proof of the disproportionality that afflicts the current system. The international community moved swiftly to return guest workers fleeing Kuwait to their countries of origin and to provide food and shelter to Iraqi Kurds in the mountains along the Turkish border. Rescuing and protecting Liberians in Monrovia and the countryside and assisting those who had fled to neighboring Sierra Leone were not a priority.

Examples of such disproportionality abound. In December 1992, when the UN Security Council authorized military action in Somalia, an equally serious situation existed in nearby Sudan. During the six months following the December landing of U.S. troops, international expenditures for military and humanitarian activities reached $1 billion in Somalia. These dwarfed comparable expenditures in the Sudan, where no fewer people were at risk of starvation. Even more striking was the fact that the protection of aid operations was the stated reason for the intervention in Somalia, which cost about ten times the value of emergency relief. Yet at the time of the December 1992 landing by U.S. troops, more humanitarian personnel already had been killed in the Sudan.

Illustrations like these identify a major weakness of the world's current humanitarian safety net. It does not have built-in mechanisms to ensure that it will respond with proportionality to simultaneous instances of human need. A decade or a generation ago, lack of adequate information about the nature and extent of the suffering or an ideologically based reluctance to act might have been at fault. Today, early warning information about explosive situations is usually available, and East-West constraints have abated. Yet the world's responses often remain uneven and disproportionate.

There is every reason to construct a system to handle major crises simultaneously. After all, the world's military establishments prepare for multiple crises in very different parts of the world. Comparable humanitarian infrastructure could be designed to respond with balance and dispatch to concurrent challenges. If such an infrastructure were in place, activities around the world would not suffer when, as in 1992 and 1993, UNHCR committed about half its annual budget to the former Yugoslavia, or when, as in 1991 and 1992, ICRC earmarked half of its total resources to Somalia.

It would be gratifying to report that based on the world's accumulated experience, humanitarian action has become more proportionate and measured over time. The passing of the Cold War was expected to make it easier to allocate resources in accordance with human need; however, two factors have frustrated such hopes.

First, the easing of East-West conflict has left the world with a monumental backlog of unfinished and long-delayed humanitarian business. The enormous suffering of civilians and the massive destruction of economic and social resources in the places where the Cold War was played out are now evident beyond any doubt. During the war, the human consequences of superpower jousting was downplayed by an overriding focus on political considerations; now, the human damages and the looming cost of reconstruction are beyond dispute.

Before he assumed his current position as U.S. national security advisor, Anthony Lake edited a review of the devastation of Cold War–related destruction and the companion costs of reconstruction in Afghanistan, Indochina, Central America, southern Africa, and the Horn of Africa. "In these five areas," he wrote, "more than 15 million people have left their homes to become internal or external refugees. … [T]he devastation includes not only the dead and displaced people, but also livestock lost, schools and clinics destroyed, and many missed years of economic production," Lake called for an international fund for reconstruction on the order of the Marshall Plan.[9]

Ironies abound. During the Cold War, there was no shortage of funding for land mines and other antipersonnel weapons. Today, millions of unexploded land mines dot the landscape of developing countries, from Cambodia to Angola, from Afghanistan to Mozambique. Yet the resources for the more expensive and more laborious task of demining, a prelude to agricultural reconstruction and social rebuilding for the affected societies, are proving elusive.

Second, reduced tensions between Washington and Moscow have been followed, paradoxically, by growing violence. Reduced East-West rivalry has ushered in more overt expression of historical grievances. "It is a wonderful thing that the Cold War is over," stated U.S. President Bill Clinton. "But the end of the bipolar world has made it possible … in some parts of the world for people to be starved, brutalized and killed with much greater abandon."[10]

Changes in the former Soviet Union and Eastern Europe have led to a massive expansion of the human suffering to which the international community is obliged to respond. The U.S. government estimates that the geographical area potentially served by its international disaster office has expanded by one fifth since the end of the Cold War. The new areas include an additional 1.2 billion potentially vulnerable people.

Of course, a measured response to suffering should take into account the resources available locally. The resources on hand to address emergencies in Tajikistan and Azerbaijan may exceed those available within less economically advanced settings such as Eritrea and Mozambique. The principle of proportionality does not mean that victims of urban violence in Los Angeles and Belfast exercise the same claim on international resources as their counterparts in Colombo or Kigali. The respective wealth and wherewithal of the United States, United Kingdom, Sri Lanka, and Rwanda have a clear bearing on the residual responsibilities of the international community. Despite infant mortality and life expectancy rates in sections of Washington, D.C., that are worse than those in Port-au-Prince, Haitian suffering should obviously exercise a greater claim than American suffering on international action. Even so, the competition for international attention and assistance is heightened by cataclysmic geopolitical changes, which are stretching the already overextended humanitarian safety net virtually to the breaking point.

Responding with proportionality also requires difficult choices regarding competing claims on limited resources for emergency assistance and for poverty alleviation and development activities. In recent years, donor governments have shown greater inclination to respond to the "loud" emergencies. In 1992, U.S. emergency assistance for the first time exceeded U.S. development assistance to Africa.[11] It is standard practice for a crisis in country $x$ to receive reduced allocations because of pledges to country $y$. UN efforts receive fewer resources from governments because of efforts that they prefer to make on a bilateral basis. International needs receive less because of the claims of hungry people at home in donor countries and because of efforts by industrialized nations to reduce spending.

A further deterrent to proportionality is the increasing pressure for triage, as noted throughout this book. With resources growing tighter and donors feeling overwhelmed, the apparent need for selecting among the needy escalates. It is costlier to aid people in civil wars and less sure that they will be spared later violence. Proportionality thus involves considerations beyond the application of a standard per capita expenditure in crises around the world.

In sum, the idea of proportionality may make eminently good sense, but the allocation of humanitarian resources according to the severity of human need is an exceedingly complex challenge. A mathematically precise division of all international resources among those at risk would not do justice to different levels of suffering and to varying local capacities. Yet a division strictly according to where investments could be used most effectively would not be just, since it would penalize persons in dire straits due to factors beyond their control.

There is no "invisible hand," either within a given agency or among humanitarian institutions as a whole, that ensures equitable resource distribution among the world's armed conflicts. The solution, however, is not to abandon the effort but to put in place arrangements to achieve greater proportionality taking these key variables into account.

### Nonpartisanship

If the relief of life-threatening suffering is undercut by disproportionate allocations of limited resources, it is also compromised when political considerations are injected into lifesaving ministrations. A third guiding principle is that humanitarian action responds to suffering because people are in need, not to advance political, religious, or other extraneous agendas. When human need results from internal or international strife, humanitarian agencies should not take sides in the conflict.

In an interview in early 1993, the Commissioner of Refugees of the Republic of Serbia, Dobrica Vulovic, offered a telling illustration of how outside agendas can infiltrate humanitarian activity. As a government official operating in the highly politicized atmosphere of the conflicts in the former Yugoslavia, Vulovic nevertheless sought to carry out his humanitarian responsibilities with dispassion and professionalism. Yet politicization abounded.

The government of the Federal Republic of Yugoslavia, headed by Slobodan Milosevic, denied refugee status to Bosnian Serbs of military age while granting it to their wives and children. The regime feared that once they qualified as refugees, these men would be lost to the

Serb cause. But the international community, too, politicized refugee issues by providing less assistance to the Bosnian Muslim refugees who fled east to Serbia than to similar refugees who sought asylum to the west in Croatia. In that 1993 interview, the commissioner told the story as he and many other Serbs saw it:

> Serbia had offered hospitality to refugees fleeing the war in neighboring Bosnia, Muslims and Serbs alike. The refugees, though victims of the same war, are punished for the very simple reason that they've escaped across the Drina River to Serbia and Montenegro. The children are suffering, the elderly are suffering, and they are still forgotten. Even the international organizations of the UN could not help them because the countries financing those agencies have insisted on a very restrictive approach. Those countries have decided to assist the refugees with their own hands, taking such persons into their own homes and providing them with the available social services.

The commissioner was unhappy on several counts. First, refugees in Serbia and Montenegro had received far less attention and succor than other victims of the breakup of the former Yugoslavia. Second, the world was making the Federal Republic of Yugoslavia suffer for a war for which other parties—the Croatians in Croatia and Bosnia, the Bosnian Muslims, and the Bosnian Serbs—also bore responsibility.

Moreover, by levying economic sanctions against Serbia and Montenegro in May 1992 and tightening them in April 1993, the international community sought to force the Milosevic government to change its policies of "ethnic cleansing." Although the arms embargo of September 1991 had benefited the Serbs, who controlled the bulk of the military assets of the armed forces of the former Yugoslavia, the economic sanctions were seen as singling them out for punishment.

The impact on humanitarian activities of the perceived anti-Serb animus was demonstrably negative. The strategy introduced what the UN chief of humanitarian operations in Serbia and Montenegro, UNHCR's Judith Kumin, termed "a fundamental contradiction: trying to implement a humanitarian program in a sanctions environment." The UN was, in effect, trying to deny assistance and to provide it at one and the same time.

UN schizophrenia was felt with particular intensity by its own humanitarian agencies, which sought to provide nonpartisan assistance

Refugees from Bosnia arrive in Serbia in May 1992 in a wagon that also serves as their shelter. (UNHCR Photo/22036/05.1992/A. Hollman)

to people whose needs were adversely affected by economic pressure meted out by the same United Nations. In fact, at a time when UN humanitarian activities were geared toward reaching about 500,000 beneficiaries, the population whose health status was imperiled by the UN embargo was several times that number. Similar dilemmas have been created for the UN's humanitarian agencies in northern Iraq, Haiti, and other such locations.

Commissioner Vulovic viewed "donor fatigue" as a pretext for political animosity. Governments whose politics had overridden their sense of humanity were using an alleged shortage of resources to rationalize limiting assistance. As a result, even the aid provided was viewed with suspicion and disdain.

Despite the fact that Vulovic worked for a pariah state, his outrage reflected a sentiment widely shared in Serbia, among other government officials and the public: "The injection of politics into humanitarian matters," said a senior Foreign Ministry official, "represents a violation of all humanitarian norms and of even the most elementary moral and ethical standards that an individual is entitled to." The point is legitimate. One clear test of the integrity of the world's humanitarian system is precisely whether it treats distressed civilian populations in pariah states as fairly as it does civilian populations elsewhere.

The fact that the principle of nonpartisanship is regularly abused does not mean that it should be abandoned. In debates in the UN General Assembly in late 1991, Brazilian Ambassador Ronald Mota Sardenberg made an eloquent appeal of preserving the apolitical nature of humanitarian assistance. "Humanitarian activities," he said, "must by definition be disassociated from all shades of political consideration. They are, by definition, neutral and impartial." The ambassador observed:

> Not by chance was the notion of humanitarian activities developed in connection with situations of armed conflict. The secret of effectiveness in the humanitarian field is that even when nations disagree on everything else, even when they clash, they can still agree that the wounded must be assisted, that the sick must receive adequate care, that suffering must be relieved. That is a minimal straight line drawn in the crooked timber of humanity. It is the fact that agreement on such a core of minimum values is discernible ... that makes humanitarian action possible.[12]

To emphasize the apolitical essence of humanitarian action is not to deny that relief and protection have political ramifications. International humanitarian activities sometimes affect delicate political and military balances. They may relieve political authorities of their responsibility for meeting the needs of their populations, afford them greater freedom to use existing resources for other purposes, and help them win enhanced respect at home and abroad. Such political repercussions may often be unavoidable, but humanitarian organizations need to anticipate, acknowledge, and monitor them.[13] Yet the likelihood of such political impacts do not constitute grounds for refraining from action, any more than the likelihood of such an impact should constitute grounds for taking action.

Views of the relative importance of nonpartisanship differ among humanitarians. A central factor in all wars is that warring parties seek to press all available instruments into the service of their cause. The instruments at their disposal include financial and human resources from their own citizenry, domestic and international public opinion, and, of course, outside humanitarian assistance.

In fact, many civil wars find the protagonists using not only humanitarian aid but also access to populations in need of such assistance as weapons in their struggles. The more intense and desperate the battle, the greater the perceived importance of harnessing outside humanitarian resources, access, and agencies for their cause.

From the standpoint of such agencies, there are practical reasons to avoid being drawn into the conflict and taking sides. Taking sides identifies agencies with a political agenda, such as liberation from oppression, or with a political strategy, such as the use of violence, and thus may undermine humanitarian principles.

Faced with the denial of access, some organizations will not provide aid to persons in areas controlled by any side unless and until they can provide aid to those on all sides. Others are prepared to help in one area even if they are not granted access elsewhere. The experience of two organizations in the Sudan's civil war illustrates the differing approaches and results.

The International Committee of the Red Cross carried out painstaking negotiations from March through December 1988 with government authorities in Khartoum and the insurgent Sudanese People's Liberation Movement. Finally it won agreement to make relief deliveries to an equal number of locations on both sides. Negotiations occurred at a time when both sides were fully prepared to deny assistance to civilians in areas that they controlled in order to prevent aid from reaching people in areas controlled by their opponents. Now as then, the ICRC considers the principle of impartiality so important that it waits to begin humanitarian activities until all parties agree to cooperate. The pursuit of this principle is not without costs. During the year consumed in negotiating the necessary agreement, an estimated 250,000 persons died from war and famine.

Catholic Relief Services, a U.S. NGO confronting the same suffering at the same time, took a different approach. It believed that making efforts to reach people within the insurgent-controlled areas of the southern Sudan contingent upon prior agreement with Khartoum would reinforce the logic of the civil war and the use of food as a political instrument. CRS therefore mounted a relief operation from neighboring Kenya and Uganda, crossing into Sudanese territory without

Khartoum's permission. The scale of its efforts and those of other church-related organizations was modest, but it did succeed in preventing some starvation. Building on its experience, CRS subsequently approved a new policy that states its preference "to assist victims on both sides of the conflict unless needs on one side are met by other groups or unless operational considerations preclude working on both sides."[14]

From the beginning of time, belligerents have used civilian access to essential food and medicine as a weapon in their political and military arsenals. They also have denied or granted access according to whether doing so served their short-term objectives. Civil wars are by definition situations in which countries are divided against themselves. Thus, humanitarian actors should anticipate efforts to manipulate their activities and to align them with one or another belligerent, however scrupulously evenhanded they try to be. Yet as a matter of principle and practicality, humanitarian action should not promote a particular political, religious, or ethnic agenda, solidify the loyalty of a particular group or geographical area, dampen disaffection, or preempt insurrection.

### Independence

To be effective, humanitarian action should be able to respond to life-threatening suffering without interference. Independence is required from political authorities in areas where activities take place and from those in donor countries. Independence is needed not only for government and intergovernmental aid organizations that express the will of political constituencies. It is also indispensable for private organizations that are motivated by people-to-people impulses.

Belligerents have found various ways to harness humanitarian activities for immediate political benefit, just as outside groups have found ways to maximize their own independence. In fact, the conflicting dynamics of political and military actors often lead to an ongoing contest of wills within the larger context of a given war.

Seated governments normally turn first to existing ministries for services to people in the areas that they control. In its war with the Contras, the Nicaraguan government did this through the ministries of health, education, and agriculture. In addition, early in the war it created the Nicaraguan Social Security and Welfare Institute (INSSBI) to

maintain contact with the more than 150 private organizations providing aid. Through the INSSBI, nongovernmental organizations coordinated their work with the respective government departments that
were active in the field.

While engaged in intense fighting with the Contras, the Sandinista
regime also reached out to meet civilian needs, except among the Mi-
skito Indians along the Atlantic coast and in areas controlled directly
by the Contras. The social policy of the government corresponded to
the philosophy and inclination of many NGOs, which therefore
cooperated closely with government ministries at the national and local level. As a result, NGOs became identified with the government's
programs and implicitly accepted the restrictions on their ability to
function in areas where the government was suspect.

Late in the 1980s, as the civil war grew in intensity and the competition for the loyalty of civilian populations increased, government policies and tactics became more politicized and less humane. Many NGOs
realized that their sympathy with Sandinista social objectives had in
fact blinded them to the need for greater independence. In retrospect,
many participants hold that humanitarian organizations must strive
to maintain autonomy even from regimes that seem well intentioned.

The contrast to the situation in neighboring El Salvador was stark.
Salvadoran government officials sought from the outset to press international aid more thoroughly into the service of their political-military game plan. In 1982 the National Commission for the Displaced

(CONADES) sought and received international resources to promote activities situated firmly within the military's counter-insurgency strategy. There was such an obvious lack of convergence between humanitarian objectives and government policies that private agencies had every reason to establish their independence from the start and to guard it zealously from day to day. Equal vigilance was called for in dealing with the insurgencies in each country.

A comparison from the Horn of Africa dramatizes differing approaches to maintaining space for independent action. Each of the insurgencies battling the Ethiopian government created a civilian agency to coordinate outside aid groups and to work with the relevant ministries to facilitate assistance.

Although each organization reported to insurgent political authorities, each also enjoyed a certain degree of freedom. Believing that their cause would be served if the needs of civilian populations were effectively met, the insurgents allowed ERA and REST considerable autonomy. A recent evaluation has concluded that even though more independence would have been desirable, ERA was an effective and businesslike operation that was granted a certain humanitarian space by the EPLF.[15]

The contrast nearby in the Sudan was dramatic. SPLM, which declared war on the Khartoum government in 1983, formed the Sudan Relief and Rehabilitation Association to provide a point of contact with outside aid organizations. The SRRA had a division of labor among its officials, with duties throughout SPLM-controlled regions in the south parceled out in such areas as health, agriculture, and education. The absence of local government revenue heightened the importance of outside aid to the conduct of social services.

The SRRA was staffed with officials from the military, was continuously subject to pressure from insurgent commanders, and was rife with mismanagement and other abuses. It never achieved anything like the minimal independence requisite for serious humanitarian activity. When a fissure developed in the SPLA and a new faction emerged, it rescinded the need for such an instrument and created the Relief Association of the Southern Sudan (RASS). The new humanitarian focal point, however, has not been without problems of its own.

Earlier, humanitarian space was seen to be constrained by such government practices as visa requirements, travel permits, exchange regulations, rules governing hiring local staff, and concurrence regarding the location and nature of program activities. Such regulations may be imposed by insurgencies as well as by recognized governments. Although some such movements may be more dependent on outside support than governments, they are not necessarily more ready to provide independence to aid agencies.

The Red Cross and Red Crescent family of agencies illustrates both the difficulty and the desirability of preserving independence. Independence is, in fact, one of its seven articulated principles. In actual practice, however, independence is difficult to establish and maintain, especially at the national and local levels. As civic institutions, national Red Cross and Red Crescent societies normally include government representatives on their boards of directors. Eight of the fifty members of the American Red Cross Society board serve by virtue of their positions in the U.S. government. The president of the Red Cross in the Federal Republic of Yugoslavia is the mayor of Belgrade; in Montenegro, a well-known politician famous for his inflammatory rhetoric on ethnic issues holds the post. Although government connections do not necessarily make Red Cross activities an extension of the political process, independent humanitarian action may become more problematic as a result.

The International Committee of the Red Cross has a comparative advantage within the movement in this respect. Its home base in Switzerland and its reliance on Swiss nationals as heads of country delegations underscore its independence. So important is the perception of independence that some ICRC officials questioned whether their effectiveness would be undercut when Switzerland voted in 1992 for association with the European Union.

Independence is a perennial challenge for other NGOs as well. Many groups such as Doctors Without Borders, Save the Children, and CARE receive funds and supplies not only from publics in their own countries but also from donor governments and intergovernmental organizations. Such funds may have their own sets of policy or political constraints, reporting requirements, program inflexibilities, procurement restrictions, and other procedures that directly or indirectly influence NGO program priorities.

For example, U.S. assistance to Afghan refugees along the Pakistan border (and, for that matter, Soviet aid to Afghanis who remained within Afghanistan) was an extension of the superpowers' confrontation. Humanitarian groups working in refugee camps along the border and carrying out cross-border operations functioned very much as well within the framework established by the various *mujaheddin* groups, whose principal activity was, of course, military resistance to the Kabul regime and its Soviet patrons. The dramatic decline in aid by the United States and the USSR in the wake of the Cold War's end underscored the extent to which humanitarian efforts all along had been an extension of the broader global political-military struggle, not an independent humanitarian initiative in its own right.

Even in the early post–Cold War era, the independence of humanitarian action underwritten by donor governments is not assured. Some NGOs therefore continue as a matter of principle to refuse all contributions from governments. Similar considerations in the past have led other agencies to fix an upper limit on the value of contributions from governments in proportion to those received from other sources. Other NGOs have no fixed percentages but make decisions on a case-by-case, country-by-country, government-by-government basis. Still others find no difficulties in having governments function as their majority stockholders.

Although the passing of the Cold War has freed humanitarian action from traditional East-West constraints, most humanitarian organizations are aware of the need to keep their relations with all political authorities, donor and host, government and insurgent alike, under continuous review. Ongoing vigilance is in order since political and humanitarian agendas will never permanently converge, however compatible they may appear at a given point in time.

## Accountability

The fifth guiding principle is that humanitarian actors must be fully accountable to sponsors and beneficiaries for their activities. Once again, however, this apparent common-sense principle has far-reaching consequences.

Virtually all humanitarian organizations consider themselves accountable for the resources with which they are entrusted. United Nations organizations report to member governments that make up their governing boards. Donor governments see their parliaments and taxpayers as their primary overseers. Private agencies have their own policymaking entities that exercise control. The core issue is not whether activities should be accountable but rather how such accountability should be defined, implemented, monitored, and enforced.

In its most obvious sense, accountability means that humanitarian organizations are financially responsible for their expenditures. Humanitarian assistance should reach those for whom it is intended without diversion, graft, or corruption. Action to protect human rights should be mounted in efficient ways that reduce the actual or potential abuse of those rights.

That said, assisting and protecting people is not an enterprise like manufacturing cars, producing airline meals, or publishing books. Try as they may, few humanitarian organizations can say at year's end that they have provided $x$ number of people with emergency food and shelter and have prevented human rights abuses to $y$ number of people at cost per person of $z$ dollars.

Humanitarian "bottom lines" are problematic for several reasons. First, it is difficult to determine how many people are in need and how many of them have been reached with assistance. Organizations often are denied access to conflict zones or detention centers to assess the numbers and conditions of those to be assisted and protected. Field conditions make it difficult to get pertinent data and keep it current.

Second, there are trade-offs between good faith efforts to relieve suffering and to ensure appropriate accountability. Lifesaving action may not leave the desired audit trail. Organizations that repatriate refugees or run health programs in relatively stable situations may be expected to keep accurate beneficiary tallies, but how would it be possible to evaluate the number of people benefiting from high-altitude airdrops of food and medicine into Muslim enclaves in eastern Bosnia? In settings where humanitarian action is most urgently needed, it may be virtually impossible to determine precisely what goes where. A slavish adherence to strict standards of accountability could be the enemy of creative action.

In fact, rigorous standards sometimes have been imposed specifically to curtail the flow of resources. In the 1980s, the U.S. government often demanded the most detailed accounting of its resources in government-controlled parts of Nicaragua where it preferred not to see them used. At the same time it accepted more relaxed standards for NGOs working in Contra-controlled areas or with refugees outside of Nicaragua altogether. Annual reports by the U.S. State Department reviewing human rights violations on a country-by-country basis have on occasion been less critical of abuses by friendly governments than of those by others.

There are serious difficulties even when politicization does not skew accountability. In late 1992, when deaths from starvation in Somalia had climbed to an estimated 3,000 per day, news organizations reported that only about 10–20 percent of relief supplies were reaching famine-affected people. Whether the leakage was 50 percent or 80 percent, substantial amounts of food ended up in the wrong hands while it was being transported from the port of Mogadishu to warehouses in the city and beyond. Large quantities went to the now infamous "technicals"—armed local gunmen who were hired to accompany relief personnel on their rounds—and to violent elements who wrested food from recipients at feeding centers. Some ended up in local markets as well. Had normal accountability been required, many feeding activities would have been suspended.

Third, carrying out programs during armed conflicts is far more expensive than in natural disasters or in development settings. In Operation Lifeline Sudan, the cost of transporting relief supplies, normally about $300 per ton, climbed to as much as $2,000 per ton. Costs were high because a late start required the use of planes instead of barges or trucks. The approaching rainy season meant that supplies had to be moved quickly. Suspicious of relief shipments, the warring parties insisted that all supplies going to areas they controlled originate in those same areas. Operations in active war zones raised not only transport costs but also such items as insurance for equipment and personnel. Most important for accountability, activities required much greater monitoring and thus generated much higher personnel costs. That is only one of the ways in which humanitarian organizations working in conflicts pay a kind of war tax. Small wonder that assistance in active war zones is often ten to twenty times more costly than elsewhere.

Many humanitarian organizations do not have clear ground rules on such matters. A carte blanche approach—that is, that saving lives is of such importance that no expense should be spared—may be justified in exceptional circumstances. However, as conflicts become more endemic and the cost of lifesaving ministrations escalates, contributors and agencies alike need clearer terms of reference. The lack of comparable data from various crises to establish a reasonable range of expenditures complicates the situation.

In addition to quantitative and financial issues, accountability involves complex policy judgments. Should aid organizations be accountable for assuring that only civilians benefit from relief supplies? A reasonable expectation on its face, the proposition becomes difficult when wars are waged by individuals who are farmers one day and warriors the next. How should aid officials be expected to respond to the Bosnian military officer who scoffed at the idea that the beneficiaries of UN food would be limited to women and children? "Our fighting men are the hope of our women and children," he insisted.

Should aid agencies be held accountable for violence associated with their activities? In Somalia, evidence suggests that food aid inserted into an otherwise nonfunctioning economy became the major form of currency. Humanitarian groups, which were also paying protection fees, appear to have contributed to the prevailing violence, even carrying it with them as they moved into the countryside. Such negative side effects may be beyond the power of humanitarian actors to avoid altogether, but they do have a certain responsibility to anticipate and minimize them. There may even be occasions when they should be expected to reduce or suspend activities. Some agencies believe, in retrospect, that they should have done so in Somalia.

One of the essential ingredients of accountability is transparency, a quality very much in keeping with humanitarian action itself, which by definition has no secret agendas and nothing to hide. Given an atmosphere in armed conflicts characterized by suspicion and intrigue,

Patients wait in a medical center in Jilib, Somalia, operated by Doctors Without Borders. (UN Photo 159776/M. Grant)

transparency is a safeguard against the perception, sometimes used to discredit aid activities, that humanitarians are working hand in glove with political or military authorities.

Humanitarian groups differ on the relative value of transparency. Few are comfortable with covert action, but some believe that on occasion secrecy is essential. There may be occasions when transparency would limit the ability of agencies to assist or protect civilians. Had the cross-border activities of NGOs into insurgent-controlled Liberia been publicly known, their efforts in Monrovia might have been jeopardized. Acting openly is important, but saving lives is more so.

Accountability involves responsibility not only to providers of international resources but to the intended beneficiaries. "For accountability relationships to work in practice," concluded a 1982 set of UN guidelines for assistance after disasters, "donors and recipients alike must acknowledge their mutual responsibilities and all that this implies."[16]

Practitioner organizations have found various ways to involve beneficiaries or their representatives in humanitarian activities. Intergovernmental organizations such as the UN High Commissioner for Refugees have boards of governors who review policies and programs. Yet the governments that sit on the boards represent beneficiary groups only in the most general sense. In fact, in civil wars they frequently view dissident populations with suspicion, and the distrust is often mutual.

At the program level, the UN often seeks to enlist beneficiaries in program design, execution, and evaluation. This can be a tricky process even where the setting is relatively stable, but it has proven to be even more troublesome in the confusion of active conflict or post-conflict adjustment. Thus, in the years 1991–1992, UNHCR consulted with refugees in camps along the Thai border about whether they would like to return to Cambodia and where they would like to resettle. A set of options was devised (and later revised) based on the preferences of the early returnees.

Private relief groups generally have an easier time in forging two-way links with populations at risk. In addition to shaping local activities in response to the needs articulated by the people themselves, some NGOs have also included on their governing or advisory boards representatives of the communities in which they are working. Some have heeded the requests of their counterparts in crisis areas and have moved away from operating their own programs, working instead through local implementing organizations. However, there are still serious limits on the extent to which inside actors exercise accountability over outside resources.

Many grass-roots communities, refugee groups, and internally displaced persons have come to insist on a new kind of accountability, organizing themselves to make their views, needs, and demands known to outside agencies. A prime example involves Salvadorans, both within their own country and in refugee camps in Honduras. Their home-grown organizations served as channels for outside aid, helping to ensure the survival of war-affected communities and encourage populations to shape their own futures. When UN organizations proved reluctant to encourage people to return to an El Salvador that was still at war, local leaders themselves initiated a series of repopulations that resettled nearly 30,000 refugees.

In January 1993, Guatemalans in Mexico staged a highly visible return to Poligono 14, ignoring the expressed wishes of government authorities. Having learned from experience in El Salvador, UN organizations played a role in Guatemala that was more supportive of refugee aspirations. Throughout Central America, to a degree untypical of Africa or Asia, civilian victims of the wars succeeded in extracting a new responsiveness from humanitarian organizations.

In fact, the civil war experience in El Salvador was reflected in a dramatic recommendation to the U.S. Agency for International Development as early as 1984. A team of experts urged, "The overriding principle of all humanitarian assistance must be the recognition that ultimate accountability is to the displaced persons and not to the host government, the donors, or other benefactors of the humanitarian assistance programs."[17] Ten years later, the approaches of most NGOs, and even more so of most governments and UN organizations, still fall short of that mark.

Despite uneven progress, humanitarian action is becoming somewhat more mutual in accountability. Recipient countries and beneficiary groups have become increasingly insistent that humanitarian action proceed only with their approval, that such initiatives respond to the immediate crisis but also address underlying problems, and that local resources be used and developed in preference to imported ones.

These views have been forcefully articulated on behalf of developing countries by Ghana's ambassador to the United Nations, Kofi N. Awanoor. "Are we the peoples of the so-called Third World so helpless that we can only be portrayed as eternal objects of pity?" he asks. "The real stunt is to accept the humanity of those who inhabit the poor nations and to marshal the energy to eliminate the incubus of their underdevelopment. ... The time has come for efforts made by disaster-struck countries and their neighbors to be recognized as a valuable and laudable component of global humanitarian relief work."[18]

A final aspect of accountability concerns the performance of individual humanitarian officials. The occasional disciplinary action—whether transfer, resignation, or firing—tends to be for misuse of privilege or abuse of standard operating procedures rather than for lack of program effectiveness or dereliction of humanitarian duty. The underlying question concerns whether aid agency executives and their boards of governors should be held accountable in some way for their decisions.

For most of 1991 and 1992, the famine in Somalia went almost unnoticed by the United Nations, whose humanitarian personnel had been removed from the area for security reasons. Remaining behind were a hardy but tiny band of intrepid staff from private groups such as the ICRC, Save the Children, the International Medical Corps, Doctors Without Borders, and SOS Kinderhof. Their attempts to goad the world into action fell largely on deaf ears.

In August 1992, two officials from Africa Watch leveled an impassioned indictment at the United Nations, calling upon the secretary-general to launch an independent review of the situation. "All files must be opened, and all responsible officials summoned to testify," wrote Rakiya Omaar and Alex de Waal. "The proceedings must be made public. Those responsible must be called to account and punished, and if necessary prosecuted. Western citizens would demand nothing less if their children were dying."[19]

Although several UN officials were nettled by the charges, the recommended inquiry was never launched. Even as those who were accused went back to their labors, however, the challenge reverberated, particularly because of the indispensability of public trust to their continued efforts. These charges and counter-charges lent urgency to the creation of a privately funded and independently governed "Aid Watch" to monitor the performance of humanitarian agencies and encourage higher standards of accountability, qualitative and quantitative, individual and institutional.

### Appropriateness

The sixth guiding principle is that humanitarian action should be tailored to local circumstances, enhancing rather than supplanting local resources. For all of its apparent logic, however, this principle, too, faces a host of political, institutional, and cultural dilemmas in its implementation.

When disasters strike, the most available resources are generally those nearest at hand, as Ambassador Kofi Awanoor's statement also indicates. A review of responses to recent emergencies demonstrates the pivotal importance of such resources. In crisis after crisis, it is the deployment of these resources that, in the all-important initial phase of a disaster, have made impressive contributions. The forward line of the world's humanitarian defense is local people themselves and their immediate neighbors.

Evacuees started arriving at the Jordanian-Iraqi border within days after Iraq's invasion of Kuwait in early August 1990. Soon they were crossing into Jordan at the staggering rate of 14,000 per day. By the time the influx ended, the tally stood at about 1,150,000. About 850,000 were from places like Bangladesh, the Philippines, Egypt, and Yemen. They had gone to Kuwait and Iraq seeking economic opportunity and were leaving in haste. The remainder were Palestinians from Jordan hurriedly returning home.

The response of Jordanians when, literally over night, hundreds of thousands of people showed up on their doorstep was instantaneous. People in Amman donated bread and tomatoes from their own tables to share with the new arrivals. Local NGOs, backed by international counterparts and the ICRC, set up camps near the border and stocked them with locally donated or purchased supplies. The government formed a high-level emergency committee and advanced the first of what would become $55 million to buy food, shelter materials, and transport. Most of the action was well under way by the time Western governments and the UN's agencies—the vaunted "international community"—swung into action.

The response was repeated elsewhere around the region. When Iraqi Kurds began to converge on the Turkish border in April 1991, the first assistance came from local communities and the Turkish Red Crescent Society. In Iran, the initial assistance came from national, provincial, and local governmental authorities. There and in Jordan, governments shifted personnel from less essential tasks to address around-the-clock needs for shelter, sanitation, immigration processing, and security.[20]

Local responses in the former Yugoslavia were equally dramatic. Of the half-million Muslims and Serbs who fled from eastern Bosnia into Serbia and Montenegro, the vast majority were welcomed into people's own homes.[21] Muslims and Croatians who fled west or south into Croatia received an equally personal welcome. The provision of shelter proceeded initially without reference to the ethnicity of guests or hosts. All told, about 95 percent of the newcomers to Serbia, Montenegro, and Croatia were accommodated in private residences rather than in the more traditional reception centers and refugee camps. Yet, as in the Persian Gulf crisis, the astonishing generosity of ordinary people was largely lost on the outside world.

Eventually, the international community responded, and fortunately so, since the extremity of the crisis soon overwhelmed local resources. However, the responses that eventually materialized in the emergencies in the Persian Gulf, the former Yugoslavia, and elsewhere lacked appropriateness, not to say urgency.

By the time the international agencies gathered to take stock of the situation in Amman, almost a week had passed. It was several weeks later before their organizations met in Geneva—the so-called humanitarian capital of the world—to coordinate a global response that took almost a month to put in place. Of the resulting 23,000 tons of food pledged for the emergency, less than 1,000 tons arrived during the first month and only 9,000 tons by a full six weeks later. "The United Nations took some time to organize itself," concluded a UN review, with studied understatement. "If the Jordanian Government had not decided to use its own resources to provide food and shelter to the evacuees, it would have taken several days, if not weeks, for the international community to provide the same sort of services."[22]

To add insult to injury, international responses, once forthcoming, were tight-fisted. Western governments proved unwilling to reimburse Jordan for much of its generosity. The funds advanced and the purchases made by the Jordanian authorities, Western governments claimed, lacked proper documentation. In order to qualify for reimbursement, they said, the amounts spent required preauthorization. As a result, only $18 million of the $55 million the Jordanian government spent was ultimately reimbursed, adding yet another contentious issue to the highly charged relations between Jordan and the international community.

"Humanitarian gestures can place a burden on the host country," one high-level Jordanian official commented with a certain resignation. "Unless there is a mechanism that recompenses and replenishes, many countries will think very hard before allowing their facilities to be used." His opposite numbers in Teheran and Damascus, Zagreb and Belgrade, would emphatically agree.

The appropriateness of international responses was also marred by political calculations. Donor governments were not prepared to be generous with the government in Amman, which they perceived as sympathetic to Iraq's Saddam Hussein in the issues of the war. They reacted much the same way to the authorities in Teheran, which, despite Iranian hospitality to the Iraqi Kurds who fled there, remained a pariah state for Western donors.

A recurring problem in the area of appropriateness is that international responses have often been insensitive in their approaches and have preempted local efforts. Examples abound in which winter clothing was shipped to hurricane victims in the Caribbean, summer clothing to landslide victims in the Himalayas, ready-to-eat meals containing pork to Muslim populations, and medicines that arrived after their expiration dates. These snafus offer dramatic proof that the international humanitarian system is driven by outside forces to the detriment of local needs and resources.

Equally unfortunate, and equally avoidable, have been recurrent instances of inappropriate behavior by international personnel. One incident in the Persian Gulf crisis involved the violation of local Iranian mores by the wife of a senior French official, whose appearance in public with her head and arms uncovered affronted accepted standards of female behavior and brought controversy to the presence of international humanitarian and diplomatic personnel associated with the relief effort.

More serious incidents involved sexual misconduct by UN peacekeeping troops in Cambodia, who took repeated liberties with the local population. Initially dismissed by senior UN officials, who explained jocularly that "boys will be boys," the behavior eventually was taken more seriously as undercutting the professionalism of the UN operation.

Although efforts to tailor outside contributions and presence to local resources and mores are indispensable, it is also necessary to avoid romanticizing the indigenous or accommodating local preferences un-critically. What is local, experience suggests, is not necessarily right, particularly when local values conflict with international norms.

Should humanitarian workers arm themselves in societies where car-rying weapons is standard practice? Not doing so may be seen as a sign of weakness and undercut local credibility. Doing so, however, may vi-olate an organization's humanitarian principles and the deeply held beliefs of individual staff. Should an agency tolerate graft and corrup-tion among government officials and businessmen? Refusing to play the game according to local rules may complicate efforts to gain access to civilian populations or to purchase or import necessary relief items. Acquiescing in the local ways of doing business may cause a donor backlash.

In a society that favors males over females, should an outside agency insist on equitable distribution of relief food? Should an organization involved in the teaching of literacy insist on including primary school–age girls where they would otherwise not qualify to attend? To what extent should agencies providing outside resources insist that maternal and child health centers challenge local practice by provid-ing birth control devices or by discouraging female circumcision—in Western health and legal parlance, "genital mutilation"?

The World Conference on Human Rights, held in Vienna in June 1993, illuminates some of the conceptual dilemmas and political con-troversies involved in achieving international consensus on what is appropriate and designing action strategies accordingly. At the first such meeting in almost fifty years, "the argument of some authoritar-ian Asian governments that different cultural norms should exempt their countries from the universal application of international human rights instruments was one flash point of discussion," reported Hu-man Rights Watch.

"There was also a perception, among countries of the South," the group's report continued, "that the UN had not adequately addressed their human rights priorities where those priorities involved eco-nomic, social and cultural rights but had rather responded to an agenda of the developed, westernized North which emphasized pre-dominantly civil and political rights."[23]

External actors that seek out local counterparts in an effort to ensure the appropriateness of their initiatives frequently face difficult ques-tions of policy and practice. Should outside organizations enter into partnerships with groups that have political agendas or ethnic constituencies of their own? What about counterparts who have their roots deep in graft-ridden or patronage-oriented societies? Should allocations of food in a conflict such as the one in Afghanistan be delegated to or arranged in collaboration with a council of local male leaders whose stated preference is for distribution to men, many of whom are soldiers from their own families? Given the state of inside institutions, outside organizations committed to appropriateness may have difficulty finding suitable local counterparts.

When criticized for bypassing local institutions, humanitarian organizations acknowledge trade-offs between acting quickly on the one hand and enlisting and strengthening local partners on the other. In the frenzied scramble to assist the victims of war, the principle of appropriateness, unobjectionable in theory, often is a casualty. The clear and immediate challenge of saving lives usually wins out over the more ambiguous and longer-term task of empowering local people. Agencies, whose raison d'être is emergency relief, are especially prone to act without reference to issues of appropriateness.

Commenting on the U.S. government's all-out effort to keep people from starving in Somalia late in 1992, one AID official observed emphatically, "We're rightly indifferent to people's cultural needs and to appropriateness issues." Whatever else is happening, said another in charge of logistics, "I want to hear the airplane engines running." The dramatic logistics challenges upstage the more subtle—and ultimately more demanding—tasks of institution building and empowerment.

In a perfect world with sufficient resources, there would be no trade-offs between saving as many lives as possible and strengthening local abilities to cope more adequately with disasters. But a perfect world would also be one without conflicts, famines, and the need for lifesaving ministrations.

In the final analysis, trade-offs between rapid responses and longer-term benefits may be more theoretical than real. Relief and development activities that enlist local populations and institutions generally prove more successful than those that do not. In addition, lifesaving efforts themselves may be undertaken in ways that empower local people without major delays.

With these considerations in mind, more attention is now devoted to local institution building. The International Federation of Red Cross and Red Crescent Societies, for example, carries out extensive programs of staff and program development for national chapters in developing countries. These training activities paid off handsomely during the Persian Gulf crisis, when outside assistance, channeled through and coordinated by the Iranian Red Crescent, proved particularly effective.

In today's global village, localized suffering has wider international import. Yet in the process of turning a basic human impulse into a complex international enterprise, humanitarian instincts need not sacrifice spontaneity, authenticity, or appropriateness.

### Discerning the Context

The seventh guiding principle is that effective humanitarian action should include a comprehensive view of overall needs and of the impact of outside efforts. Rather than operating in a vacuum, it is important to address the underlying causes of conflicts and to encourage respect for human rights.

Two vignettes regarding the use of the military in Central America to improve the life of civilian populations illustrate this point. In January 1993, visitors to the Chaletenango area of El Salvador interviewed people from humanitarian organizations who, having been active during the civil war, were turning their energies toward postwar reconstruction. Encountering a brigade of soldiers digging a ditch in the provin-

cial capital city, the visitors were impressed. How gratifying that soldiers from a nearby outpost, which had been the scene of countless human rights abuses and deaths, were now engaged in helping rebuild society. This civic action project seemed to make eminent good sense. Further investigation indicated, however, that the soldiers were not welcome among the civilian residents and were tearing up cobblestones that recently had been laid to sink a sewer pipe that people had not requested. The entire exercise proved more cosmetic than constructive.

By contrast, the first organized repatriation of Guatemalan Indians from camps in Mexico was taking place at that time. The role of the military, which had carried out or encouraged many of the human rights abuses that had spurred the exodus in the 1980s, was extremely limited. Reflecting years of official policy, the armed forces saw the returnees as revolutionaries and terrorists. They were not enthusiastic about the refugees' return, which was supported only by Guatemala's civilian leadership and a handful of senior military officers who took a longer perspective. Giving the army a pivotal role in the process of repatriation and reconstruction would not have been constructive.

Although each of these initiatives has a certain obvious and immediate social utility, they deserve review in a broader context. However urgent it may be to build roads and schools and return refugees to their homes, having the local military play key roles in these tasks may be unwise. Although it would be wrong to assume that every such civic action project is completely without merit, a fair assessment of such efforts also must take into account their full context and their likely indirect as well as direct consequences. If the longer-term objective is the building of a civil society that is more just, pluralistic, and accountable, then ways need to be found to shift responsibilities from military to civilian institutions at the earliest possible moment.

One major recurring lesson from recent armed conflicts is that humanitarian organizations need to look beyond their immediate activities to the wider context in which they are functioning. Are the effects of their efforts as positive as possible, or at least more positive than negative? Is humanitarian action implicated in fueling conflicts or perpetuating human rights abuses? The record is not particularly reassuring. "The time has come for us in the Horn of Africa," says Kenyan Professor Kabiru Kinyanjui, "to ask whether the efforts of relief agencies are contributing indirectly or even remotely to an escalation of the wars or to a peaceful resolution of the conflicts."[24] Linkages deserve scrutiny in other areas as well.

On the plus side of the ledger, the role of the churches in the Sudan and their international support network exemplifies a positive potential connection between delivering relief and fostering peace. Building upon relationships with the largely Muslim authorities in Khartoum and with insurgent leaders in the south who practiced Christianity and traditional African religions, the World Council of Churches in 1972 helped broker peace accords that brought a seventeen-year civil war to a temporary halt. In the decade before hostilities were rekindled in 1983, the churches also provided reconstruction assistance to solidify the peace and make perceptible changes in the day-to-day lives of the southern Sudanese.

Conversely, the UN's Operation Lifeline Sudan, which helped ease the conflict for half a year in 1989, bears some responsibility for its continuation thereafter. Asked whether an agreement between the warring parties on relief efforts might have contributed to a longer and more enduring peace, the UN official in charge of humanitarian efforts, UNICEF Executive Director James P. Grant, explained that "there was nothing in my mandate at all" to resolve the underlying conflict.[25] By not approaching the war in its totality, the UN no doubt missed opportunities to provide more lasting benefits.

External aid efforts for Afghanistan have received the same mixed reviews. Massive aid to Afghan refugees in camps along the border improved the quality of their lives while war raged within their country during the 1980s. Yet the aid contributed to the jockeying among various *mujaheddin* factions that continued even after the withdrawal of the Soviet Union in 1989.[26] Moreover, the most combative and cutthroat factions, which attracted the largest amounts of outside military and economic aid, proved least committed to peace even after it arrived. Favoring the groups along the border rather than directing aid through Kabul also made humanitarian assistance an extension of the war rather than a contribution to peace and reconciliation. A more clear-cut separation of humanitarian and other objectives, however difficult, would have had more lasting value.

The challenge of countering "ethnic cleansing" in the former Yugoslavia offers another dramatic example of the worrisome ethical issues confronting serious humanitarian efforts.[27] "In the context of a con-

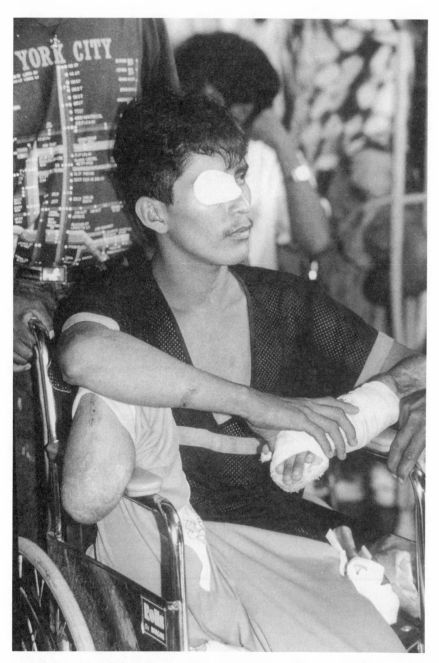

A victim of a land mine in El Salvador's twelve-year war waits to receive an artificial limb. (UN Photo 159531/M. Bleibtreu)

flict which has as its very objective displacement of people," said United Nations High Commissioner for Refugees Sadako Ogata in November 1992, "we find ourselves confronted with a major dilemma. To what extent do we persuade people to remain where they are, when that could well jeopardize their lives and liberties? On the other hand, if we help them to move, do we not become an accomplice to 'ethnic cleansing'?"[28]

The dilemma represented, as do all dilemmas, a lose-lose situation, one altogether without a satisfactory solution. United Nations policy sought both to bring safety to people where they were and, in situations in which that was impossible, to bring people to safety. The UN was criticized both for not protecting people adequately in their own communities and for not being quicker to rescue them when their lives were threatened.

"If you rally around besieged minorities when they are initially under attack," said Mohammed Sacirbey, Bosnia's ambassador to the United Nations, in an interview in 1993, "they're victims only once. If you move them out of harm's way, you find yourself moving them again, and again, and again. The solution adopted thus becomes part of the problem."[29]

UN officials agree that the first line of defense should be to assist and protect people as close to their homes as possible. However, rallying around besieged Muslims in Gorazde, Croats in Vukovar, or Serbs in Tuzla may victimize them a second time by accepting their use as human shields. "I prefer 30,000 evacuees to 30,000 dead bodies," José Maria Mendiluce, the UN High Commissioner's special envoy in the former Yugoslavia, said in May 1993 in defense of the UN's policy.[30]

Humanitarian action must thus be mounted—and evaluated— within a given context. Many would therefore agree with UNHCR's conclusion that "evacuation is a last resort, in that it acquiesces in the very displacement that preventive efforts aim to avoid. But in some circumstances it is the only way to save lives. There is a very fine line between refusing to facilitate ethnic cleansing and failing to prevent needless deaths."[31] Some, however, would question whether the United Nations and the international community more broadly were as resourceful as they might have been in the former Yugoslavia in preventing needless deaths.

Discerning the context does not mean that relief agencies themselves can monitor all human rights abuses or intercede with governments on behalf of victims of such abuse. It does not necessarily mean that aid practitioners, who arrange for corridors of tranquility for relief supplies and personnel, will negotiate cease-fires or durable peace agreements. But the compartmentalization that has frequently characterized relief and development activities and has driven a wedge between assistance and protection is not helpful. Unless humanitarian activities are seen in broadest compass, at best they fall short of their potential and at worst they stumble on the treacherous terrain where humanitarian action takes place.[32]

After all, assistance activities position aid personnel to serve as the eyes and ears of the international community, alerting the world to violations of human rights as they happen or threaten to happen. The presence of such sensory capacities in El Salvador in the 1980s, for example, moderated or deterred human rights abuses by political and military actors, government and insurgent alike.

Conversely, protection activities give human rights personnel an excellent opportunity to document humanitarian assistance requirements. Human rights organizations monitoring the plight of Guatemala's Indian population have described their desperate needs for emergency assistance. Human rights workers in the West Bank and Gaza Strip have flagged the need for short- and long-term aid. Undertaken in a vacuum, humanitarian action may not necessarily be advisable. Despite strenuous efforts by humanitarian organizations in the former Yugoslavia to urge more vigorous diplomacy, assistance activities became what amounted to a substitute for, rather than a springboard to, conflict resolution initiatives.

Discerning the context, then, is a necessity, not a luxury. This is why the advice in the *Handbook for Practitioners,* reflecting the experience also chronicled in the present volume, advises, "Don't just do something, stand there!"[33] Doing no harm may seem too modest and inglorious an objective for those committed to doing good. However, a comprehensive view of the complexities of humanitarian action suggests that a sturdy sense of realism is essential if well-meaning efforts are to avoid being hijacked or turning counterproductive.

Contextualization also means greater understanding of the reservations held by poorer countries about humanitarian action. Many believe that the international community is promoting emergency responses at the expense of longer-term assistance. The "relentless human tragedy," chronicled in such detail by a relentless media, Ghana's ambassador to the United Nations has said, "is grounded in one grim and merciless reality—underdevelopment. ... Development is the only instrument that will remove the stigma of charity that accompanies all humanitarian relief efforts." Yet development will require fundamental changes in the international economic system, which richer nations are demonstrably unprepared to make.[34]

Poorer nations also see their own obligation to be law-abiding as unfair in the light of the abrogation by wealthier countries of their own responsibilities. The Independent Commission on International Humanitarian Issues articulates the concerns as follows:

> Where was the outrage of the international community, whose norms we are now being asked to respect, during the crises that imprisoned us in poverty, ignorance and oppression, that killed our children through malnutrition and diseases, that despoiled our lands? The keen sense of structural violence on the part of its victims and their determination to resist it is the link that joins long-term issues of poverty and injustice to the breakdown of humanitarian norms in wars or violent internal struggles. The contenders in such struggles are not likely to observe the norms set by the international community until they are acknowledged to be a part of it themselves.[35]

Conscientious efforts to frame humanitarian initiatives in this larger context may not produce clear courses of action. Agencies that understand the contextual complexities may not always make the right choice. Indeed, what is right may be difficult to identify even in retrospect. However, those in need of lifesaving ministrations deserve activities not only impelled by good intentions but informed by contextual savvy.

### Keeping Sovereignty in Its Proper Place

The eighth and final guiding principle addresses the perennial tension between the rights of sovereign political authorities and the claims of the suffering to humanitarian aid. Humanitarian action should keep sovereignty in its proper place. When sovereignty and suffering clash, the latter should prevail.[36]

What constitutes sovereignty's "proper" place, however, is hotly contested. This principle, therefore, requires more extended discussion than its predecessors. Like its predecessors, however, it needs to be

approached not only from the basis of moral philosophy and political theory but also from the standpoint of real-world experience.

An early but well-remembered clash between sovereignty and the relief of life-threatening suffering occurred in the Nigerian civil war of 1967–1970. In response to an effort by the Ibo-led territory of Biafra to achieve independence, the federal government in Lagos imposed an economic blockade around the breakaway area and fought a fierce war against it. Staggering loss of life was accompanied by fierce tribal bloodletting. The impact on civil society was devastating.

In spite of dramatic media images of warfare and attendant starvation, governments were paralyzed, acceding to the pleas of Nigerian authorities to respect their sovereignty. One ICRC staff member, Bernard Kouchner, thoroughly frustrated by the prevailing inaction, founded a new organization, Doctors Without Borders (in French, Médecins Sans Frontières, or MSF), whose name and marching orders reflected impatience with the elevation of political borders over the needs of civilian populations. A number of existing NGOs also stepped into the breach, mounting an airlift whose nightly flights from Sao Tomé into the small landing strip at Uli brought supplies that stanched the worst of the bleeding.

In the intervening quarter century, Kouchner has applied his energies both outside and within governments. He served in several French governments under President François Mitterrand as the world's only minister with a portfolio exclusively of humanitarian affairs. More recently, Kouchner founded a new organization, Association pour l'Action Humanitaire. He sees the Biafra initiative as the first step in a series of crucial developments that have since established the proposition that the prerogatives of sovereign governments do not include the right to abuse their own citizens. The point is a critical one in that in their political, military, and humanitarian dynamics, post–Cold War conflicts are more like Biafra and less like World Wars I and II.

In Kouchner's view, the ICRC's efforts in the nineteenth century represented a good start at controlling the carnage of warfare, but they required the active cooperation of territorial states and the discretion of outsiders. By 1968, it had become high time to abandon discretion in favor of more forceful protests against abuse, motivated by *le devoir d'ingérence*—the "duty to interfere." The end of the Cold War has brought the third stage in this evolution. The new era involves not simply a private duty to help suffering civilians but the specific right of outsiders—states as well as humanitarian organizations—to intervene against political authorities who flout international norms.[37]

Not all observers agree with Kouchner about the evolution of a more assertive and effective humanitarian system. In fact, Aengus Finucane, chief executive of CONCERN, who was himself on the front lines in both Biafra and Somalia, feels that the first response was far more impressive than the second. Recalling the Biafra airlift, he holds, "helps put the belated and pathetic efforts to get assistance to Somalia in perspective." In his judgment, the international community demonstrated its will to cushion the tragedy in Biafra. "Twenty-five years later, there wasn't a will in Somalia until very late in the game, and even then it was lukewarm for too long."[38]

As it turns out, both Kouchner and Finucane are right.[39] However unsatisfactory the humanitarian outcomes, the world has intervened in a number of humanitarian crises, overriding protestations of sovereignty from the authorities involved. In the brief space from 1990 to 1993, Security Council resolutions and follow-up actions by the United Nations system sought to protect vulnerable populations in northern and southern Iraq, Somalia, and the former Yugoslavia.

In the first instance, the Baghdad authorities objected and were overruled. In the second, the preexisting breakdown of law and order rendered any such objections moot. In the third, the international community eventually embraced enforcement action using UN-blessed NATO troops, even though the stationing of UN peacekeeping forces remained subject to the consent of the parties to the conflict. In each instance the exercise of sovereignty was subjected to international scrutiny and drew international rebuke, but in no single instance did sustained activities address the underlying social and economic causes of the conflicts.

Thus, tension persists between sovereignty and suffering. Politicians whose authority is being tested by civil conflict are anxious to have their authority respected. Governments that lack financial resources, political influence, and international standing jealously guard their sovereignty, which remains one of their few possessions. Even governments with greater wealth and power are anything but cavalier about it.

For better or worse, sovereignty remains the cornerstone of the present, but it is steadily evolving. Government officials of all stripes still seek to construe narrowly the situations that comprise threats to international peace and security and thus legitimize Security Council action. Politicians and diplomats would prefer to finesse clashes over sovereignty, agreeing with the former Sudanese Prime Minister Dr. Gazuli d'Faallah that "the solution to the tension between sovereignty and humanitarian concern lies in redefining the sovereignty issue. Within the sovereignty of states, all these humanitarian concerns can be addressed."[40] When a sovereign state acts responsibly, there is no need for the world to pick a fight.

Operation Lifeline Sudan demonstrated the prime minister's point. In early 1989, this UN initiative persuaded both the Khartoum authorities and the insurgent SPLM, then locked in a bitter and bloody struggle, to allow an international presence and humanitarian activities in areas that they controlled and not to contest these activities in enemy areas. The government, said a senior Sudanese official who negotiated the arrangements, had "conceded sovereignty over a large part of our territory to the UN."[41] The insurgents followed suit.

According to close associates, Sudanese Prime Minister Sadiq el Mahdi genuinely felt that victims of the war had a right to international assistance. His opposite number, Commander John Garang, also affirmed the right of war victims to such aid. Lifeline programs accomplished their goals during the first six months, although with changes in leadership and the military positions of belligerents these arrangements and activities have been under duress since late 1989.

In many other circumstances, however, authorities acknowledge no humanitarian obligations in their exercise of sovereignty. Swearing on the holy writ of the Geneva Conventions provides no guarantee. Once governments become directly or indirectly involved in armed conflict, they often elevate state interests and sovereign prerogatives over acknowledged humanitarian obligations.

In fact, the Geneva Convention ban against the use of food as a military weapon or the guarantees in the Universal Declaration of Human Rights of the "dignity and worth of the human person" are invoked more often to frustrate rather than to fulfill humane objectives. Recent egregious examples include Ethiopia during the Mengistu years, Cambodia under the Khmer Rouge, Peru under the Shining Path, junta-led Myanmar, and armed forces–dominated Guatemala. The invocation of sovereignty is the last line of defense for repressive regimes.

Upon reflection, the idea that nations would impose and respect limits on their mutual brutality is startling. A relatively modern phenomenon, the idea is, in fact, fundamental to the laws of war. Designed to preserve a sense of humanity during conflict, laws to limit brutality have even evolved over the past century to keep abreast of modern military tactics and technology. The fact that the corollary proposition—insurgent forces, frequently ragtag bands operating without clear chains of command and accountability—can be placed in a similar straitjacket is more astonishing still.

"If insurgent movements expect to be dealt with in the same way as governments when it comes to humanitarian assistance," said Barbara Hendrie, a close analyst of humanitarian initiatives in the Horn of Africa, "then they must also expect to be bound by international law regarding the treatment of civilians."[42] The experience of insurgents in Sri Lanka, Mozambique, Angola, and Liberia bear out her experience. Since today's insurgents are sometimes tomorrow's governments, eliciting their cooperation on humanitarian concerns has the further value of preparing them for their international obligations once they come into power.

Even the strong, whether governments or insurgents, benefit from limiting random or lawless violence. The most callous parties are not beyond appeals to humanity, particularly since their own self-interest may be involved. In fact, recognized authorities and major powers have a great deal to lose from a world in which stated obligations are ignored. More vulnerable to hit-and-run terrorism, they have a greater stake in a functioning international system in which the rule of law is respected and order and predictability prevail.

Pariah states may be less open to international persuasion than lawabiding ones. Confronting the world's Muammar Qaddafis and Idi

Amins, international leverage is clearly limited, although not altogether absent. Someone in the global family may have a way of engaging the wayward uncle—perhaps even of bringing him to heel. At the same time, some of the more impatient family members may decide to proceed, with or without having extracted his consent.

Sometimes persuasion fails. Former Sudanese Prime Minister D'Faallah would have been more accurate had he said, Within the sovereignty of states properly exercised, all these humanitarian concerns can be addressed. It does not follow that just because states have made a commitment at a treaty conference in Geneva that they will respect their obligations when they perceive their own security challenged.

At that point, the international community is faced with a series of options for keeping sovereignty in its proper place. These options include economic sanctions and military force, each with consequences for humanitarian activities that will be examined later.

A quarter century after Biafra, however, these choices are made in an overall context in which a better balance is being struck between the claims of those who suffer and the responsibilities of those who claim sovereignty. Louise Fréchette, the Canadian ambassador to the United Nations, is clearly right when he says, "The first lesson that I would draw from the UN's new ventures is that the principles of sovereignty and nonintervention in internal affairs of states no longer reign supreme in the UN."[43]

Humanitarianism across borders seems to be the direction of the future, even though the territorial state remains the cornerstone of world politics. Meanwhile, ground rules for political-military intervention and for humanitarian action in situations of overridden sovereignty are still evolving. The UN Security Council, the world's highest political body, has awakened from its Cold War slumber to discover its humanitarian responsibilities. But it has not yet found a way of systematically putting sovereignty in its proper place and ensuring that human life everywhere is treated with equal seriousness.

Bernard Kouchner's promised land remains distant, but it is now more apparent than in the days of the Uli airlift that humanitarian action takes place within an altered context of law, politics, and history. Humanitarian action involves not only feeding people but educating donor publics. It requires not only protecting people from human rights abuses but supporting pluralistic institutions and an investigative media. It necessitates not only coming to people's rescue but guarding against prolonging conflicts.

Whether the situation is one of anarchy, acquiescence, or resistance, recent international action puts states on notice that major violence against their own populations is no longer exclusively a matter of domestic jurisdiction. Similarly, international access no longer depends exclusively on sovereign discretion or on national decisions, which may themselves now be subjected to other standards. Boundaries are still relevant but are becoming more porous and subject to outside influences and intervention.

In the final analysis, political authorities who control access to civilians in war zones are more likely to meet their humanitarian responsibilities to the extent that others throughout the world meet theirs. International humanitarian law, reinforced by diverse ethical and religious traditions, imposes obligations on all parties. This includes those who have acknowledged their duty to provide aid no less than those whose cooperation is needed for such aid to be effective. All parties to the Geneva Conventions and Protocols are pledged to insist on, and assist in, their full implementation.

**Conclusion**

This review of the eight guiding principles of humanitarian action leads to a number of observations. First, the principles identified are at best signposts, not a gyroscope for putting the humanitarian aircraft on automatic pilot. The challenges faced by individual humanitarian organizations are imbedded in complex historical, political, and cultural realities. Individual agencies read the same situations differently and choose different strategies.

Second, tensions and contradictions are present between and among the stated principles. Efforts to relieve suffering without discerning the context can add to the prevailing violence. Saving as many lives as possible in one conflict may generate disproportionality toward another. Insistence upon accountability can retard or impede lifesaving action. Again, differences in perspectives and priorities lead humanitarian organizations to chart different courses.

Third, fidelity to principles may—or may not—make for more effective action. Humanitarian activities are mounted and maintained in highly confused and idiosyncratic situations. Success may involve improvisation and adaptation. However, guiding principles may provide a necessary framework and may represent an alternative to make-do or opportunistic strategies.

Finally, principles are routinely at risk of being undercut or infiltrated by politics. A better humanitarian system requires a clearer understanding of positive and negative interactions with the political realm. Given the impossibility of isolating humanitarian action from politics, principled pragmatism may offer a middle course between humanitarian naïveté, which denies the inevitable intersections with politics, and humanitarian realpolitik, which champions the overt manipulation of humanitarian action to achieve political ends.

# 3
# Challenges

Armed conflicts present humanitarian actors with seven common challenges: assessing the severity of a particular crisis, negotiating access to affected populations, mobilizing human and financial resources, delivering services, ensuring coordination, pursuing education and advocacy activities, and looking beyond the emergency.

Illustrations of each of the seven challenges abound in many recent theaters of operations. The focus here is on two regions: the Horn of Africa for the first four tasks and Central America for the final three. The tasks to be performed, the plan of action for accomplishing them, and the conditions under which operations proceed constitute what may be called the humanitarian terms of engagement.

In the Horn of Africa, four major conflicts have been played out during the past fifteen years. The government of Ethiopia was locked in combat with the secessionist Eritrean People's Liberation Front, which sought independence, and with the Tigrayan People's Liberation Front, which sought greater power within the recognized borders of Ethiopia. Eventually the two joined forces to oust the Mengistu regime. A UN plebiscite held in Eritrea in 1961 to determine the future relationship between Eritrea and Ethiopia endorsed secession.

In the Sudan, civil war originally broke out in 1972. From 1972 to 1983 the country was tense but relatively peaceful. Since 1983 virtually uninterrupted warfare has pitted a succession of Sudanese governments in Khartoum against the Sudanese People's Liberation Army. The conflict gained a third party when a second insurgent faction splintered off in August 1991. This new group subsequently has fought against both the Sudanese army and the SPLA. At issue have been competing visions for the country and the southern region, reflecting an amalgam of political, religious, tribal, and economic differences.

Civil war in Somalia began in mid-1988 with battles in the north between the government and the Somalia National Movement. In 1990, the central regions of the country became involved. This was capped by a popular uprising in Mogadishu late in the year against government repression by the United Somali Congress. In late 1991, fighting increased between rival USC faction leaders General Mohammed Farrah Aidid and Ali Mahdi Mohammed. With the flight of President Siad Barre in April 1992, the country descended into virtual anarchy, accompanied by widespread famine born of drought and war.

In Central America, civil wars raged during the 1980s between governments and insurgents in Nicaragua, El Salvador, and Guatemala. In the case of Nicaragua, war between the U.S.-backed Contras and the Sandinista regime lasted more than a decade following the overthrow of the Somoza regime in 1979. In El Salvador, conservative governments faced a challenge from the Farabundo Martí National Liberation Front. In Guatemala, warfare that had been sputtering for three decades between the Indian population and a succession of regimes was heightened by tensions across the region.

Following the Esquipulas Accords in 1987, tensions in all three countries began to ease. The Sandinista government was replaced by an elected regime in 1991. El Salvador held its first postwar elections in early 1994. In Guatemala, the civil war continues, although the first organized returns of refugees from neighboring Mexico took place in late 1993 and early 1994.

**Assessment**

A clear picture of the nature and extent of human suffering is the basis for effective humanitarian action. The complexity of the assessment task is demonstrated by three cases. The difficulty of establishing the nature of the problem emerged in the Ethiopian famine of 1984. The difficulty of determining the magnitude of the crisis was illustrated in the Sudan in 1988 to 1989. The challenge of making seasoned assessments when international personnel are largely absent occurred in Somalia in 1991.

In the age of satellites, computer data bases, and CNN, why is it difficult to figure out what causes a given crisis, how many people are affected, and what sort of assistance is needed? In many natural disasters—hurricanes, cyclones, floods, tidal waves, and the like—

assessments can be quickly made and conveyed to those who wish to help. For example, within hours after a cyclone and follow-up tidal surge in the Bay of Bengal hit low-lying areas of Bangladesh on April 29, 1991, efforts to survey the damage and respond were under way. An estimated 130,000 people had lost their lives; property damage was placed at $2–4 billion.[1]

While a quick tally of the extent of need may prove difficult at such times, the task is usually much more complicated in wars. In 1984, when groups of refugees began straggling into the eastern Sudan from northern Ethiopia, the Horn had endured a drought for more than a year. There had been warning signs that people's resources were being drained—they were selling off some of their livestock and family possessions—and that they might flee in large numbers in search of sustenance.

Alarmed by the influx, some aid groups began publicizing the famine and encouraging governments and Western publics to contribute to what would become a major relief effort. They calculated how many people lived in the affected area, how many might need assistance over how long a period, and planned accordingly for operations in the eastern Sudan and northern Ethiopia.

Other organizations took a more probing approach. After interviewing refugees, a U.S.-based organization, Cultural Survival, confirmed that although many persons had fled in search of food, their departure was triggered more by the policies of the Ethiopian government than by the drought itself. The Mengistu regime had discouraged price incentives for farmers, systematically abused human rights, and spent heavily in the war against secessionist Eritrea at the expense of social sector investments.

To complicate the situation further, the famine was more a product of human choices than lack of rain. As noted earlier, even such "acts of God" as classical natural disasters are increasingly understood to bear the marks of conscious governmental policies and the practices of ordinary people themselves. According to current disaster thinking and research, the real culprit is often people, who overtax the land's carrying capacity with too many people or livestock. Human settlements and agricultural technology often are implicated in natural disasters.

But what difference does it make to understand the causes that trigger emergencies? Although people will require emergency food, shelter, and medicine regardless of the causes, the framing of a problem

Sacked quarters of the Red Cross of Liberia in Monrovia, January 1991. (ICRC Photo/LIBE 91-11/30/R. Sidler)

has a direct bearing on the responses made. What good does it do to rush emergency food to a distressed area if governmental pricing policies discourage agricultural production? Does it make sense to mount a major refugee effort if continued abuses keep the flow of people coming?

In the Ethiopian crisis of 1984, many humanitarian groups took the easy way out, for a number of reasons. They realized that Western publics and parliaments respond more generously to natural disasters than to those whose roots in politics and internal conflict defy easy explanation and more quickly to visible, short-term crises than to more complex and intractable long-term problems. The unpopularity of the Mengistu regime during the Cold War made it all the more tempting for the West to ignore the roots of the problem. Aid and human rights groups also were reluctant to mount a public campaign against the regime's policies: some of them were already working, or might someday wish to work, in Ethiopia.

The prevailing approach was simply to respond, not to probe underlying causes. The assessment process was driven by institutional politics and fund-raising, by the need for agencies to respond quickly, and by the desire to keep appeals to the donor public simple. Emphasis was placed on the gravity of the people's suffering, not on the complex web of historical, social, economic, ethnic, and political forces that were implicated in the tragedy.

Experience from the Sudan illuminates the difficulty of assessing the severity of need. During 1988, a combination of drought and civil war claimed roughly 250,000 lives, almost all of them civilians. Most outside humanitarian agencies were unable to provide assistance because Khartoum's authorities barred international access to the hard-hit areas in the south, where the war was being fought.

In a breakthrough in early 1989, UN officials prevailed on both sides to allow relief operations to get under way. In preparation for a high-visibility international pledging conference in Khartoum in March, the United Nations hurriedly compiled rough estimates of how many people were affected by food shortages and how much tonnage would be needed over how long a period. They calculated that a relief operation would require 107,000 tons of food and more modest amounts of medicines, seeds, and agricultural implements before the rains returned in September.

UN officials agreed upon and eventually exceeded those quantitative targets, although the process took longer than they anticipated. By year's end, international donors had committed 111,654 tons of food, of which 98,500 tons had been moved and 89,750 tons distributed. About 3,760 tons of nonfood items also had been provided. With its emergency food assistance reaching an estimated 1.5 million people, the United Nations could report with accuracy and satisfaction that the massive starvation of the previous year had been avoided. Yet the data on which the whole enterprise had been based were flimsy and reflected the very problem that had contributed to the earlier deaths: the lack of international access to the famine areas.

In an exercise of their sovereignty, government authorities had barred UN officials from rebel-held areas where the suffering was worst and had strictly limited access even to government-controlled areas. As an organization of governments that takes its marching orders from officials of recognized regimes in power, the United Nations was unwilling to challenge the exclusion of its officials. As a result, assessment data on which UN relief efforts were based were highly conjectural. Operation Lifeline Sudan became, said one UN official who had helped plan it, "a voyage of discovery."[2]

The United Nations believed, with some further justification, that it was more important to reach people quickly than to count them first. It placed a premium on averting massive starvation rather than on confronting the restricted access of such governments as the United States and the United Kingdom and such intergovernmental organizations as the European Community to famine areas. At the same time, UN officials did not systematically solicit data from NGOs that had entered the Sudan illicitly from Kenya and Uganda and had better information about civilian suffering in insurgent-controlled areas in which they were engaged.

Given the difficulties of data gathering and the pressure to launch a major appeal, it is remarkable that UN estimates were not more off the mark. These estimates filled the immediate gap in reasonably solid numbers on whose basis much-needed international resources could be mobilized. Simultaneously, the estimates also exposed the UN to a series of controversies that embroiled the aid program and eventually undermined its effectiveness.

Because of the UN's own emphasis on the magnitude of the need, Lifeline's ability to meet its tonnage targets became the single benchmark by which the media judged its success. As a result, the fact that its other contributions far outweighed the many logistic difficulties of delivery was obscured. Moreover, the belligerents later questioned the accuracy of the needs assessment data, each of the belligerents alleging UN bias in dividing resources between government- and rebel-held territories. Needs assessments conducted in 1993 to 1994 have sought to address the problem by using teams that include the UN, donor governments, NGOs, and the respective political authorities in whichever areas are being sampled.

In Somalia during the period 1991–1992, UN responses were hamstrung because of the relative absence of UN officials throughout the country as the crisis unraveled. Concern about the security of staff in a setting of worsening civil strife—and about the application of existing life insurance coverage in a war zone—led UN headquarters in New York in January 1991 to order the evacuation of personnel. The absence of staff on the scene contributed to delayed responses from the

United Nations, which lacked the means of evaluating the distress calls received from the ICRC and NGOs over a period of months as the situation deteriorated.

The challenge of assessing needs among the Horn of Africa's wars demonstrates the importance of devising creative ways to obtain the most reliable assessments possible of the nature and extent of suffering. In the confusion and suspicion of civil wars, the task of establishing and monitoring needs is both more complex and necessary.

### Negotiations

Once the nature and severity of a crisis are known, humanitarian organizations confront another formidable task: negotiating access to those who require help. Vignettes from the Horn of Africa illustrate recent efforts to do so. One highlights an initially successful UN undertaking to solicit cooperation from belligerents in the Sudan. Two examples from Ethiopia showcase efforts by the Untied Nations World Food Programme and a coalition of national church organizations to open channels for relief. A final example from Somalia demonstrates the difficulties of negotiating access when there are many feuding parties.

The UN breakthrough in persuading the Sudan's warring parties to grant access in early 1989 reversed a sequence of demoralizing failures. Two UN officials who had sought to reach people in the south in 1986 and 1988 had been declared *persona non grata* and forced to leave. Four NGOs associated with similar efforts in 1987 had been expelled: the Lutheran World Federation, World Vision International, Association of Christian Resource Organizations Serving Sudan (ACROSS), and the Swedish Free Mission. The ICRC, which began negotiations with both parties in March 1988, finally reached an agreement in December for relief activities in three limited areas on each side.

The agreement on Operation Lifeline Sudan represented a remarkable breakthrough. It required negotiations not only with the Sudanese government but also with the insurgents. Once the authorities in Khartoum had consented to the undertaking, an agreement was hammered out between the UN Secretary-General's Special Representative James P. Grant and Sudanese People's Liberation Army Commander John Garang. Even though UNICEF, which Grant served as executive director, had a tradition of dealing with antigovernment forces on humanitarian issues, negotiations between the UN's political department and insurgent forces were largely unprecedented.

Despite the success of the UN's negotiations with both belligerents, the resulting agreement soon became an item of contention among humanitarian actors. The United Nations proceeded to work out arrangements with the warring parties, largely without consulting NGOs on the scene, many of whom were not invited to the Khartoum pledging conference in early 1989 that marked the kickoff for the new effort. To make matters worse, the plan of action assumed—but failed to enlist—NGO participation. NGOs were particularly outraged that, after not having consulted them, the UN would count the relief supplies they delivered toward Lifeline's tonnage targets.

Some NGOs went public with their displeasure. They saw the difficulties experienced by the first Lifeline convoys as confirming their suspicions that the United Nations was more interested in a media caper than serious humanitarian action. UNICEF became a particular target. NGOs credited its special goodwill ambassadors, such as actress Audrey Hepburn, with helping put the Sudan crisis on the world map, but they saw the heavy emphasis on publicity as interfering with day-to-day relief tasks.

NGOs also saw the arrangements negotiated by the UN with the Khartoum authorities as a recipe for future difficulties. Management by UN officials raised serious policy concerns among NGOs, which worried that the government would expect the UN to police NGO activities. Some NGOs chose to keep their distance from the UN-negotiated relief effort.

In insisting on independence from Lifeline, one NGO official, ACROSS Executive Director Dan Kelly, observed, "Let not the bias of the UN be the means of frustrating or constraining NGOs, which need not have that bias themselves." As the situation developed in late 1989 and thereafter, the Sudan government did, indeed, look to the UN to rein in freewheeling NGOs in insurgent-controlled areas of the south.

Viewed from outside the warring humanitarian camps, the UN's efforts in negotiating arrangements with both sides produced sizable benefits for all. The ICRC was able to expand its activities significantly. The increased international personnel in the south and the expanded communications and transport associated with Lifeline enhanced the security of NGO staff and the efficiency of NGO programs. Western

Dr. John Garang, chairman of the SPLM, confers in April 1989 in Kongor with James P. Grant, personal representative of the UN secretary-general. (UNICEF/3573/Hartley)

governments no longer risked the displeasure of Khartoum authorities by participating actively in relief work.

Maintaining the access provided in the original Lifeline agreement and in subsequent extension of it has proved to be a perennial problem since late 1989. Complicating factors have included changes in the perceived interests of the belligerents, the emergence of a second set of insurgents, and a waning of international attention. Negotiations carried out first by UNICEF's Grant and then by other Lifeline officials have become the responsibility of the UN's Department of Humanitarian Affairs, whose missions to both north and south have encountered difficulties.

In Ethiopia, two sets of negotiations provide an interesting counterpoint to those in the Sudan. One involved an initiative by Ethiopian national NGOs to mount relief activities from Addis Ababa into an insurgent-controlled area; the other concerned arrangements in 1990 to reopen the port of Massawa as a staging area for international relief operations.

The Joint Relief Partnership (JRP) was an initiative of three national church bodies—the Lutheran Church Mekane Yesus, the Catholic Archbishopric, and the Orthodox Secretariat—and two international church organizations—Catholic Relief Services and the Lutheran World Federation. Their undertaking followed years of limited access from the capital of Ethiopia and other government-controlled areas to civilian populations experiencing great deprivation in the north.

The three national church bodies approached Ethiopian authorities with a proposal to mount a "cross-line" feeding program. That is, they would move convoys from Addis Ababa and other government-controlled areas into rebel-held portions of Tigray. After protracted negotiations with both the government in Addis Ababa and the TPLF in Khartoum, they reached an agreement with the warring parties that enabled them to move food across the front lines of the war zone to the great benefit of civilians in Tigray. A cross-line operation of major proportions resulted.

Positive outcomes notwithstanding, the undertaking was subsequently criticized by both sides. The TPLF believed that the operation allowed too much oversight and control by the Ethiopian authorities and failed to meet agreed tonnage targets. The regime, meanwhile, saw the political cause of the insurgents as the major beneficiary. For its part, JRP leadership emphasized its humanitarian objectives and results: People in need who would not otherwise have been reached benefited from an initiative that succeeded in carving out the requisite independence from both sides.[3]

Indeed, the role of national NGOs, with support and encouragement from international friends, was pivotal. They filled a gap created by the unwillingness of the Ethiopian authorities to negotiate with or through the UN. Doing so, the regime feared, would acknowledge its own limited reach and give international legitimacy to the TPLF. The NGOs were able to accomplish what they did by building on working relationships established with the insurgents over the years in a variety of human needs collaborations.

The second illustration involves the use of the port of Massawa, which had been captured in 1990 from the Ethiopian armed forces by the Eritrean insurgents, who eventually ousted the government after thirty years of armed struggle. Massawa's harbor facilities had been used by the Ethiopian government as a staging area for relief to the city of Asmara, which it had also controlled, even though the city was under EPLF siege. The port was also strategically and militarily important. The EPLF hesitated, not wanting to undermine its strategic advantage by opening the port to international humanitarian operations. The Mengistu regime, for its own tactical reasons, sought to monitor offshore what passed through the harbor and Asmara. The UN lacked the confidence of the Eritreans because of its failure to carry out the plebiscite promised in 1962.

Negotiations on behalf of the UN with the warring parties were carried out by James Ingram, then executive director of the WFP. Looking back, he discounts the assumption that "wearing a UN hat was a decisive factor" in their eventual success, although he concedes that "the explicit backing of the UN Secretary-General was very helpful." Ingram believes that another organization with comparable political support could have done the job as well, or better. "If political factors play a part in negotiations over access," he asks, "isn't the United Nations the appropriate agency to carry out the negotiations? I think not." Expressing some of the same concerns articulated by NGOs in the Sudan, Ingram said, "The United Nations is too political. Even if [it is] acting impartially, the parties will tend to see the UN as having goals that go beyond saving lives and that threaten their interests. The United Nations is above all an organization of states, and even its humanitarian agencies are not apolitical."[4] Ingram's choice for such mediation efforts in the future would be the ICRC, which lacks the political baggage of the UN and enjoys credibility with all sides in most conflicts.

A final example is drawn from the years 1991–1992 in Somalia, where negotiations of humanitarian access took place in a situation in which civil society had virtually broken down. There were multiple political protagonists, among them the undisciplined forces of former President Siad Barre, General Mohammed Farrah Aidid, and Ali Mahdi. If smaller groupings of armed subclans are included, the number of these actors neared one hundred. Hampered by the lack of an on-the-scene presence noted earlier, the United Nations was divided about the relative merits of continuing negotiations and forcing its way into the country with military force.

Throughout 1992, a series of mediation efforts by UN Under Secretary-General James O.C. Jonah were unsuccessful, although they resulted in a paper agreement between Aidid and Mahdi in February

1992. In the face of recurring difficulties in negotiating and protecting access, Jonah came to embrace the view that it was useless to negotiate with people he publicly called thugs. An alternative approach was taken by former Algerian Ambassador Mohamed Sahnoun, appointed in May 1992 as special representative of the secretary-general, who attempted to negotiate an end to the fighting with the main belligerents through a series of confidence-building measures, including discussions at the local level.

To increase the security of humanitarian workers and their activities, Sahnoun sought permission for deployment of a UN battalion of Pakistani soldiers and the expansion of the UNOSOM I forces by 3,500 additional soldiers already approved by the Security Council. His more inclusive and deliberate approach to negotiations and his unvarnished criticism of the UN system eventually cost him the support of the secretary-general and led to his forced resignation in October 1992.

The merit of the various approaches to negotiating humanitarian access was mooted with the introduction in December of UN-approved and U.S.-led military forces. In the intervening years, a number of studies have retraced the ground in an attempt to identify the necessary lessons to be learned from the Somalia debacle.[5]

The moral of these tales from the Horn of Africa is that the process of negotiating the nuts and bolts of access is as complex as it is indispensable. The organization or individual best positioned to pursue negotiations for access may vary from situation to situation. It should not be a foregone conclusion that any single actor—including the United Nations—is the preferred vehicle for all occasions. Whoever takes on the task should consult as widely as possible to ensure that the voices and resources of all potential outside contributors are appropriately engaged. Attention also must be paid to protecting and nurturing the access once granted because it can easily erode, whether from the pressure of events or from the decisions of belligerents.

## Resource Mobilization

Responding to war-induced humanitarian emergencies requires significant human and material resources. Judgments about the potential availability of resources from the public or private sector figure prominently in decisions by various organizations on whether to become involved, and if so at what level. Meeting the obvious requirement of paying the bills is not becoming easier as budgetary and recessionary pressures inhibit contributions while war-induced crises proliferate.

Two vignettes illustrate the complexities of this third challenge. The first concerns Somalia and the Sudan, where consolidated appeals have been launched under the auspices of the United Nations to counter the effects of recent warfare. The second involves Ethiopia, where the use of funds mobilized from the general public during the emergency of 1984 were used for longer-term development purposes, causing something of a scandal.

Reflecting the diversity of the humanitarian community, individual organizations traditionally have raised funds to support their own activities in individual crises. Separate appeals would be launched for Somalia or the Sudan by, for example, Catholic Relief Services, the American Red Cross, the International Committee of the Red Cross, UNICEF, and the World Food Programme. Bilateral donor organizations such as AID might approach the U.S. Congress for a supplemental appropriation to deal with a particularly overwhelming emergency.

Although individual organizations have the value of mobilizing a range of different constituencies, they risk confusing donors with multiple requests. Resources might flow from individual donors in the American public to specific NGOs and, through the U.S. government, to NGOs, the ICRC, UN agencies, and AID's own bilateral programs. Individual appeals also place a premium on identifying activities in various crises with particular agencies. This linking of certain activities with certain agencies may work against developing concerted strategies that maximize available resources.

A step in the direction of more coordinated and cost-effective resource mobilization was taken in the 1980s with the creation by the United Nations of the Office of Emergency Operations in Africa (OEOA). Faced with widespread famine in many sub-Saharan countries, the international community decided to conduct periodic appeals for the subcontinent as a whole. By putting into a common framework the requests of the various UN organizations, dynamic OEOA leaders prevailed on strong-willed individual UN agencies to limit their individual appeals. Donor governments welcomed the approach, and NGOs, too, benefited from heightened international awareness of the dimensions of the need.

One reason for the creation of the new UN Department of Humanitarian Affairs was donor government interest in institutionalizing on a global basis this ad hoc OEOA arrangement for Africa. Using the mechanism of an interagency standing committee staffed by the DHA, system-wide requests are now routinely prepared and forwarded to governments and the responses tracked accordingly. The arrangement meets the expressed interest of donors for a more coordinated approach to resource mobilization.

The effort has been disappointing in two respects, however. First, recent appeals have been less a consolidation of the requests of individual agencies, screened to establish priorities and to avoid overlapping activities, than a summary of their individual wishes. Second, the response of governments has been disappointing. Consolidated appeals issued during the initial two-year period were reported to have requested a total of $2,094,851,008 on behalf of ten UN organizations, the International Organization for Migration (IOM), NGOs, and others. Contributions and pledges of only 25 percent of that amount had been forthcoming, ranging from 32.6 percent of UNHCR's askings to 5.7 percent of the Food and Agriculture Organization's (FAO). The UN's Consolidated Appeal for Persons Affected by the Crisis in Burundi had been subscribed at 32.5 percent; the companion appeal for Liberia at 1.9 percent.[6]

The second illustration of resource mobilization comes from the NGO community and its occasional joint efforts by agencies to raise funds for a particular emergency. During the 1980s, U.S. Roman Catholic, Protestant, and Jewish organizations joined in a common initiative for the Horn of Africa, taking out newspaper advertisements to publicize their undertaking. For the most part, however, individual NGOs raise their own funds from their own constituencies for programs.

In 1984, as public awareness of the Ethiopian famine increased, Catholic Relief Services mounted a major effort through diocesan publications and newspaper advertisements to raise funds. It succeeded in mobilizing more money than CRS could use through its own staff and its Ethiopian partner organizations. Looking to the time when public interest would ebb and its own and other fund-raising efforts would become more difficult, CRS set aside funds for reconstruction and development needs, which would necessarily take longer to organize and be used over a more extended period.

Its action became a source of considerable controversy. The following year, this set-aside that CRS had viewed as the strategic use of resources came to be viewed by some as a betrayal of donor intent. After all, critics pointed out, the outpouring had been unleashed by BBC and other portrayals of famine scenes in northern Ethiopia, and it was immediate hunger that people wished to alleviate.

The incident became a sobering object lesson for humanitarian organizations, governmental as well as private, in responding to complex emergencies. There may be compelling reasons to look and plan beyond the immediate emergency, however, contributors must be educated to the need for doing so. Moreover, public interest in famine alleviation may not automatically transfer to the underlying causes of food shortages, be they war, drought, government policies, or human settlement practices, even though addressing them might help prevent future crises.

### Delivery

The fourth challenge—the most obvious, but hardly the easiest—is the physical provision of humanitarian relief and the protection of human rights. Again, experiences in the Sudan, Ethiopia, and Somalia illustrate the essential aspects: who does the actual work, how it is managed, how the necessary ethical choices are made, and how security is assured.

Operation Lifeline Sudan illuminates the necessary decisions regarding who would carry out its lifesaving ministrations among civilian populations. UNICEF, tapped by the secretary-general to become the lead UN agency, began by immediately transferring experienced hands from its posts around the world. They were reassigned on an urgent basis to New York, where the overall program was managed from UNICEF headquarters, to Khartoum, the base for activities in government-controlled areas, and to Nairobi, the center for UN operations in areas controlled by the insurgents. Food and its transport were entrusted to the World Food Programme, whose headquarters staff in Rome soon established operations bases in Khartoum and Nairobi.

UNICEF moved quickly to mobilize people to design, train, and monitor health programs. By November, its programs in insurgent-controlled areas alone had protected an estimated 115,000 children against measles, polio, diptheria, and tuberculosis and 30,000 women of childbearing age against tetanus. UNICEF also recruited agricultural specialists to mastermind the selection and distribution of hand tools

Villagers in Polje, Bosnia, load relief supplies for local distribution in January 1994. (ICRC Photo 152/5/J. Barry)

and seeds and enlisted hydrologists to provide potable water by rehabilitating hand pumps, wells, and electric generators, benefiting from a nearby airstrip.

Although its budget personnel procedures were less flexible than UNICEF's, WFP mobilized experienced logistics personnel to organize and accompany barge convoys down the river from Khartoum to Malakal and truck convoys overland from the Kenyan port of Mombasa into the southern Sudan. WFP and UNICEF staff also established and operated an expanded base of operations at Lokichoggio in northern Kenya that included warehouses, vehicle maintenance facilities, a telecommunications post, training rooms, and staff accommodations.

Within months, about 175 UN staff were working full time on Operation Lifeline Sudan. Other agencies had their own staffs. The ICRC contingent included 95 expatriates, 41 Sudanese from the national Red Cross/Red Crescent Society, and 867 local personnel. International and national NGO staffs further swelled the aid ranks.

Problems were created by the sheer size of the Sudan, Africa's largest country, with an area approximating that of the twelve countries of the European Union or of the continental United States. Given the prevailing political and military situation, careful monitoring was a necessity. The high international profile of the Lifeline operation led to the deployment of more UN and other staff than in most war zones, with an unusually large number of them stationed in the hinterlands. Criticized for relying too heavily on expatriates, some of them Westerners without prior relief experience who happened to be in the area, the UN responded that at least 90 percent of the Lifeline staff were non-Westerners hired from the region. In 1994, Lifeline operated in more locations than at earlier points in its history, with a large contingent of UN staff still deployed at the district and local levels.

A second issue concerned the best location for the program's management. Initially, Lifeline was managed from New York, with field representatives in Khartoum for government-controlled areas and in Nairobi for the south. This seemed logical since UNICEF, which had the lead responsibility among UN organizations, was based in New York. The location benefited from access to senior UN officials, diplomats, and New York–based media.

The New York location also had a largely unanticipated advantage. Since activities based in Khartoum and Nairobi both reported to New York, the geography symbolically underscored the UN's intention that its activities be strictly evenhanded. In October, when the United Nations shifted its base of operations to Khartoum, its image as an honest broker suffered. The insurgents complained that the change had lodged management of the program firmly in enemy territory. After all, UN officials with responsibilities in SPLA-controlled areas reported to UN superiors in Khartoum. Despite periodic meetings with both sides in Nairobi designed to correct the impression that the program was under Khartoum's thumb, the earlier image of nonpartisanship was never recaptured.

From a management perspective, it would appear highly questionable to establish a command center 10,000 kilometers from the scene of a crisis. On the contrary, reform efforts within the UN system over the last two decades have urged that decisions be delegated as fully as possible to the country level. However, in civil wars the importance of preserving nonpartisanship may outweigh the value of decentralized decisionmaking. That was the approach of the ICRC, whose activities on each side of the war reported separately and directly to its Geneva headquarters. In fact, the ICRC guarded its impartiality so assiduously that its program staff in each area were unfamiliar with operations by colleagues on the other side.

A third aspect of the operational task concerned thorny ethical choices. As an illustration, an aid worker from the British agency Oxfam and a group of national Ethiopian colleagues were monitoring activities during the 1984–1985 famine at a food distribution point in northern Ethiopia near the town of Korem. They witnessed uniformed army personnel rounding up male villagers who had come to pick up rations for their families. As the men were being led away and shot, a senior Ethiopian army officer took aside and threatened the expatriate. If word of the incident surfaced, he warned, the Oxfam worker and his local counterparts would meet the same fate.

At its country office in Addis Ababa and its headquarters back in Britain, Oxfam management pondered what to do about the incident. The roundup posed a serious threat to the integrity of humanitarian work. How could Oxfam continue a food distribution program that served as bait for men who were then killed? The incident secured a clearly documented violation of human rights by identified members of the armed forces that demanded exposure.

At the same time, the threat against aid staff also had to be taken seriously. Although the expatriate status of Oxfam's country director provided him with some protection, Oxfam's national staff and their families were considerably more vulnerable. A public denunciation of the Ethiopian army's culprits also could lead to closing Oxfam's countrywide operations, bringing down the curtain on its ability to serve as a channel for resources being energetically mobilized back in England to counter the famine.

Oxfam's decision remained strictly confidential at the time. After a discrete interval, details of the incident were released to the press in Nairobi on the condition that it be reported without reference to the location within Ethiopia or the specific agency involved. This alerted the international community to what was taking place without directly jeopardizing the future of personnel or programs. Personnel delivering assistance can play an indispensable role as the eyes and ears of the international community, but there are real dangers in doing so, particularly for national staff.

Life-and-death security issues, not on an exceptional basis as in Korem but in the routine conduct of day-to-day business, are a critical element in relief delivery. This was apparent from a visit in mid-November 1992 to Mogadishu, where, at the airport just outside the capital and throughout Mogadishu itself, violence hung heavy in the air. "Technicals," young men with machine guns at the ready, escorted visitors between the airport, relief offices in the city, and beyond. The relief offices themselves, set behind fences topped with concertina wire or broken glass, were heavily guarded inside and out by armed men. Walkie-talkies and radios crackled with constant transmissions as aid staff confirmed their whereabouts or requested instructions. A trip from one office to another for an ordinary meeting, or to the aid compound for a meal or overnight accommodations, required elaborate prearrangements and confirmation in the highly volatile situation.

Although they were alarmed by the prevailing insecurity in Mogadishu and the outlying countryside, humanitarian organizations were deeply divided about what could be done to make the overall atmosphere more conducive to humanitarian action. Some held that the security situation was deteriorating to the point that substantial military force was required if humanitarian operations were to continue at all. The International Rescue Committee and CARE took the lead in promoting this view. Other practitioners such as MSF and Oxfam-UK reacted quite differently, contending that the introduction of more armed soldiers would escalate the possibility of violence without necessarily increasing existing security. They also argued that outside military forces could even make aid workers more vulnerable to targeted or random incidents.

In November, U.S. agencies signed a letter to President George Bush's national security advisor, General Brent Scowcroft. "An end to the fighting is the ultimate solution to the Somali crisis, and we strongly support UN mediation efforts under way," the groups wrote. "However, humanitarian agencies cannot work effectively in Somalia without greater security. We believe that appropriately armed UN security forces tasked with protecting emergency supplies and staff may actually decrease the likelihood of conflict."[7]

Organized by InterAction, the professional association of U.S. NGOs, the letter illuminated deep divisions among aid providers. Some organizations did not sign, and others did so without consulting their representatives in Somalia or against their recommendations.

Similar divisions between supporters and opponents of more military muscle to support humanitarian operations existed elsewhere within the international community.

The NGO letter figured in discussions at the weekly coordination meeting in mid-November in Mogadishu. The first item on the agenda, as usual, was a security briefing by the head of the UN peacekeeping operation in Somalia (UNOSOM I), Pakistani Brigadier General Imtíaz Shaheen. After reviewing the week's security incidents, he turned to what he described as a matter of great importance. He had just been asked by the local media about reports that humanitarian organizations had requested reinforced security. "I took the liberty of denying that the reports contained any truth whatsoever," General Shaheen said, looking around the circle for any indication of disagreement. Despite nodding of heads, the situation was too highly charged to be debated before the general.

At issue was the advisability of a higher element of force, not the weakness of the existing UN peacekeeping force. Everyone, including UN military officers, agreed that the UN's military presence was feeble. After four months, the 500 poorly equipped members of the Pakistani battalion still were not deployed. An additional 3,500 troops had been approved by the Security Council, but they awaited agreement from belligerents.

Major transformations in the political and military landscape took place in the ensuing weeks. A UN Security Council resolution in late November authorized military action. U.S. President Bush, then a lame duck, authorized a U.S. contingent to come ashore in Mogadishu in early December 1992, as the first of an eventual 37,000 troops from some twenty countries. A strengthened UNOSOM II would take over in May 1993 to ensure humanitarian access and to disarm the warlords, the first Chapter 7 operation unambiguously under the direct control of the UN secretary-general.

Yet the jury remains out regarding the net value to humanitarian activities of the resulting military operations. The implications of a more assertive military presence remain to be reviewed.[8] Most of the immediate effects were positive. Within weeks, food distribution efforts proceeded more smoothly, and death rates among Somalis in several of the worst areas were reduced to an estimated 10 percent of previous levels. However, violence also claimed the lives of two aid workers. In

Somalis walk to a UN-supported feeding center near Bardera in April 1993.
(UN Photo 159849/M. Grant)

fact, there were more casualties and deaths among aid workers and journalists in the three months following the launching of Operation Restore Hope than in the preceding twelve.

Over time, insecurity also increased as UN-associated military personnel drew—and returned—fire. U.S. gunships attacked selected areas of Mogadishu controlled by Mohammed Farrah Aidid in June and July to avenge the killings of Pakistani, Italian, and U.S. peacekeepers and local aid personnel. Riots and the immediate assassination of four journalists began an unfortunate downward spiral that led eventually to the withdrawal of U.S. and other forces in early 1994. The longer-term costs and benefits were far less positive.

**Coordination**

Shifting from the Horn of Africa to Central America, the fifth challenge involves orchestrating collaboration among the many aid actors.[9] That was the task of the International Conference on Refugees in Central America. (Its Spanish acronym, CIREFCA, is also used in English.) This organization illustrates the various aspects of the coordination task and the difficulties encountered in war and immediate postwar situations.

CIREFCA was born toward the end of a decade of bitter internal conflicts that had left a broad swath of human debris in their wake. The conflicts also exacerbated the problems that had caused the tensions in the first place: widespread economic and social inequities, land shortages, and disenfranchisement of the poor from the established political institutions and processes. A durable peace would require resettling uprooted populations into situations that held promise for a better tomorrow. Discussions of reconstruction and development, which began while the conflicts still raged, were an integral part of the broader process of establishing reconciliation and peace.

At the regional and national levels, CIREFCA served as the specific institutional mechanism for the challenging task of coordination. Poor coordination is a chronic shortcoming in the international response to many major emergencies. The three essential elements of the task—in Central America as elsewhere—are establishing priorities, achieving an effective division of labor, and promoting accountability. CIREFCA's contribution to the first two elements was strongly positive;

it did less well with promotion of accountability, although its short-comings were eventually redressed.

At the first CIREFCA meeting in May 1989, governments, UN agencies, and NGOs endorsed a plan of action whose priorities were embraced by all outside humanitarian organizations. In fact, CIREFCA's inclusion of all the major interests within the region made it possible for the voices of governments, representatives of the armed opposition movements, and nongovernmental organizations to be heard systematically.

The most important policy decision to emerge from the CIREFCA coordinating process was that programs would be directed toward all people displaced by the conflicts. Distinctions were no longer attempted among refugees, returnees, the internally displaced, and the externally displaced (the latter being those who had left their country but were not formally recognized as refugees). Institutional learning took place and creative adaptation to the evolving situation continues.[10] One consortium that emerged, Coordinación, remains an effective advocate for the uprooted, enjoying open channels of communication to civilian and military officials.

The process also enhanced the credibility of UN organizations, whose traditional close working relationships with governments were viewed initially with suspicion by some NGOs, both outside and inside, and by local populations. Guilt by association is hard to overcome in civil wars, but ways have been and must be found to move beyond suspicion if meaningful coordination is to occur. Basic contact is a minimal requirement, and in El Salvador contacts have expanded.

The United Nations Development Programme had little experience with NGOs during the conflict. Yet as it assumed its normal role as coordinator of UN efforts for reconstruction, UNDP facilitated greater involvement for NGOs than the Salvadoran or other governments in the region might have proposed. The CIREFCA process introduced these organizations to each other and encouraged the development of constructive relationships based on a certain mutuality and division of labor.

CIREFCA's impact in terms of accountability has been less satisfactory. The initiative by Central American authorities in taking their fate into their own hands injected a positive sense of regional ownership of international activities. Beginning with the Contadora process and continuing with the efforts for which former Costa Rican President Oscar Arias won the Nobel Prize for Peace in 1987, governments in the area took the initiative and found ways to sustain regional leadership and momentum.

The basic agreement reached in Esquipulas served as a mechanism through which the region's regimes were able to hold one another's feet to the fire, while the international community was also pressing them to meet their stated obligations. That pressure has been significant in both Nicaragua's and El Salvador's wars. Guatemala's conflict has proved the most intractable to pressure from inside and outside the region alike.

Regarding the resources mobilized by and committed through CIREFCA, some $360 million were made available from 1989 through 1992, the largest single part provided by the Italian government to the Development Program for Displaced Persons, Refugees, and Repatriates (PRODERE), an activity managed by UNDP. Although CIREFCA played a noteworthy role in generating these resources and in directing them into well-formulated activities, their ultimate uses and effects are less clear. CIREFCA has not yet served to foster program or financial accountability, the third element in successful coordination.

A recent review of CIREFCA faults the mechanism for not keeping better track of the contributions that it helped mobilize. This study also notes that donor governments partially undercut CIREFCA's ability to monitor performance by providing funds through their own channels, bypassing CIREFCA when it was convenient to do so. As a result, although CIREFCA's overall results were demonstrably positive, the accomplishments on the ground at the local level resulting from CIREFCA-supported projects were more difficult to assess.

The performance of CIREFCA in these three major respects compares favorably with Operation Lifeline, its counterpart in the Sudan. Through a strategy of careful discussions and collaboration, CIREFCA included the full range of actors from the start. The collegiality it built avoided the sense among NGOs of being taken for granted by the UN, which had soured NGO participation in Lifeline. CIREFCA also contributed to a more effective division of labor among organizations, sidestepping the jockeying in Lifeline for position at the local level.

When it comes to orchestrating coordination, a harmonious performance does not occur simply because talented musicians show up for an emergency. Satisfying harmony requires specialization among the instrumentalists—be they governmental, nongovernmental, or inter-governmental, from inside or outside the area of conflict geographically. Harmony also requires reading from the same sheet of music, that is, following an agreed-upon plan of action. A successful conductor produces a professional ensemble sound by eliciting outstanding contributions from the players based on leadership and respect, not simply by virtue of the title "maestro." Effective coordination is the result of collegial cooperation, not fiat.

### Education and Advocacy

The sixth challenge involves two related sets of activities. The first concerns education, that is, familiarizing publics in donor countries with the crises and their solutions to nurture continued public support. The second has to do with advocacy, that is, efforts to generate pressure on donor governments to improve their policies toward people in crisis. An example from Nicaragua illustrates the work of NGOs and solidarity groups in educating Northern constituencies. An example from El Salvador highlights a largely successful effort by NGOs to bring about specific changes in U.S. policy toward the civil war.

In the case of Nicaragua, American public opinion, reflecting U.S. government policy, was generally hostile to the Sandinista regime throughout most of the 1980s. Portrayed as a foothold for the Soviet Union in the Western Hemisphere, the regime was the subject of a U.S. economic embargo and of a destabilization effort through U.S. support of the Contras.

Educational initiatives by U.S. NGOs and solidarity groups sought to dramatize the needs of ordinary Nicaraguans and to moderate the prevailing demonization of the Sandinista government. Study tours to San Salvador and rural areas, sister city exchanges, and support for grass-roots development projects were launched to overcome the prevailing ideological divide. The success of such efforts was modest at best. Public opinion remained skeptical, if not hostile, throughout the decade, accepting the anti-Sandinista tenor of U.S. policies in the areas of foreign relations, humanitarian assistance, trade, and immigration.

Educational efforts by European NGOs were more successful, although the task was probably easier there than in the United States. The prevailing political sentiment toward the Sandinista regime in Europe was generally more moderate. Connections between progressive forces such as labor unions and the media there and their counterparts in Nicaragua were closer. Flows of humanitarian assistance and personnel from the Nordic countries and the Netherlands were particularly large.

NGOs were more effective in bringing about changes in U.S. policy toward El Salvador. Pivotal events in their ongoing campaign for change occurred in late 1989. In the aftermath of an FMLN offensive on San Salvador on November 11, the government mounted a series of attacks on religious and humanitarian aid workers and activists suspected of sympathizing with the insurgents. The most publicized was the murder of six Jesuit priests, their housekeeper, and her daughter. In the month that followed, more than fifty-four searches of church facilities and homes of church workers by government forces were documented. By year's end, more than half of the existing expatriate aid workers had left the country.

In response, NGOs around the world quickly put into place an effective emergency support network. Working out of the Lutheran Council in Washington, workers from a variety of religious agencies maintained daily contact with groups in El Salvador, reported late-breaking developments to the State Department, and kept the media apprised of the rapidly changing picture. On November 30, twenty-five U.S. NGOs sent a letter to President Bush calling for "an immediate end to Salvadoran government and army interference with humanitarian relief operations, their personnel, their property, and their access to civilians in need of assistance." Citing the reluctance of the U.S. ambassador to criticize the harassment taking place, the group urged that the envoy be instructed "to actively defend humanitarian work and personnel."[11]

At the international level, the December meeting of the International Council of Voluntary Agencies called on NGOs throughout the world to intervene with their governments to press for a cease-fire and negotiated settlement to the conflict. ICVA also sent a delegation to meet with the Salvadoran president, defense minister, and other senior officials to express outrage and with relief organizations to express solidarity. The group called on governments to stop all arms shipments to the region and to condition economic aid on an immediate cease-fire and on support for a political solution to the conflict.

Returning through Washington in January, the delegation met with U.S. officials and gave interviews to publicize the situation. "We were shaken and profoundly dismayed by the constraints and interference with the legitimate operations of humanitarian organizations imposed by the military, and the extent and impact of this curtailment of humanitarian aid," the group reported. "This interference has the characteristics of being more systematic than simply a series of excesses in the heat of battle at the time of the FMLN offensive."[12] Although U.S. policy did not change at once, increased public and political pressure played a role in helping to limit abuses by the military and to bring the perpetrators of the killings to justice.

These examples of education and advocacy suggest an evolving division of labor within the larger NGO community, North and South, which has major implications for the world's humanitarian system. In recent years NGOs of the South have been saying with increasing eloquence and urgency that they intend to be the main actors in humanitarian and development programs in their own countries. Northern NGOs are encouraged to focus their energies on educating their own publics and improving the policies of their own governments.

The assertion of greater responsibility, operational and otherwise, by Southern institutions is indeed a welcome development. In fact, it illustrates the empowerment to which people-to-people organizations are avowedly committed. At the same time, the change raises serious difficulties for Northern organizations that traditionally have showcased their hands-on programming overseas, shying away from more complex educational and public policy issues on the home front. The message of the day is that Northern agencies that do not enhance their humanitarian activities abroad with education and advocacy activities at home can expect to command less respect in progressive quarters.

### Looking Beyond the Emergency

The seventh and final challenge is often lost in the day-to-day scramble to carry out humanitarian relief. Earlier examples have conveyed how difficult it is to look beyond an emergency while helping to mitigate acute war-induced suffering. Three situations highlight the problem and confirm that ignoring the impact of emergency strategies can undercut the effectiveness of humanitarian action.

The first example, taken from the Central America–wide experience of the 1980s, concerns anticipating the negative impact of humanitarian efforts, however unintended. The second is drawn from the UN

UN soldier from Kenya with Croatian children. (UN Photo 159256)

peacekeeping initiative in El Salvador, where the central lesson is more positive and suggests the value of keeping the overall picture in mind while carrying out emergency programs. The third, again drawing examples from the region, involves bringing those who suffer into the structure of emergency activities. Their participation represents an essential ingredient in ensuring adequate links between emergency action and the next steps of reconstruction and development.

First, the importance of anticipating the negative becomes obvious from a growing number of instances in which efforts to address urgent problems create still other problems. Rushing international food aid into a famine area may fend off starvation, but it also may undermine the incentives available to local food producers. Bypassing national and local channels may expedite relief, but it may squander an opportunity for enlisting them in the process. Commandeering outside troops to transport relief supplies may get the job done quickly, but it may strengthen the status of nondemocratic institutions on the receiving end, such as local armed forces.

Experts label such developments negative externalities, reflecting the reality that humanitarian action introduces into local situations resources, personnel, and other outside elements that may have unexpected and unhelpful consequences. Negative externalities are not associated exclusively with emergency aid; they often accompany longer-term development activities. Recurrent infusions of outside aid may undermine local self-reliance and impede rather than facilitate longer-term economic viability. Externalities are so important that aid practitioners, however well intended and initially successful, as noted earlier, need to embrace the Hippocratic watchword to "do no harm," or at least as little harm as possible.

Central America during the 1980s—including Honduras, Mexico, Costa Rica, Belize, and Cuba, in addition to Nicaragua, El Salvador, and Guatemala—was thoroughly politicized. Global geopolitics infiltrated national political and economic life in what was traditionally considered the back yard of a superpower. The confrontation between the United States and the Soviet Union cast a long shadow, affecting the conduct of even humanitarian action.

One of the unfortunate effects of politicized aid was that the wars lasted longer for some institutions than for the belligerents themselves. Even as the armed conflicts diminished, organizations had enormous difficulty in shedding their wartime ideological baggage and ridding themselves of the accompanying obsession with emergency aid. Those that had played active roles in providing relief were reluctant or unable to shift gears and address reconstruction challenges. Perhaps most difficult, reaching out across political divides required aid workers to establish trust in quarters where they had been viewed as partisan.

Looking back on the decade, even seasoned veterans are struck by how much most humanitarian agencies became identified with one side or the other. This is not to say that they feel that any other approach or result would have been possible. "It was simply a question of whose side you were on," recalled one U.S. activist. "You could either ally yourself with the forces of justice and social change, or with the status quo. There was no middle alternative."

UN organizations were generally perceived as working hand in glove with the region's recognized governments. In contrast, many NGOs were viewed as having close ties to the uprooted. Donor governments divided their sympathy with one side or the other, depending upon geopolitical interests. As a result, the humanitarian associations and activities of outsiders were seen as expressing political biases.

In this context, the activities of solidarity groups deserve attention. Like all NGOs, they were involved in providing outside resources directly to communities in the region. Like many other NGOs, they frequently worked with indigenous counterparts whom they sought to encourage and strengthen. Unlike most other NGOs, however, they fervently embraced an explicit political agenda, such as resistance to government control over the rural poor. NGOs may sometimes have been inattentive to the perception that they were supporting a particular political cause, but the presence of solidarity groups made such a pretense particularly unrealistic.

For all the difficulties, however, less politicized approaches and alternative strategies were probably more possible than many activists thought at the time. For example, the ICRC diligently pursued efforts to bridge the prevailing divides. In El Salvador, its representative recalls holding scores of meetings during the decade with the government, and an equal number with insurgents, to arrange access for its delegates to civilian populations and to visit prisoners of war. Among all the actors, the ICRC worked hardest at keeping its efforts depoliticized and was perhaps the most successful at doing so. As a result, it emerged with the widest respect of all parties. Yet, although ideally placed to help in reconstruction, it left El Salvador soon after the peace treaty was signed in 1992 because its mandate was limited to countries experiencing internal armed conflict.

NGO officials acknowledge in retrospect that they paid too little attention to nonpartisanship. They also concede that their identification—mostly with populations in insurgent areas in El Salvador and in government-controlled areas in Nicaragua—prevented them from being trusted by officials and communities identified with the other side. While NGOs often criticize solidarity groups for a highly political agenda, they themselves did not succeed in assisting on both sides of the conflicts.

In short, neither UN organizations, governments, nor NGOs emerged from the war with the trust of all civilian populations. Politicization of emergency relief slowed reconciliation and limited the number of institutions involved in it from the outset.

If emergency lifesaving activities have negative consequences that must be minimized, a second illustration suggests that they also have a hidden potential for positive spin-offs that must be augmented. Ill-conceived and well-conceived responses to a crisis may also produce positive synergisms. A case in point is the UN Observer Mission in El Salvador (ONUSAL), a comprehensive and visionary instrument designed to anchor a shaky peace agreement and to help a battered country move beyond conflict to reconstruction.

The Security Council established ONUSAL in July 1991, when the United Nations was playing an active role in peace negotiations between the government of El Salvador and the Farabundo Martí Front for National Liberation. Initially charged with monitoring human rights performance, its duties expanded with the implementation of a cease-fire on February 1, 1992.

The peace agreement represented an opportunity to implement the vision of "peace-building" articulated in the UN secretary-general's important public document, *Agenda for Peace*.[13] Activities spanned many mutually reinforcing sectors. In addition to a mission to protect human rights that began even before the official cease-fire took hold, ONUSAL's multifaceted efforts included demobilizing regular and irregular forces and confiscating their weapons, monitoring elections, reforming government institutions, establishing law and order, and training the personnel necessary to preserve it. Also integral to the peace agreement and ONUSAL's mandate were humanitarian activities already under way under the auspices of UNHCR and other UN organizations. The overall success of ONUSAL had a positive impact on the pace and success of all activities.

ONUSAL opened up the process of reconstruction by negotiating the return of mayors to municipalities in conflict zones from which they had been barred. It was in a position to insist on including all persons, not just those of one political persuasion. ONUSAL's reporting of human rights abuses laid the groundwork for the findings of the Truth Commission. In a courageous report that highlighted links between human rights protection and longer-term requirements for peace, this three-person tribunal called for purging over 100 persons clearly implicated in earlier official repression. This, in turn, helped highlight links between human rights protection and longer-term requirements for peace. The presence of 1,000 outside personnel, fanning out across the relatively small country and conveying a sense of the world's commitment to the peace process, also exercised a stabilizing influence at a politically sensitive and potentially volatile moment of transition.

Despite these accomplishments, the synergism could have been greater still. ONUSAL staff members met weekly with UN humanitarian personnel, but their contacts were not as productive or interactive as they could have been. They saw themselves with a limited, focused, and political task, which they approached as superior to the work of UN staff engaged in less critical activities. Conversely, UN humanitarian officials, whose work had preceded ONUSAL, viewed the last arrivals as interlopers and latecomers. Although both sets of UN staff were international civil servants, they tended to go their separate ways. This lack of collegiality and vision diminished the reinforcement potential of separate but related activities.

Many key activities were carried out largely in isolation from ONUSAL, including UNHCR's nationwide project of documentation and refugee resettlement, UNDP's country-wide development programs, and the everyday work of other UN organizations such as UNICEF, WFP, and World Health Organization/Pan-American Health Organization (WHO/PAHO). The mutual reinforcement that did take place between these efforts and those of ONUSAL tended to reflect the creativity of individual UN officials in given locations rather than policy decisions taken in San Salvador, New York, or Geneva.

A specific example of missed opportunities emerges from the conflicting approaches to land transfers, a critical area since the equal distribution of land had been a key problem underlying the conflict. In an effort to proceed with reconstruction after the wars, claims to land seized during the war required prompt and fair adjudication as uprooted populations returned home.

Before deciding on the ground rules for land transfers and providing for them in the ONUSAL budget, the UN secretary-general received detailed estimates from UNDP and FAO personnel in El Salvador of the number of people who would qualify for such transfers and the work involved in completing the necessary paperwork. The final figures in the ONUSAL budget, however, reduced the number of cases, the cost per case, and the numbers of transfers that would be completed by ONUSAL before it concluded its work.

The secretary-general's desire to keep the cost of ONUSAL down made sense, but his approach deferred a critical political issue that could destabilize the peace agreement itself, particularly given stringent demands by international lenders to keep Salvadoran government spending in check. The burden of funding such activities shifted accordingly from ONUSAL to individual UN organizations, which are less well endowed by governments and which will have to pick up the unfinished business after ONUSAL's departure. The decision also eased pressure on the Salvadoran government to fund a major share of land transfers and to expedite the process.

Some analysts—including Alvaro de Soto and Graciana del Castillo, who were involved in the UN's mediation efforts—have argued convincingly that the UN system is encountering great difficulties in El Salvador, where they say the UN's efforts in the politico-military field "could be on a collision course" with the stabilization program and other economic adjustment activities by the International Monetary Fund and the World Bank.[14]

Whatever else was implied when the UN secretary-general wrote of an "integrated approach to human security" in *An Agenda for Peace*,[15] he clearly intended the international community's activities in the political-military and development realms to work in tandem rather than at cross-purposes. At a minimum, the Central American experience suggests structural difficulties in the UN's playing a leadership role in two essential components of human security.

In spite of such difficulties, the UN has made a major contribution to humanitarian action in El Salvador. Although more time should be allowed to elapse before ONUSAL's success is considered durable, the UN initiative has already helped turn former adversaries into stakeholders in the elections of April 1994. ONUSAL also served as a model for another comprehensive effort, the United Nations Transitional Authority in Cambodia (UNTAC). There, however, in the absence of viable national political and administrative structures after the civil war, the UN received an even more intrusive mandate and faced even more difficult challenges.

A third illustration suggests that an indispensable feature in international humanitarian initiatives should be the involvement of the people affected by crises. The strength of indigenous organizations in refugee camps, repatriated communities, and among internally displaced persons was a major factor in tailoring emergency assistance and assuring that it served reconstruction objectives in Central America. Victims of crises emerged as a fundamental resource in alleviating suffering and in working for political solutions. Salvadoran refugees in Honduras and Guatemalans displaced to Mexico set their own agendas, sometimes ignoring or overruling expatriate advice and plans.

Over time, the CIREFCA process also contributed to the efficacy of humanitarian operations. UN agencies forged new relationships and assisted governments in reaching out to a wider range of private groups that had been encouraged to organize themselves.

The guiding principle of appropriateness highlighted the importance of resisting the temptation to treat saving lives as an end in itself, isolated from the involvement of local institutions and leadership. The tendency to do rather than to facilitate is an unfortunate hallmark of many outside-led approaches to humanitarian action.

Judgments must necessarily be framed in tentative terms when reviewing a decade of armed conflicts so soon after they have begun to wind down. Yet it seems clear that when humanitarian endeavors take their guidance from beneficiary populations at the earliest possible moment and enlist them in creative ways, they will prove more durable than efforts, however efficient, that are managed by outsiders for "target populations."

That has been the stated philosophy of the UN Development Program. "An essential part of any political process to benefit the poor is a high degree of participation," observes its *Human Development Report 1991.* "Encouraging the autonomy of citizens is, indeed, an end in itself. And participation is a means to ensure the efficient provision and more equitable distribution of goods and services." The report concludes, "If people are involved in decision-making, policies and projects tend to be more realistic, more pragmatic, and more sustainable."[16]

This approach has been validated, in UNDP's view, by recent experience in Central America, where UNDP spearheaded an agricultural training program for ex-FMLN combatants supported by various donor governments and international organizations. Using forty-nine training centers around the country, the initiative was designed with the active participation of the government of El Salvador and the FMLN to facilitate the reentry of more than 6,000 recently demobilized soldiers into the agricultural sector.

Training courses held during a five-month period in late 1992 and early 1993, a delicate time in the transition of the country from civil strife to peace, sought to make erstwhile insurgents stakeholders in a productive and peaceful El Salvador. "As social, political and economic exclusion are often at the root of deadly civil strife," observed UNDP in a review of the experience, "the participation of the historical parties to the conflict in designing the reintegration programmes is clearly a key step toward addressing this historical source of conflict."[17]

## Conclusion

This overview of the seven challenges of humanitarian action underscores the complexity of the tasks confronted by humanitarians venturing into war zones. Many of the tasks need to be performed concurrently, an added complication.

As with the guiding principles discussed earlier, the seven individual challenges intersect and overlap. Perhaps the most important and overarching, however, is the seventh: the need to take a comprehensive approach that charts humanitarian action within its broader political, military, and developmental contexts. It provides the framework within which the other individual tasks may be tackled.

The enumeration of these challenges is not intended to imply that each organization should tackle each humanitarian task. Some organizations are clearly better able to meet particular challenges than others. To expect each agency to carry out each of the tasks would be a recipe for confusion and waste, as well as overextension and superficiality.

Chapter 4 examines how various humanitarian organizations interact as they carry out their tasks. It seeks to assess their comparative advantages, identifying what each does best and least well. In this way, strengths may be reinforced and weaknesses offset within a more effective global humanitarian community of the future.

# 4

# Interactions

The eight sets of major humanitarian actors interact with each other in responding to the seven challenges faced in conflicts. Since each has its own strengths and weaknesses, identifying who does what best in particular circumstances can help improve the humanitarian system of the future.

Staff of international organizations based in Europe—for example, at the Palais des Nations in Geneva and the headquarters of the European Union in Brussels—often display a favorite poster on their walls. "Heaven is where the police are British, the cooks French, the mechanics German, the lovers Italian, and it is all organized by the Swiss." On the other hand, the poster continues, "Hell is where the chefs are British, the mechanics French, the lovers Swiss, the police German, and it is all organized by the Italians."

However stereotyped, the message contains a deeper reality. Some individuals and organizations are better at doing certain humanitarian tasks than others. The global humanitarian community of the future needs to harness the energy, qualities, and creativity of all the major actors. The better the fit and the less chafing under the harness, the more efficient the utilization of scarce resources.

## Outside Resources

Outside resources are made available for humanitarian purposes through five major channels: intergovernmental organizations, the bilateral agencies of donor governments, NGOs, the ICRC, and outside military forces.

Faced with such a plethora of actors, the public often wonders, Why are there so many humanitarian groups? Is relief reaching the people who need it? Which outfits are doing the best job? Do tax dollars need to underwrite this? To whom should I make my private donation?

The donor public is not alone in its bewilderment. Political authorities in conflict areas often are similarly befuddled. A senior Jordanian coordinator of relief efforts for those fleeing from Kuwait and Iraq in 1990 became exasperated at having to distinguish "the charlatan from the humanitarian." He complained of having spent valuable time with "so many who gave empty promises and were never seen again." Before granting a visa for interviews in Belgrade in June 1993, an official of the Federal Republic of Yugoslavia in Washington expressed unhappiness at the number of humanitarian organizations seeking permission to enter his country. "Why are there so many? What do they all do? Why can't they get together? Which ones are serious? Why haven't they made a difference yet?"

These questions recur with each new emergency and each time an ad hoc constellation of organizations assembles at the scene of a new disaster. Why do all these organizations exist? Is one better than the next? Are they all necessary and useful? Do they somehow fit together into an organized whole, or is the whole less than the sum of its parts?

At a time when international crises are legion and the world's humanitarian resources overstretched, such questions assume new urgency. The various actors deserve discussion, each in its own right and in their interaction with each other.

## Intergovernmental Organizations

The United Nations system consists of many different organizations.[1] They share a common UN connection, are staffed by international civil servants who travel on the United Nations' own passport, or *laissez-passer*, and enjoy certain perks as international civil servants, including a common retirement system. Yet each United Nations organization has its own set of objectives, style of operation, board of governors, constituencies, accountability, and culture. An examination of the four major UN entities with humanitarian assistance and protection responsibilities—UNICEF, UNHCR, WFP, and the Centre for Human Rights which functions less as an operating agency and more as a system-wide monitor—illustrates this diversity.[2]

The first three are operational agencies, oriented to the field where emergencies occur. The United Nations Children's Fund, with origins

UN high commissioner for refugees visits Sarajevo. (UNHCR Photo/E. Dagnino/L. Ronchi/07.1992)

in World War II, has in the intervening years provided assistance to women and children for emergencies and for longer-term development. While the "E" in its acronym originally referred to the "emergency" represented by the world cataclysm that ended in 1945, UNICEF in recent years has sought to direct more resources to longer-term development. Emergencies nevertheless continue to clamor for attention, placing UNICEF front and center in many of today's major conflicts.

Three characteristics distinguish UNICEF from other UN agencies. The first is its well-established tradition of operating in civil wars without supporting the cause of one belligerent or another. Building on a history of involvement in internal armed conflicts such as China (1946–1947) and Nigeria/Biafra, UNICEF has developed a capacity for functioning in highly politicized territory where other UN agencies, more attuned to the sensitivities of sovereignty, hesitate to tread. Second, UNICEF has developed more presence and name recognition in crisis-affected areas, both through its own staff and through links to nongovernmental partners active at the grass-roots level. Third, UNICEF has devoted considerable resources to publicizing human needs through extensive fund-raising, education, and advocacy activities in developed and developing countries. Its success and visibility in these three areas have made it perhaps the most widely known entity around the world and have led to criticisms in some quarters of self-promotion.

UNHCR also grew out of World War II and the needs of its victims. The focus of its staff at its headquarters in Geneva and in many countries around the world remains the victims of war, violence, persecution, and other human rights abuses. Like UNICEF, it subcontracts many of its service provision activities to NGO operational partners while maintaining working relationships with both donor and recipient governments.

As the R in its acronym implies, UNHCR's normal mandate is for what have traditionally been defined as refugees. The agency does not normally work with internally displaced persons, unless specifically requested to do so by its governing board or by the United Nations secretary-general. Unlike the situation in earlier years, when most displaced persons crossed national borders and therefore qualified as refugees, many today remain within their countries of origin but find themselves nonetheless in refugee-like conditions. Since these persons now exceed the number of traditional refugees, there is growing pressure to find an institutional home among the existing UN agencies for such concerns or to create a new one.[3]

As lead UN agency for the international response to the humanitarian crisis in the former Yugoslavia, UNHCR has assumed responsibility for those who have remained within their countries of origin as well as those who have crossed an international frontier. Faced with policies of "ethnic cleansing" by the belligerents, UNHCR has been given the further task of seeking to prevent persons from becoming either refugees or internally displaced.

The World Food Programme is the UN organization that specializes in the provision of food aid for relief and development. In natural disasters and war-related emergencies, it handles the logistics of food delivery. When efforts turn to reconstruction and development, WFP provides commodities and technical assistance for "food for work" programs. Founded in 1963 and based in Rome, where it is now related to but independent of the UN Food and Agricultural Organization, WFP has a cadre of international staff posted in countries around the world. It channels substantial amounts of commodities received from individual governments such as the United States and Canada and from intergovernmental organizations such as the European Union. It also receives cash contributions to underwrite food transport costs and to purchase additional food. In recent years WFP has emphasized the purchase of commodities where possible in developing countries themselves and has assisted governments to develop national resources and to manage their food stocks effectively.

For many years, WFP tended to be bureaucratic in its approach and relationships, dealing for the most part with government ministries in developing countries on a fairly circumscribed set of food distribution issues. In recent years WFP has decentralized some of its decisionmaking and worked more closely on humanitarian issues with insurgent groups to respond more effectively to a growing number of civil war-related emergencies. The importance of providing food effectively in a growing number of armed conflicts has given new importance and visibility to its activities.

Compared with these three UN organizations and with the UN Development Program—whose operational mandate in humanitarian emergencies is limited, but whose country representatives often coordinate the response of the UN system—the UN Human Rights Center is conspicuous by its modest size. The Geneva-based agency is the program arm of the UN Human Rights Commission, a body made up of fifty-three member governments that meets in regular sessions twice a year. Unlike more operational UN agencies, the commission traditionally has had no international staff resident in countries in crisis. Instead, it dispatches special rapporteurs that report back to the commission on alleged human rights abuses.

In recent years, Human Rights Commission rapporteurs have been sent to such hot spots as the Sudan, northern Iraq, and Haiti, often in response to pressure from member governments and human rights groups. The human rights community, which has pressed the UN system, the center, and its parent commission to be more assertive, has encouraged and welcomed the development of a more field-oriented UN human rights presence in Cambodia, El Salvador, Haiti, and other crisis situations as well, although it has been critical of the ways human rights issues have been managed within UN peacekeeping operations.[4] A number of innovative and possibly precedent-setting steps also have been taken in the former Yugoslavia, although their implementation in that setting has left much to be desired.[5]

More human rights assertiveness often has been resisted by the governments of some developing countries. As noted earlier, some governments at the Vienna conference on human rights in June 1993 questioned the universality of civil and political rights and discouraged international scrutiny of treatment of civilian populations. Nevertheless, the General Assembly decided later that year to elevate human rights issues and approved the creation of a UN High Commissioner for Human Rights, who is now charting his course on these matters.

From the outside, one might conclude that the UN secretary-general was master of these four organizations and of the wider UN family. In fact, however, his executive responsibilities are limited to managing the UN Secretariat, a far more limited staff with carefully delimited functions. Although the secretary-general has a certain broad political authority over the UN's humanitarian activities, that authority is mainly legal and constitutional rather than actual.

Within the UN system as a whole, the secretary-general is *primus inter pares* (first among equals), with the emphasis on *pares* rather than *primus*. The heads of UNICEF, UNHCR, and WFP manage annual budgets that approach in size the resources over which the secretary-general has direct control. Their resources, which emanate from governments that supervise their organizational performance through separate governing boards, are neither channeled through the UN's CEO nor, strictly speaking, accountable to him. Autonomy and independence are the hallmarks of individual UN organizations, not integration or collaboration.

If the UN secretary-general has very limited authority over the UN's humanitarian activities, his under secretary-general for humanitarian affairs has even less. The post was an outgrowth of General Assembly resolution 46/182, adopted in December 1991 to avoid another stumbling UN performance in crises like that in the Persian Gulf. The UN's first humanitarian maestro, Jan Eliasson, a respected Swedish diplomat who negotiated the end to the Iran–Iraq War in 1987 and helped shape the General Assembly consensus in favor of creating such a position, organized the new Department of Humanitarian Affairs and saw it through its infancy.

With New York staff numbering about fifty, DHA has been involved in promoting humanitarian concerns in discussions with the secretary-general and other major UN departments, and through "humanitarian diplomacy" has sought to negotiate access to people trapped in civil wars around the world. DHA's Geneva staff of about 100 helps coordinate the work of the UN's many humanitarian organizations, launch coordinated appeals for emergencies on their behalf, and provide a point of information and accountability for UN activities.

The UN's first humanitarian maestro brought more coherence to its often disorganized response to major crises. Yet DHA, sometimes for reasons beyond its control, has made very little practical difference in major headline crises in places such as Somalia and Bosnia. DHA has been even less successful in internal lobbying on humanitarian issues with the secretary-general, the Security Council, and those in charge of peacekeeping and political affairs. Even admirers concede that at a time when the infant DHA was experiencing natural teething problems, Eliasson needed to bare more teeth.

The deck remains stacked against his successor, a Dane with considerable UN experience named Peter Hansen, who assumed his duties in March 1994. Faced with unresolved problems in preexisting crises and with the difficulties experienced by the UN in new flashpoints in Rwanda and North and South Yemen, Hansen will need to take the weak bureaucratic hand he has been dealt and persuade and cajole UN aid agencies to function more efficiently and collegially. In a somewhat pro forma review of DHA's work in November 1993, the UN General Assembly encouraged it to be more assertive but dealt it no new cards and certainly no trumps.

The UN's humanitarian organizations interact not only with each other but also with the political and military side of the United Nations. As the UN has become more active in what is now called peace enforcement, a widening cleavage has developed between UN organizations whose tasks are humanitarian and other parts of the UN operational apparatus whose preoccupation is for "peace and security." As a result, the UN is suffering a serious case of schizophrenia.

As noted earlier, the visibility and relative importance of humanitarian crises have increased in the post–Cold War era, along with the UN's role in addressing them. During the heyday of superpower confrontation, the world's highest political body—the UN Security Council— was largely marginalized. Reflecting a more collaborative spirit between the former superpowers, the council now construes its responsibility for maintaining international peace and security more broadly. In fact, international peace and security have become what Harvard historian Stanley Hoffman calls an all-purpose parachute. The potential spillover of domestic instability and internal migration, both associated with war-related humanitarian crises, thrusts matters earlier described as purely domestic clearly into the international domain.

The UN General Assembly, the world's representative political body, has also turned its attention increasingly to humanitarian concerns. In the mid- to late-1980s, it discussed the proposal of some governments and NGOs to establish a new international humanitarian order. In 1991, it held a wide-ranging debate on humanitarian intervention that resulted in the recommended creation of a new position of under secretary-general for humanitarian affairs at a level comparable to the existing positions of under secretaries-general for peacekeeping and political affairs. Humanitarian concerns, subordinated to East-West geopolitics during the Cold War, have attained a new level of importance.

Welcome in principle, the elevated priority of humanitarian interests has been a mixed blessing. The UN's humanitarian organizations and officials have experienced considerable difficulty in carrying out their mandates in armed conflicts by virtue of their closer association with punitive economic and military actions taken by the Security Council.

Commenting at the time of the Persian Gulf crisis in 1992 on the tension, an informed Jordanian stated, "It is hard for people on the ground who see punitive actions, which harm people more than their leaders, not to be emotional about the role of the United Nations." Referring to the UN's twin roles in northern Iraq—blessing military action and then providing mop-up humanitarian aid—a senior staff member from a Jordanian NGO observed with evident sarcasm, "The United Nations kills, and then hurries to walk in the funeral."[6]

There also have been problems in other settings in which the UN has provided humanitarian relief after—and to offset the effects of—economic sanctions. A study released in 1994 by a Harvard team caused a stir with its assertion that UN sanctions had caused the deaths of 1,000 children a month.[7] Sanctions imposed by the UN Security Council on the Federal Republic of Yugoslavia also worked great hardship on civilians and undercut the credibility of the UN's humanitarian organizations.[8] As in Haiti, humanitarian items were exempt, but the case-by-case review imposed by the Security Council's Sanctions Committee

Girls peer out through a fence near Aranos, Namibia. (UN Photo 159330/E. Debebe)

on relief shipments by the UN's own humanitarian agencies caused major delays.

In late 1990 and early 1991, when the Security Council was debating whether economic sanctions against Iraq were working or military force should be applied, the views of well-placed UN humanitarians were not solicited. WFP staff in Baghdad were in an ideal position to assess the effectiveness of the UN embargo on Iraqi food supplies but were not consulted. UNICEF, familiar with the status of the groups most vulnerable to the impacts of sanctions and war, was not consulted by the Security Council either.

The existence of regional organizations, some of them members of the UN system and some separate, adds another interactive element to the intergovernmental framework. The secretary-general's *Agenda for Peace* recommends a greater role for them, as does the UN Charter itself.

Each region has a United Nations–affiliated organization, with corresponding acronym: Economic Commission for Africa (ECA), Economic and Social Commission for Asia and the Pacific (ESCAP), Economic Commission for Europe (ECE), Economic Commission for Latin America and the Caribbean (ECLAC), and Economic Commission for Western Asia (ECWA). Based in Addis Ababa, Bangkok, Geneva, Santiago, and Baghdad, respectively, each is constituted by and accountable to a board made up of government representatives. Although perhaps not directly active in humanitarian assistance or protection, UN regional entities carry out relevant policy work and offer selected support services.

Thus, the UN meeting on peace and reconciliation in Somalia, called by the UN secretary-general and chaired by the under secretary-general for humanitarian affairs, took place in December 1992 at ECA headquarters in Addis Ababa and with its administrative support. Other regional commissions are studying the impact of wars on economic performance and lobbying member states to respond.

Regional intergovernmental organizations without an institutional UN connection do not normally carry out their own humanitarian activities, with the notable exception of Europe discussed below.[9] Two prominent organizations are the Organization of African Unity, also based in Ethiopia, and the Nigeria-based Economic Community of West African States. Both monitor economic and political developments and undertake initiatives with a bearing on humanitarian concerns. The OAU played a key role in the adoption of the 1967 African Refugee Convention, which affirms the crucial principle that hospitality to refugees will not be considered an unfriendly political act. In 1990, ECOWAS dispatched a regional peacekeeping force to contain Liberia's civil war, which had displaced 1.5 million refugees throughout the region. Earlier the OAU had attempted unsuccessfully to send military forces to Chad and had considered action in numerous civil wars. In the Liberia and Rwanda conflicts, the OAU had also played a "good offices" role.

Those who urge a larger role for regional bodies argue not only that the UN as a universal organization is overextended in the face of a sea of challenges but also that regional approaches to conflict management have a special logic and urgency. Regional stakeholders often have the most to lose from the consequences of wars in their areas—both direct (in the form of refugee flows) and indirect (through plummeting trade and investment transfers). The current institutional capacities of most regional organizations, however, remain extremely feeble. They normally have been unable to protect peace and security or to launch major humanitarian initiatives. The stated advantages of proximity to crises are offset by practical disadvantages such as partisanship, local rivalries, and a lack of resources.

An exception to these generally negative views about the poor performance of regional institutions in humanitarian disasters is found in Europe, although there, too, the actual results have been disappointing. Confronted by the crisis in the former Yugoslavia, European diplomatic and military dithering in the form of largely unsuccessful efforts by NATO, the Western European Union (WEU), and the European Community (since November 1993, the European Union) has already been noted.

Interestingly, as in the West African response to the Liberian crisis, the difficulties of hammering out a common regional position and the problems presented by the differing sets of existing relationships with the belligerents complicated joint regional action. As was also the case in West Africa, diplomatic initiatives joined regional European and universal UN approaches.

Whatever the problems on the political-military side, the European Union has become a more prominent intergovernmental player in world humanitarian affairs. Since its early years, the EC, and more recently the EU, has coordinated bilateral development aid from member governments and financed projects agreed to by the twelve-member group.

To deal with the special challenge of the former Yugoslavia, the EC created a European Community Humanitarian Office, with emergency resources, activities, and personnel of its own. Its performance exemplified both strengths and weaknesses. In 1991, following recognition of Croatia first by Germany and then by the entire European Community, ECHO provided bulk food aid directly to the Croatian government. The EC seemed largely unconcerned whether food deliveries supported the broader international effort (they did not) or even whether they reached those who needed them (EC food aid was alleged to have been diverted to support the Croatian government's war effort). The overriding concern at the time was that the EC be perceived as "doing something."

In the Federal Republic of Yugoslavia, by contrast, EC food aid was carefully designed to supplement other international assistance. Directed to host families and their refugee guests, it complemented other food relief provided through UNHCR. The striking contrast to the difficulties in Croatia reflected both applicable ECHO policies and the personalities entrusted with managing the interactions.

The Geneva-based International Organization for Migration is an intergovernmental agency in something of a class by itself. Formed in 1951 as the Intergovernmental Committee for European Migration to help resettle displaced persons in Europe, IOM has since received a mandate "to ensure, throughout the world, the orderly migration of persons who are in need of international migration assistance."

With fifty-two member states and forty observers, IOM carries out activities through its headquarters in Geneva and seventy-three field offices and a staff of more than 1,000. In the early 1990s, it facilitated the return of about 700,000 people to their homes in Asia, Africa, and the Middle East following Iraq's invasion of Kuwait. In the former Yugoslavia, IOM has assisted in the evacuation of Muslims detained in concentration camp–like settings, helped refugees and displaced persons reach countries offering temporary or permanent asylum, and evacuated serious medical cases. IOM has the advantage of a well-recognized and global mission without the unwieldiness of universal membership and a large governing board.

What, in sum, are the strengths and weaknesses of assistance channeled through intergovernmental organizations? The overarching strength of UN institutions is their universality. As expressions of global solidarity, they form a network that leaves virtually no corner of the world unreached. Within that network, individual UN agencies, each with its own mandate and ethos, make distinctive contributions. The global reach of UN organizations, however, may involve liabilities, including larger bureaucracies and correspondingly slower responses, lessened effectiveness, diffused accountability, and greater difficulties achieving consistent policies and results.

Compared with the intergovernmental organizations of the UN system, regional organizations at their current stage of development are of secondary importance within the humanitarian arena. Nevertheless, their assertion of leadership can be positive if they assure regional ownership of activities and provide a point of entry for the larger international community. Yet regional political agendas and personalities often present problems that universal organizations are better able to avoid.

## Bilateral Agencies

In addition to contributing to the work of intergovernmental organizations, donor governments are direct participants in their own right in international humanitarian activities. Most donors have their own bilateral aid agencies that provide grants to the poorest countries and loans to those more able to afford them. For the U.S. government, the bilateral channel is the Agency for International Development; for the United Kingdom, the Overseas Development Administration (ODA); for the Netherlands, the Netherlands International Development Agency; and so on.

Donor governments make up a twenty-one–member Development Assistance Committee (DAC) of the Paris-based Organization for Economic Cooperation and Development (OECD). Although not a donor itself, the DAC provides broad analytical support and information-sharing services to its member governments.

"Nontraditional donors"—countries whose oil wealth and new-found international standing propelled them in the 1970s into aid activities—have their own bilateral aid programs and also have joined in efforts supported by the Organization of Petroleum Exporting Countries (OPEC).[10] The oil-producing countries, whose contributions have tapered off in recent years, have generally underwritten development rather than relief activities. Although some have expressed a sense of solidarity with fellow Muslims, OPEC countries have not been major humanitarian actors in recent crises such as in Somalia and Bosnia.

Donor governments attach different priorities to contributions channeled through their own bilateral agencies as against funds they provide to multilateral organizations. The United States historically has attached greater importance and resources to its own bilateral programs than to the work of intergovernmental organizations, although it is the largest single contributor to many of them as well. By contrast, Scandinavian governments, with less ambitious bilateral programs and a greater philosophical commitment to the UN system, often commit a far larger share of their resources multilaterally. The contribution of Scandinavian governments in the form of "official development assistance" exceeds that of the U.S. government, but the per capita giving of the American public to private rather than government aid organizations exceeds that of Scandinavians.

Countries on the receiving end of humanitarian assistance also have diverse judgments and preferences regarding the various aid channels available to them. Many have a long-term preference for multilateral rather than bilateral because the world organization is seen as attaching fewer political and other strings to its disbursements. Some recipient governments also have strong preferences for some bilateral donors over others. A comparison of recent bilateral aid to El Salvador by the U.S. and Canadian governments indicates some important differences in purpose, style, and effectiveness.

Assistance from Washington to the government of El Salvador during the 1980s reflected ideology, not importance. For most of the decade, tiny El Salvador was the fifth largest recipient of U.S. aid, exceeded only by Israel, Egypt, Pakistan, and the Philippines. Transfers included military assistance, managed by the U.S. Defense and State departments, economic assistance from the State Department (including AID), and humanitarian assistance from AID via its Office of Foreign Disaster Assistance.

Humanitarian assistance in the form of food, medicine, and other emergency support made up a significant portion of U.S. economic aid but by no means the lion's share. The largest single aid component was balance-of-payments support—that is, checks written by Washington to the Salvadoran treasury as an investment in building a hemispheric bulwark against communism, particularly that emanating from Castro's Cuba and Sandinista Nicaragua. In 1992, El Salvador received a total of $400 million in such aid.

Canadian bilateral assistance to El Salvador, managed by the Canadian International Development Agency, differed both in scale and objectives. It was more modest, and it focused on identifiable human needs activities. Rather than being transferred to the Salvadoran treasury, it was channeled through specific ministries and NGOs for use in specific projects.

With the war over and attention turning toward social and economic reconstruction, the contrast between AID and CIDA activities in El Salvador in the early 1980s was dramatic. The AID mission was part of the U.S. embassy, an imposing and tightly secured fortress just outside of town on land especially provided for that purpose. Entrance required running a gauntlet that included electronic checks at the gate house and the inside entrance. Having obtained the necessary visitor's badge by sacrificing a passport or other important identity document, the visitor was escorted to the desired destination.

The CIDA mission occupied a two-office suite on the second floor of the Canadian embassy, a modest and unprepossessing building in a predominantly residential part of town. Entrance required identifying oneself at the outside telephone and at the desk downstairs. CIDA staff from the region consisted of one expatriate and several Salvadorans. There were no Canadian nationals, soldiers, or escorts to greet visitors.

The contrast between the two bilateral programs and styles was particularly striking because of the physical proximity of both the United States and Canada to El Salvador and because of the association of each with long traditions of generous humanitarian support. Both saw themselves reflecting historical relationships between their respective nations. They also sought to advance their respective political interests, which in terms of hemispheric relations were not much different.

After the war, AID actively promoted large-scale projects to foster reconciliation and economic development between the FMLN and the government. AID also pressed local NGOs, which it had either created or heavily subsidized during the 1980s, to mobilize private funds or be cut off from additional U.S. government support. However supportable its reconstruction and development aims, AID seemed a prisoner of its own largesse and of its heavily politicized relationships born of the conflict. AID staff seemed miffed about the FMLN's unwillingness to cooperate more actively with Washington to advance the process of social reconciliation. Officials of other governments were also puzzled—not over the FMLN's reticence but over Washington's short memory and political insensitivity. After its heavily partisan involvement in Salvador's bloody civil war, U.S. overtures could hardly have been warmly reciprocated.

CIDA, too, was committed to fostering reconciliation and development but went about the task differently. It took a lower-key, smaller-scale approach, emphasizing local projects designed to build bridges directly between former protagonists. CIDA officials conceded that the process was moving slowly but indicated that a priority to nurture social and attitudinal change rather than to disburse resources rapidly would take time.

CIDA's efforts to facilitate reconstruction thus seemed intrinsically more in keeping with the requirements of the postwar moment than

156

Women and children await medical care near San Isandro, El Salvador, in
October 1983. (ICRC Photo SALV 83-16/13/E. Winiger)

AID's well-financed and more visible contributions. In one respect, however, Washington had a clear advantage over Ottawa. Having bankrolled so much of the government and the military during the 1980s, the United States had greater leverage to exercise and more debts to call in. To its credit, the United States used these late in the decade to moderate human rights abuses and press for peace.

The Salvadoran situation contrasted markedly to that in Guatemala, where the United States had less influence because its resource transfers during the 1980s were smaller. (The Carter administration had cut off aid to the Guatemalan military as a reaction to human rights abuses.) Of course, not all bilateral influence is tied to financial aid flows, and reductions in aid levels can be important in their own right. By the end of the decade, direct U.S. leverage over civilian and military officials was considerably limited. The recognition of the legitimacy of Guatemalan Indian aspirations through the 1992 Nobel Prize for Peace awarded to Rigoberta Menchú ultimately may have exerted more constructive and effective pressure on the Guatemalan government than aid from any bilateral donor.

In sum, bilateral humanitarian aid embodies the distinctive ethos and expertise of individual donor countries that are sometimes lost when such aid is channeled through a multilateral agency. On the more negative side, bilateral aid may also inject unhelpful political agendas, involve excessive national flag waving, and pose serious problems of coordination.

## Nongovernmental Organizations

The sheer diversity of external NGOs—a universe in its own right—is mind-boggling. At one end of the spectrum are "mom and pop" operations that provide limited assistance to individuals affected by a specific war. Among the external NGOs responding to the crisis in the former Yugoslavia, for example, were British Direct Aid, which mobilized and operated a transport fleet of nine trucks in central Bosnia, Edinburgh & Lothans Direct Aid, which arranged food convoys from Great Britain to Sarajevo, The Serious Road Trip, a London-based organization with eight trucks for moving food into Sarajevo, Helping Hands, a German group whose contribution included a warehouse in Munich, an armored truck, and several drivers, and Love in Action International, which channeled assistance from its base in Garland, Texas, to local organizations in the region. Even more ad hoc arrangements were made by local groups, such as one in Strasbourg, France, which collected used clothing and transported it by rented truck to Zagreb.

At the opposite end of the spectrum are private groups that are operational in a wide variety of conflicts in many different regions and multisectoral in their activities. They have substantial annual budgets, global personnel and communications networks, special expertise in areas such as agriculture, health, refugee resettlement, and monitoring human rights abuses, and staffs with differentiated responsibility for planning and evaluation, operations, and promotion. Those organizations, which played a major role in the former Yugoslavia but at the same time were active in many other humanitarian crises as well, included the International Rescue Committee, the Caritas network, the Danish and Norwegian Refugee Councils, the Lutheran World Federation, Oxfam-UK, the Save the Children and Doctors Without Borders families of organizations, and Amnesty International.

Whether an external nongovernmental organization is small or large, focused or far-flung, its activities tend to concentrate on the practical needs of ordinary people. The prevailing grass-roots or people-to-people approach means that NGOs emphasize local links and endeavor to customize their activities to the grass-roots level. NGO aid is sometimes called retail to distinguish its community-level focus from "wholesale" assistance provided by governments and UN agencies.[11]

Resources of external NGOs vary widely from crisis to crisis. On some occasions, a single truckload of relief supplies may be involved. On others, the amount amassed may exceed that available through AID or UNICEF. Government and UN officials in countries struggling with emergencies or longer-term development challenges often envy the scale—and the flexibility—of international NGOs. They often are able to act without elaborate bureaucratic procedures and clearance processes. As they have evolved in recent years in response to major emergencies, however, some NGOs have less in common with one another than they do with bilateral and UN agencies. That is, there may be more similarity between Save the Children-UK and UNICEF than between MSF and Love in Action International.

NGOs along the spectrum also differ in the sources of their revenues. Some, like the U.S.-based Mennonite Central Committee and the Unitarian Universalist Service Committee, insist that all funds come from individual contributors. Others, like CARE, the Norwegian Refugee

Council, and the International Rescue Committee receive more than half of their program funds from governments. Still others, like Oxfam-UK, set a limit, such as 20 percent, on such resources. Most make case-by-case determinations depending on the project, country, government, and funds involved.

At issue, of course, is the nongovernmental and nonpolitical nature of NGOs. Private groups that rely exclusively on private funds are generally wary of the political influence that accepting government funds might have on their activities. Those that accept funds from governmental or intergovernmental sources do so to expand the scale of their programs, usually with a knowledge of the level of political risk involved. If U.S. government funds become less infused with short-term political objectives in the wake of the Cold War, NGOs may become more willing to accept these funds.

Experience suggests the importance of nongovernmental revenue sources and accountability for establishing the bona fides of independent, people-to-people organizations. That identity is particularly indispensable in civil wars, when outsiders are often suspected of harboring political agendas. Of course, even in the absence of government funds, some external NGOs have their own political and other biases.

Over the years the NGO community has devised terms to describe organizations that masquerade as NGOs but fail critical tests. A government-organized NGO (GONGO) reflects the interest of a government, whether in a donor or a developing country, in having an ostensibly private organization to carry out certain tasks. Similarly, a QUANGO is a quasi-NGO, a term developed to describe NGOs set up by Communist or Socialist governments not fully committed to private sector entities.

In the United States, NGOs are called private voluntary organizations (PVOs), to accent their civic as opposed to tax-supported nature. This occasionally leads PVOs to be described as volunteer organizations, giving the false impression that their staffs donate their time. U.S. government policy itself is not particularly strict or rigorous in defining "private," reflecting a certain ambivalence among U.S. private groups themselves. Organizations that receive as much as 75 percent of their resources from governments or UN organizations may still qualify as "private" for U.S. government purposes.

Human rights groups are a special category of international NGOs active in armed conflicts. Although not involved directly in relief, these groups often mitigate immediate suffering and help to develop the foundation for a more viable society when wars wind down. They perform an invaluable function as the eyes and ears of the international community and convey an important element of solidarity on the part of the outside world.

In recent years, Amnesty International has become something of a worldwide household word. Enjoying perhaps less name recognition, still the Watch groups—Africa Watch, Asia Watch, Middle East Watch, Helsinki Watch, and Americas Watch—also have become major players. In the former Yugoslavia, Amnesty International and Middle East Watch have monitored the situation closely, documenting abuses in on-site missions and pressing governments and UN agencies to prevent violations. Human Rights Watch has published an ongoing series of reports detailing particular abuses and has urged an international tribunal and swift prosecution of violators on all sides.

The effects of two recent Nobel peace prizes awarded to prominent women suggest the importance of outsiders supporting insiders who promote and protect human rights. Myanmar's Daw Aung San Suu Kyi and Guatemala's Rigoberta Menchú received international recognition in 1990 and 1992, respectively, as defenders of human rights. Both the awards and their recipients were viewed with suspicion by government authorities. However, the recognition brought important benefits to human rights work by international and local organizations and individuals in both countries and beyond.

During the Cold War, outside NGOs contributed heavily to humanitarian action, partly because governments and intergovernmental organizations, prisoners of the prevailing understanding of sovereignty, found private aid channels useful. In the Sudan in the late 1980s, for example, the U.S. government often was unwilling for geopolitical and strategic reasons to put pressure on the authorities in Khartoum, whose cooperation the United States needed elsewhere in inter-Arab politics. Also unwilling to provoke the government by sending AID officials into portions of the south controlled by insurgents, Washington channeled resources through external NGOs. UN organizations labored under similar constraints until 1989. Mounting humanitarian programs in the south without the government's consent was viewed as a violation of national sovereignty.

Outside nongovernmental organizations are less constrained by respect for state sovereignty and more guided by moral imperatives. Keeping sovereignty in its proper place generally has meant giving pri-

Somali woman feeds children. (UN Photo 146504/J. Isaac)

ority to the alleviation of suffering rather than the observance of sovereignty. "We are practitioners of what is possible," Emergency Coordinator Marcus Thompson of Oxfam-UK has observed, "rather than
what is legal." His counterpart, President Reginald Moreels of MSF-Bel-
gium, has noted, "The actions of MSF rely on ethical rather than legal
norms."[12]

NGOs entered the early post–Cold War era in a strong position as a
result of their institutional growth during the previous quarter century
and the crucial role that they played during the decades of East-West
tension. Moreover, mounting skepticism of large bureaucracies has resulted in greater allocations of government funds to external NGOs.
Growing pressure for reductions in government spending also has
made organizations that mobilize private sector resources and initiatives more attractive. Governments have had successful experiences
with NGOs and are more attuned to how they work. Private contributors, too, have developed loyalty for particular NGOs.

It is also probably true that there are cost savings involved in channeling funds through NGOs. Historically speaking, the costs of stationing an NGO practitioner for a year overseas have been considerably be-

low comparable costs for bilateral or intergovernmental officials. In recent years, however, salaries in some of the more established NGOs may have risen faster than those, for example, in AID or the UN. Other factors make comparisons difficult. UN salaries are tax-free. Allowances for housing, vehicle and administrative support, and international travel differ significantly among NGOs and between them and other organizations, as may be true of program effectiveness.

In short, the greatest "bang for the humanitarian buck" may still be achievable through NGOs, although additional work is needed in this area. Certainly, considerations of cost, combined with the popularity of people-to-people programs and a disaffection with government and UN bureaucracies, are still steering a growing share of public spending through NGO channels.

The attractions of NGOs are not only their people-to-people nature but also the sense of personality and humanity epitomized by their leaders and staffs. In the Sudan, for example, the work of Norwegian People's Aid (NPA) was associated with the swashbuckling style of its country director, the late Egil Hagen. A former Norwegian army counterintelligence official, Hagen was anathema to the Khartoum authorities for his closeness to the SPLA insurgents, whom he was suspected of supplying with guns. With roots in the Norwegian Labor Party, NPA made no secret of its progressive political orientation. In South Africa, Nicaragua, and Tigray, as well as in the Sudan, NPA took the side of the underdog. As NPA representative in Nairobi, Hagen was no favorite of the United Nations, which he often openly criticized. In 1989, he publicly ridiculed UN efforts to generate publicity for its late-blooming efforts at humanitarian relief in the Sudan. If the United Nations were serious, he told the media, it would spend less time on publicity and more on logistics.

Loose cannon or not, Hagen and NPA responded to famine vigorously and creatively at a time when governments and UN agencies were largely absent. Even by 1990 and 1991, when a larger number of humanitarian organizations had gathered on the scene, he helped keep the continuing civil war in the Sudan on European television screens. Yet his style continued to fuel the suspicions of the Sudanese government about the subversive nature of all nongovernmental activities. NPA thus complicated the efforts of other external NGOs as well as the international community to hammer out and sustain more businesslike and impartial working relationships with the political authorities.

The operating style of CARE more closely resembles a bilateral or intergovernmental organization than some of today's smaller NGOs. With actual expenditures of $438,235,000 in the year ending June 30, 1993, and with activities in virtually all the world's major humanitarian crises, CARE's reach is indeed global. Its president and CEO, Philip Johnston, was a retired U.S. army and former government official from AID who spent much of his career in emergencies. In late 1992, CARE lent him to spearhead the sizable UN relief effort in Somalia, where his assignment was to put humanitarian relief deliveries on a faster track. CARE is a major implementing partner of AID and UN organizations in reconstruction and development as well as emerging theaters.

Fred Cuny is also a familiar figure in war-related emergencies. His style personifies the commitment of NGOs, even though, strictly speaking, he is not one. Dubbed Mr. Disaster and the Red Adair of Humanitarian Relief, Cuny is a private management consultant whose extended front-line assignments have included Tigray, Somalia, Bosnia, and Sri Lanka. President of a small consulting firm in Dallas, Texas, his services are regularly in demand by AID, UN organizations, and NGOs, although he can also be outspokenly critical of them. His firm, Intertect, serves as a reminder that not all private organizations engaged in humanitarian activities are "charitable" or nonprofit. He spent much of 1993 on assignment with the International Rescue Committee in Sarajevo, seeking to resuscitate the city's gas and water systems with support from private financier George Soros.

Despite this bewildering diversity of nongovernmental organisms, common elements are present. These include a strong commitment to alleviate life-threatening suffering, utilize people-to-people channels, and proceed with can-do determination, despite obstacles created by the insecurity present in active wars and by uncooperative host or home governments. In this sense, it is possible to speak of an NGO "culture" with characteristics that distinguish it from those of bilateral and intergovernmental aid agencies.

To their credit, external NGOs tend to be nonbureaucratic and innovative. They do not easily take no for an answer. Their determination leads them to take risks and to be relatively unconstrained by the insecurity of war zones or prevailing political conventions. Their ties with local communities make them better interlocutors in certain kinds of data gathering and negotiations. Their administrative structures tend to be leaner and their compensation packages more modest, with higher percentages of their budgets going directly to the needy.

External NGOs also bring certain weaknesses to their participation in humanitarian work. Their energy may lend frenzy and confusion to activities. Careful planning and evaluation are not a stock in trade. The desire to get on with the next emergency contributes to a lack of reflectiveness and an inattention to institutional learning. Impatience with well-known constraints may reflect a naïveté about the highly political contexts in which they operate and about the extent of their activities' political and humanitarian ramifications. Some NGOs guard their autonomy so closely that they miss opportunities to expand their efforts and to coordinate with other like-minded institutions.

**International Committee of the Red Cross**

With the ICRC, the bewildering diversity of governmental, intergovernmental, and nongovernmental organizations gives way to a certain refreshing consistency. The ICRC is a private entity related to the NGO genus but, by virtue of its recognition in international humanitarian law, is in a class by itself. The International Court of Justice has actually suggested that the ICRC epitomizes humanitarian action at its most authentic.

Not an organization to take its special status lightly, the ICRC has articulated a set of seven humanitarian principles that it nurtures in its daily operations around the world. In 1993, the ICRC family numbered about 6,500 worldwide. Of the almost 6,000 staff posted in the field, 862 were expatriates, 175 were provided by national Red Cross and Red Crescent societies, and the remaining 4,800 were hired locally. The ICRC's budget in that year exceeded $500 million. With over a dozen international lawyers working exclusively on humanitarian law at its headquarters, ICRC has assembled the largest cadre of international legal practitioners—more than in the UN Secretariat, the U.S. Department of State, or the law faculty of the Sorbonne. As promoter and custodian of the Geneva Conventions and Protocols, the ICRC runs an extensive array of training courses each year in various locations, not only for its own staff but also for diplomats, academics, and other humanitarian practitioners. It founded and, now in partnership with UNHCR, sponsors the International Institute for Humanitarian Law in San Remo, Italy.

The ICRC is among the longest-lived of today's humanitarian institutions. Since its beginnings in the middle of the last century, the organization has always emphasized documenting and learning from efforts to humanize war and protect its victims, both civilian and military. A few years ago, the ICRC opened a museum on its grounds in Geneva that documents ongoing international efforts to bring the ever-evolving technology and strategies of warfare under more rigorous and humane controls. In 1993, the ICRC was granted official observer status by the United Nations General Assembly, although governments indicated at the time that they viewed their decision as exceptional. The ICRC monitors UN deliberations on humanitarian and human rights issues closely and on occasion makes its own views known in one way or another in UN debates.

Over time the ICRC has elaborated the clearest set of principles and accompanying operational procedures of any humanitarian organization. It places a high premium on negotiations with all parties to conflicts, in the case of El Salvador holding about 250 meetings with the government and a similar number with the FMLN, in order to win and maintain access to prisoners of war and civilian populations on both sides. Nevertheless, it often experiences difficulty eliciting respect from governments or insurgents, receiving no more respectful treatment than other humanitarian actors. In extraordinary circumstances—and there have been significantly more of them in recent years than early on—the ICRC goes beyond private appeals to belligerents to orchestrate governmental and public pressure against the inhumane and illegal practices of warring parties.

Thus, during the period from mid-1991 until the end of 1992, the ICRC responded to the violence of the former Yugoslavia by issuing almost a dozen appeals to the belligerents and the international community, decrying violations of international humanitarian law, and pleading for its observance. In 1991 and 1992 it went to extraordinary lengths to bring together the warring parties on four separate occasions to agree on providing access to civilians and prisoners of war.

One ICRC delegate on the front lines in the former Yugoslavia recalled a tense meeting with a commanding general in the Bosnian Serb army following the still unexplained assassination of the ICRC's chief delegate in Sarajevo in May 1992, which sent a shudder through the organization and led to the temporary suspension of operations in Bosnia. Speaking for the organization, the ICRC delegate took the firm position that ICRC principles would have to be respected before it would proceed with its humanitarian tasks. "We know what you stand for," the general shot back, "but we'll make you change your principles." Reflecting on the encounter, the delegate later recalled having remarked, "Principles are indeed a handicap, but they're one handicap we don't want to lose."

Defense of ICRC principles has occasioned battles not only with donor governments and belligerents but also with other humanitarian organizations. Various groups at one time or another have sought to identify themselves with, appropriate, or misuse the Red Cross symbol. In such instances, the ICRC has challenged not only belligerents who commandeer ambulances to carry weapons or make hospitals to serve as military staging areas but also other humanitarian organizations who do not honor what the ICRC considers its principles. In the former Yugoslavia, for example, where the ICRC believes that the United Nations has become a party to the conflict, it has suggested that the Red Cross–bearing white vehicles widely used by UN humanitarian organizations be painted "UN blue" to prevent confusion with ICRC vehicles and personnel. In an effort to keep its distance from UN military operations, which the ICRC views as compromising the impartiality of associated humanitarian organizations, the ICRC does not coordinate its activities with the UN.

If the conflict in the former Yugoslavia has been trying for the ICRC, Somalia has been all-consuming. A cardinal ICRC tenet involves avoiding the use of force, even to gain access. Since access is an acknowledged international obligation of warring parties under the Geneva Conventions and Additional Protocols, the ICRC places a premium on persuasion rather than coercion.[13] "To prepare the groundwork of peace and reconciliation," one delegate observed in Mogadishu, "we do not use force." However, by late 1992, if massive numbers of starvation deaths in Somalia's civil war were to be avoided, there seemed to be no alternative even for the ICRC—short of suspending relief operations altogether.

The ICRC therefore made concessions that surprised many, including some within its own ranks. Like other agencies, it employed "technicals," gun-toting young men provided by the reigning warlords to accompany its relief vehicles and personnel. (When possible, the armed escorts were placed in separate vehicles to keep the ICRC's own vehicles weapon-free.) The ICRC also paid protection fees to ensure that its supplies got through, even though the fees—and the supplies— probably contributed to the climate of violence. Although the ICRC

UN soldiers of the British battalion on patrol in the Muslim enclave of Stari Vitez. (UN Photo 186716/J. Isaac)

did not join other groups in calling for increased protection from UN-related military personnel, it readily acknowledged that its own activities benefited from the restoration of law and order. In any event, the presence of armed men and vehicles within ICRC compounds was a jolt to ICRC staff and those familiar with its ways, and it is a decision upon which the ICRC continues to reflect.

For all its attractiveness, the ICRC is not beyond criticism. Some commentators have faulted what they consider a "gold-plated" approach to relief operations. The ICRC in turn explains somewhat higher operational costs than those of many other private organizations as investments in the professionalism of its work and ingredients in its overall success. Others have found the "Swissness" of the Red Cross offputting. ICRC policy traditionally has insisted that all ICRC delegates—that is, the ranking representatives of the ICRC abroad—be Swiss nationals. In recent years, however, it has accepted as delegates a number of nationals from other countries. Although the ICRC normally hires local staff for junior positions, the European complexion of senior staff seems questionable, particularly in the many crises whose victims are non-European.

At the level of doctrine, a frequently advanced criticism concerns the ICRC's tradition of making hard and fast distinctions between humanitarian and political issues. The ICRC describes itself as a swimmer struggling against the tide of politics. It consequently seeks to insulate itself against the corrosion of politics, on occasion placing itself above the fray and dealing itself out of the action. The organization's integrity, it explains, will be compromised if tainted.

"Despite its efforts, and those of some outsiders, to present the ICRC as a unique and completely distinct agency," University of Nebraska political science professor and former ICRC consultant David Forsythe has said, "the ICRC is inevitably and inextricably part of a global shift toward more attention to victims of war and politics by more actors on the world stage." How can the ICRC accomplish its tasks, which require continuous interaction with governments, without making choices, some of which necessarily involve compromises? Indeed, how can the ICRC present itself and its work as apolitical? "If politics is the art of the possible," concludes Forsythe, "then humanitarian politics as practiced by the ICRC is but a subset of this principle."[14]

In sum, the ICRC's greatest strength is its consistent adherence to law and principle. This is the hallmark of the organization from its hilltop perch in Geneva to outposts in Baghdad and Belgrade and to its frontline presence in Zahko and Mostar. However, its greatest weakness is perhaps the mirror image of its strength: its inflexibility and reluctance to improvise. That has limited its presence and activity in some major humanitarian crises, where it has not been able to negotiate what it considers adequate humanitarian space. To be sure, other organizations that have made such compromises have themselves encountered difficulties. Buffeted by its experiences in recent years, the ICRC has launched an in-house review of its policies and operations. Various innovations, some potentially major, are now under discussion.

**Outside Military Forces**

Military forces play expanded roles on the humanitarian front in the post–Cold War era.[15] Two roles are particularly noteworthy: assisting in the delivery of relief and the physical protection of humanitarian space. Especially important is the use of outside troops to support major United Nations humanitarian undertakings in war zones. These include the troops of NATO, which is transforming itself in the post–Cold War era into a possibly significant military player in humanitarian affairs. The use of outside military forces not authorized by the UN Security Council action and the use of inside military forces—that is, military or paramilitary contingents from within countries in crisis—is beyond the scope of this discussion.

Three war-related emergencies in which outside soldiers have served as an essential component of UN humanitarian efforts have been well documented: the allied coalition in northern Iraq, UN peacekeeping troops and U.S.-led national contingents in Somalia, and UN peacekeeping forces and NATO troops and aircraft in the former Yugoslavia.[16] A review of these examples suggests the strengths and weaknesses of military forces in the humanitarian sphere.

With respect to the physical delivery of relief items, outside military forces have played roles ranging from major to modest. In northern Iraq, crack ground troops from the United States, France, the United Kingdom, and the Netherlands swung into action in April 1991, when they were the only hope of getting timely assistance to the Kurds in the snowy mountains along the Turkish border. There were problems—for example, some airdrops caused casualties on the ground and there were some initial rough edges in relationships with the UN and NGOs. However, Operation Provide Comfort made an indisputable life-and-death difference.

By the time the relief operation was handed over fully to the UN several months later, good working relationships had been established between the military units of the allied coalition and UN and NGO humanitarian personnel. Some of the major cultural differences between the humanitarians and the military also had been accommodated. Most NGOs welcomed the added security and the firm operational anchor provided by the military in an otherwise chaotic and dangerous situation. However, several chose not to operate if this meant working within the military's terms of reference. Cooperation was enhanced because the military was so clearly identified with protecting the Kurdish population and because of the high level of professionalism among the troops, many of whom were skilled in such fields as civil administration and engineering.

In Somalia and the former Yugoslavia, the role of outside troops in actually delivering relief has been far more limited. Unlike northern

Iraq, military personnel in neither theater were given major relief chores. There were, of course, instances in Mogadishu and Baidoa when soldiers transported food to feeding centers and distributed it. There were also examples of UNPROFOR troops coming to the aid of individuals in the UN's so-called protected areas within Croatia and in the safe areas in eastern Bosnia. Yet these actions tended to be exceptions, reflecting personal decisions made on the spot rather than official duties. Generally speaking, the military did not routinely transport or distribute relief supplies or ferry civilians to safety in Somalia or the former Yugoslavia.

The various militaries in both locations, however, did associate themselves with carrying out relief activities. In the former Yugoslavia, UNPROFOR Force Commander General Wahlgren, pressed on his departure in mid-1993 to explain how his troops had made a difference, took pride in explaining, "We have been able to assist with humanitarian aid to some of the people." Yet the statement of an UNPROFOR spokeswoman at the time was closer to reality: "Humanitarian assistance is everything we are about," she said, "even though UNPROFOR troops themselves are not engaged in it. We are not engaged in any direct humanitarian activities, except of a good offices nature."

There were several major exceptions to the more limited delivery duties of the troops in Somalia and the former Yugoslavia. A major airlift of relief supplies by a fleet of U.S. Air Force cargo planes from the Kenyan seaport of Mombassa to Mogadishu moved food into position for delivery during the crucial months beginning in August 1992. Getting the food into Somalia did not solve all the problems, but when deliveries by road and sea were seemingly impossible, the airlift overcame a major impasse in the supply line.

An airdrop of supplies into eastern Bosnia, begun by the U.S. Air Force in early 1993 and later joined by other NATO nations, also helped reach people at risk whose needs at the time could not be met by overland convoys. The airdrops were discounted initially as a gesture more symbolic than serious. However, the first six months of flights by American, German, and French military aircraft provided 7,000 tons of food (9 million meals) and 144 tons of medical supplies, a major lifesaving contribution.

"There are several thousand people alive today because of the airdrops," commented U.S. Brigadier General Donald Loranger, who was in charge of the airdrops from Rhein-Main Air Base in Germany. A representative of the Bosnian Muslim government concurred. In a war in which the United Nations and the European Community have "lost every other battle," said Mufid Halilovic, "this is one of the few things that has worked."

In each of the three conflicts under review, UN-associated troops played essential roles in the second duty of outside military forces: protecting humanitarian space. But there were key differences reflecting the particular military and political dynamics of each civil war, the chemistry of coercion and consent varying accordingly.

The allied coalition in northern Iraq used military muscle to open up the necessary space for the return of civilians and the activities of aid organizations. Following Security Council Resolution 688 of April 1991, outside military troops under U.S. command and following NATO procedures invaded northern Iraq from Turkey under NATO air cover. They reclaimed the land occupied by the Iraqi army north of the thirty-sixth parallel, from which the Kurds had fled and to which they sought to return.

Following the physical withdrawal of coalition forces and the turnover of aid activities to the United Nations, the presence of Western aircraft at Turkish bases protected the access gained earlier through the presence of ground troops. The fact that the Security Council had insisted on international access to the civilian population made Baghdad's consent unnecessary. However, the UN eventually negotiated and renewed several times a memorandum of understanding with governmental authorities that detailed the terms of its operation within Iraq.

On the ground in and around Zahko in northern Iraq, the allied coalition was able to expand humanitarian space dramatically. In mid-1991, the Kurds were eager to return from the border to their homes but were hesitant because of the presence of Iraqi intelligence agents. Consequently, the coalition devised an innovative strategy. Meeting the Iraqi officials, military officers first elicited a list of the agents, ostensibly to protect the operatives from injury or reprisal at the hands of returning Kurds. Having received the list, the coalition then posted the names throughout the area. The agents fled for their lives and the Kurds reclaimed their homes.

In Somalia, there were three distinct phases in efforts by outside military forces to open and protect humanitarian space. There was the original deployment in August 1992 of UN troops under the first

United Nations Operation in Somalia. This was followed by the introduction in December of U.S.-led troops, soon joined by contingents
from twenty other countries, in what UN wordsmiths labeled the Unified Task Force (UNITAF) but what more poetic Pentagon counterparts
called Operation Restore Hope. Finally, the United States in May 1993
turned the operation over to the United Nations in what became
UNOSOM II.

A common purpose of all three phases was the protection of humanitarian operations, but the actual results were different. In the first
phase, the 500 Pakistani troops stationed in Mogadishu were by their
own admission unable to open and protect access. Despite troops
posted at the airport and in the city, humanitarian operations there
and in the countryside remained hostage. In fact, the presence of
"technicals" inside the headquarters of UN peacekeepers in Mogadishu confirmed the inability of UN forces to control even their own
space, to say nothing of the volatile area beyond.

In the second phase, the introduction of U.S. amphibious, ground,
and air power carved out space for humanitarian activities. Within
weeks of the arrival of U.S. troops in early December, starvation rates
were reduced drastically. Fanning out from Mogadishu to Baidoa,
Bardere, Kismayu, and other population centers, the troops helped restart relief operations. Although the troops confiscated some weapons,
Washington did not view disarming tribal militias as part of UNITAF's
mission, and as a result, more than enough heavy arms remained to
wreak havoc.

In the third phase, the United Nations reclaimed direct control over
outside military forces. UNOSOM II had a more ambitious mandate
than UNITAF's. Its geographical coverage was larger (all of Somalia instead of the southern half), and it was charged with disarming belligerents and protecting aid workers. This was the first-ever enforcement
activity in support of humanitarian objectives under Chapter 7 of the
United Nations Charter that was clearly under the secretary-general's
command and control. Difficulties emerged, however, over the proper
diplomatic and military responses by UNOSOM II to provocations
from supporters of General Aidid. The use of heavy firepower from helicopter gunships of the U.S. Rapid Deployment Force, which remained under direct U.S. command and control, created difficulties
with the Italian government and other UN troop contributors. U.S.-led

ground and air strikes precipitated retaliation against aid workers and journalists and eventually against U.S. troops themselves.

In August, the first three buildings taken by elite U.S. troops in their hunt for General Aidid and his key aides were the offices of the UN Development Programme and of two external NGOs. The summary arrests and detention of aid personnel by the military continue to rankle, particularly in the context of military operations supposedly undertaken to protect humanitarian activities. Continuing insecurity was implicated in the deaths later in the year of several aid workers, whose protection had been the stated rationale for the initial deployment of military personnel.

As of early 1994, the jury was still out on the overall humanitarian benefits and costs of using outside troops, despite their early contribution to reducing famine deaths. Prospects for the success of UNOSOM II appeared even more problematic in light of the withdrawal of most Western soldiers at the end of March 1994. The secretary-general was unable to recruit replacements, and the situation seemed precariously close to reverting to the status quo ante.

In the former Yugoslavia, outside military forces were challenged every day by belligerents, who successfully interrupted and derailed humanitarian activities. The calculated denial or provision of access to civilians was an element in strategies pursued by Bosnian Serbs, Bosnian Croats, and the Bosnian Muslim government, although the most routine and repeated offender was clearly the Bosnian Serb army. Neither relief deliveries, personnel, distribution points, nor vehicles received the protections specified in international humanitarian law or envisioned in the enabling Security Council resolutions. All were subject to random violence and targeted strikes.

The failure to establish the appropriate role of military force operating in the murky area beyond traditional peacekeeping (where the consent of the warring parties as required under Chapter 6 of the UN Charter was granted) but short of meaningful peace enforcement (where military personnel are imposed under Chapter 7 without consent) proved untenable for UN troops in Bosnia and Herzegovina. A UN peacekeeping force, duly authorized, lacked the military capability to coerce a solution across a wide front. Unable to create the conditions for its own success, it lost all military credibility. Shortly before resigning in January 1994 as the UN commander in Bosnia and Herzegovina, Lieutenant General Francis Briquemont lamented the disparity between rhetoric and reality: "There is a fantastic gap between the resolutions of the Security Council, the will to execute those resolutions, and the means available to commanders in the field."[17]

The United Nations was supposed to be distinguished from its defunct predecessor, the League of Nations, because it had the authority to impose economic and military sanctions to back up international decisions to counteract aggression and atrocities in such a setting. In reality, the role it played in Bosnia was aptly described by UNPROFOR officials themselves as "eunuchs at the orgy."

In February 1994, NATO's successful brinkmanship concerning the twelve-mile exclusion for artillery from Sarajevo and the subsequent downing of four Serbian aircraft finally reversed two years of saber rattling. Yet just as NATO, the United Nations, and the Clinton administration were hoping that these modest military actions would end the siege of Sarajevo and facilitate diplomacy, the Serbs moved the violence elsewhere. New "ethnic cleansing" and atrocities began in Prejidor and Banja Luka along with violent attacks against the so-called safe area of Gorazde. Two American F-16s carried out another NATO "first" in April, bombing Serbian ground positions outside of Gorazde. The stated purpose of the strikes under Operation Blue Sword was to protect the handful of UN observers and relief workers—the language of the relevant UN resolutions—but the real target was the Serbs.

However, these military actions were still more hopes than decisions because there was insufficient resolve. The air attacks were pinpricks that enraged the Bosnian Serbs, who responded by killing a British soldier, shooting down a British Harrier aircraft, detaining 200 UN personnel, and then taking over Gorazde. The Serbs once again had called the bluff offered by NATO, which remained essentially unwilling to confront the Serbian aggression for fear of all-out war between the 100,000 Serbian and 17,000 UN soldiers in Bosnia and Herzegovina. The extension of modest military protection to pockets of refugees was not unwelcome, but it also underlined how feeble earlier responses had been.

Subsequently the Serbs withdrew most of their troops from Gorazde and their weapons outside of a twenty-kilometer radius, extending this same Sarajevo-like procedure to the four other "safe areas" of Tuzla, Zepa, Srebrenica, and Bihac. Yet the vacillation about military force suggests how much the League of Nations model frames humanitarian action at the end of the twentieth century. The West clearly is unprepared to devise a credible political and military strategy to end not just the sieges of Bosnian Muslim areas but also the war.

UNPROFOR was more successful in less obvious but still important ways in expanding the space available to humanitarian organizations. From 1992 to 1994, UNPROFOR liaison officers provided regular security briefings of UN and other aid personnel in Zagreb, Split, Belgrade, and Sarajevo. To help make judgments and provide training on security matters, several exmilitary officers were seconded by governments or directly retained on the staff of UNHCR at its operational headquarters in Zagreb and around the region.

Alerting aid personnel to security problems was a more useful and easier task than the physical protection of convoys. Military escorts sometimes accompanied aid deliveries within Sarajevo and, on occasion, convoys from the Dalmatian coast into central Bosnia or from Belgrade to eastern Bosnia. However, the escort role of the troops was considerably less common than generally believed. Military officials themselves underscored the vulnerability of a line of relief-bearing vehicles to hostile fire, even with armored vehicles at the beginning, middle, and end of the procession. Armed military escorts often increased rather than eased the peril of aid operations and personnel.

UN military operations were criticized for not having provided more muscular protection for aid activities. UN soldiers never fought a battle with any of the factions to assure passage of an aid convoy. Yet some of those most closely associated with UN aid operations felt that any effort by UNPROFOR to "shoot its way through" would have proved counterproductive. "Any attempt to use force," commented a key UN logistician and strategist in mid-1993, "would have had a whiplash effect throughout the entire aid operation." Successfully running one roadblock might have caused a tightening of all other checkpoints, reducing rather than expanding access. Moreover, UNPROFOR troops, who were deployed only with the consent of the political authorities, were often unavailable when and where most needed—for example, in Bosnian Serb–controlled areas.

Many of those who advocate increased use of military muscle in aid operations were not directly involved on the ground in the former Yugoslavia. However, some on-the-spot observers felt that a larger and more robust UNPROFOR, operating from the start under more assertive terms of engagement, could have ensured fuller access to the civilian population. In their view, a larger military presence could have changed the overall dynamics and perhaps prevented the worst human suffering, even without the actual use of firepower, except on rare occasions. Moreover, they argue that applying military power at the very outset of the conflict would have benefited humanitarian operations, reducing the need for military personnel to accompany convoys and personnel.

The debacles in the former Yugoslavia and Somalia have attracted most of the attention since the middle of 1993. Contrasted to these largely negative experiences, revisiting the northern Iraq situation may rekindle an appreciation of the appropriate application of military force in support of humane values.

These three crises, all of which involved delivering relief and protecting operations, raise many fundamental questions about using military forces to ameliorate war-induced suffering. What specific support functions should the military undertake? What changes in decisionmaking and accountability are required if soldiers are to play the unaccustomed role of supporting operations instead of leading them? Can the United Nations protect humanitarian space without U.S. leadership and firepower? Are there some situations in which civilian humanitarians should not set foot, even with the best possible military protection? What accountability safeguards are in place?

However tentative the data, some of the strengths and weaknesses of outside military forces have emerged from these recent experiences. Concerning delivery, the allied coalition in Operation Provide Comfort and the U.S. and NATO airdrops into eastern Bosnia demonstrated situations in which only the armed forces of major powers have had the requisite logistic, personnel, and organizational capacities to reach civilian populations at risk quickly and effectively. Particularly in Iraq, the array of resources within the military constituted key elements for humanitarian operations in this war zone. In all these settings, clear authority and procedures were helpful.

Yet the resources deployed were extremely costly. Sending U.S. forces to Somalia under UNITAF for six months cost approximately $500 million more than what it would have cost to keep the soldiers at their home bases. This sum far exceeds the U.S. commitment to many other current humanitarian crises and, for that matter, dwarfs total international aid to Somalia over many years. Even if the military establishments of countries providing troops do not bill their respective aid ministries in full, the costs of utilizing them remain high.

The military "culture" was also in certain respects antithetical to the prevailing humanitarian one. The gap was particularly apparent in northern Iraq, where military officials, despite their qualifications in technical areas, were unfamiliar with relief organizations, lacked knowledge of relevant international humanitarian law, and showed little interest in local customs and institutions.

Outside military forces demonstrated considerable skill in opening humanitarian space but less ability in maintaining access to those at risk. Although the enforcement rhetoric used by the Security Council in all three cases was similar, the allied coalition in northern Iraq proved the most successful, both through the presence of troops on the ground and, after their departure, through the continual threat of air strikes and their actual conduct during air sorties against government targets. Troops were less successful in Somalia, where the threats to humanitarian operations were more random, especially after May 1993. In the former Yugoslavia, particularly in Bosnia, the troops were also less successful, perhaps because, faced with more persistent threats, the constellation of forces was totally inadequate. Even in Iraq, where civilian life has returned nearly to normal, so, too, have sporadic harassment of the Kurds and Shiites, arbitrary interference with aid activities, and government targeting of humanitarian personnel.

Another strength is the military's success in advising humanitarian personnel about security threats. This has been particularly useful in the former Yugoslavia. In northern Iraq, the allied coalition also advised UN and NGO personnel. In Somalia, the military seems less familiar with the terrain. These contributions correct the view that the military is powerless to contribute to humanitarian efforts short of the outright use of firepower.

Among the weaknesses is a still unresolved tension between efficiency and multilateral accountability. The most effective applications of military force were by the allied coalition in Iraq and UNITAF in Somalia. Although both were carried out under the broad authorization of the Security Council, neither was directly under UN command and control. UNOSOM I and II and UNPROFOR, all under UN command and control, were awkward and ineffective from a military standpoint.

Confusion in UNOSOM in particular raised for countries such as the United States and Italy an issue regarding the wisdom of placing their combat troops under UN command. That approach, called for by President Clinton and originally recommended in a draft presidential decision directive in mid-1993, was reconsidered in the light of the loss of American life suffered in Mogadishu in October 1993. The same tension surfaced in September in the minority report of the U.S. Commission on Improving the Effectiveness of the United Nations and in the president's maiden speech before the General Assembly.[18] The Defense Department's *Bottom-Up Review* also questioned the feasibility of multilateral military efforts in general and in particular the wisdom of sending U.S. troops as part of the UN's efforts to restore the elected government in Port-au-Prince.

In April 1993, the final presidential decision directive confirmed that U.S. forces were likely to remain under U.S. or NATO command and control for the foreseeable future. The Pentagon will cede them to the UN secretary-general only for safer and smaller operations like the one in Macedonia. In the unlikely event that a new international force materializes soon for Bosnia and Herzegovina, NATO will maintain command and control with the troops from NATO countries already in UNPROFOR that have been integrated in the new NATO command. It is even more unlikely that NATO troops will be integrated into the UNPROFOR structure.

Looking ahead, the future may hold fewer Iraqs, where the Security Council overrules a sovereign government and enforces its will, than Somalias, where a state collapses and gives way to general lawlessness. There may in turn be fewer Somalias than Yugoslavias, where the international community's unwillingness to pay the military and diplomatic price of countering the flagrant abuse of sovereign power renders humanitarian action a highly dangerous, costly, and perhaps ultimately unfeasible enterprise.

Some observers view recent experience as raising the question of whether force can be a valid instrument, even in the short run, for laying the groundwork for genuine reconciliation among warring parties. Others conclude, particularly from the experience in Iraq and the former Yugoslavia, that higher levels of force applied sooner in the service of a more coherent political strategy may help avoid much human suffering and facilitate negotiated settlements. The military will clearly be a player of importance in the humanitarian arena for the foreseeable future. Even if force is not the only way to halt genocide or break a physical impasse that prevents access to the needy, logistic support and technical expertise are bound to be a contribution of the military to an effective international safety net.

## Inside Resources

If stereotypes can be believed, societies in crisis are normally so bereft of resources that they are unable to help themselves. Experience suggests, however, that this assumption is often more self-serving than accurate. If inside institutions and capacities are lacking or incompetent, unwilling or unsuited to the challenge, outside actors are better able to move in and take charge.

At times of major emergencies, three main humanitarian resources are available to civilian populations at risk: host governments, insurgencies, and the institutions of civil society, including NGOs. These resources are fewer in number than the five external actors discussed above. Moreover, they are considerably less well known to the outside world. To the extent that they are known, they are often associated with causing rather than alleviating suffering. For these and other reasons, the humanitarian contributions, real and potential, of inside actors are normally undervalued.

Looking in from outside, external actors often are so unfamiliar with the contexts of civil wars that they are unable to identify locally available resources. They accept too easily the assumption that "failed states" such as Somalia are typical, that widespread civil wars confirm the outright inability of many poor and undeveloped nations to direct their own affairs, and that internal forces of leadership and cohesion are nonexistent in such settings.

The truth is more complex, even in the extreme case of Somalia from 1992 to 1993. To be sure, rival warlords worked their will, violence ruled the day, and such elementary features of law and order as police and sanitation were absent. Yet outside of Mogadishu there were clan elders whose leadership was respected, and even within the politicized capital there were fixed points of reference. In addition to elders with widespread popular followings and considerable experience in conflict resolution, there were also active and viable Somali NGOs, some of them with constituencies spanning acrimonious divisions among subclans. In fact, one of the most telling criticisms of the strategy followed by outside actors was that it reinforced the power of "warlords" who had a vested interest in continuing the conflict to the detriment of civil society. Some commentators have noted that for Somalis themselves the concept of warlords is more artificial than real.

In this context, it is ironic that the international intervention in Somalia, reflecting a respect for national authority even in a situation in which it had ceased to exist, riveted attention on Mogadishu, where internecine rivalries were greatest. UN efforts to bring to heel the two rival leaders in the capital were thus undercut by the UN's own strategy of channeling assistance through Mogadishu, which gave those leaders additional economic and political leverage. Meanwhile, needs elsewhere in Somalia were played down, as were existing internal forces of leadership and stability.

An alternative strategy was promoted in 1992 by some private relief groups and adopted in 1993 by UNICEF. It involved bypassing rather than showcasing the capital and its feuding leaders. A decentralized approach instead made use of the largest possible number of points of entry into the country, a widely dispersed relief distribution network, and aid workers and installations functioning in multiple locations with relative autonomy and self-reliance. An aid strategy that maximized the full array of existing inside resources early on probably would have had a far better chance of success.

Failure to make use of inside actors is also ironic inasmuch as a serious liability of outside resources, as well as a potential strength, lies precisely in their externality. In crisis after crisis, the foreignness of aid has undermined its appropriateness to local needs and mores. Frequently a negative reaction to outside humanitarian programs and personnel—in the Sudan and Bosnia, in Iran and Jordan—undercuts the value such aid might have by virtue of its independence of the parties to the conflict. Internal actors, often overlooked, represent a potentially key link between the concerned outside world and effective on-the-ground programs.

The three internal actors thus deserve closer review within the framework of their possible contributions to more successful humanitarian undertakings.

**Host Governments**

In many regions and conflicts, host governments have served as the first line of defense in responding to emergency needs. A prime example noted earlier was the quick action by the Jordanian government and by citizens of Amman when the first of several hundred thousand evacuees from Iraq and Kuwait appeared on their doorstep. Much time then elapsed before the world's more cumbersome intergovernmental machinery was mobilized and made its presence felt on the scene. Yet it was the second and less effective line of defense that captured the attention of the international media.

The resourcefulness of host governments and populations also is demonstrated by the response to those uprooted by the conflict in the former Yugoslavia. Once again, media coverage has featured the efforts of international aid personnel—French military officers, UNHCR field workers, Danish convoy leaders—to provide assistance and protection, frequently at great personal risk. As a result, the extraordinary contribution of the governments and people of the region is largely unknown and requires additional presentation here.

By mid-1993, almost 800,000 of the uprooted people who sought shelter in Croatia, displaced either from their homes in Bosnia and Herzegovina or within Croatia itself, had been accommodated by individuals. Most of the remainder were housed at government expense in hotels and collective centers. The process went forward largely without systematic discrimination, suggesting that humanitarian instincts at the outset ran deeper than political calculations. Many Bosnian Muslims became guests of Croatian families, even though ethnic tensions were playing themselves out in the war. The Croatian government incurred significant expenditures on behalf of Muslim refugees.

The Croatian experience also dramatizes how much difficulty outside agencies may have adapting to doing business in the light of local circumstances and preferences. Most previous refugee situations have involved distressed populations grouped together in camps, where their needs have been met by food prepared for them or distributed to them for their own preparation. The initial food aid to Croatia from Europe arrived in bulk shipments geared to institutional feeding; months elapsed before the requisite family-sized packages were devised and distributed.

Outside help also was largely geared toward welfare rather than self-help. "With funds you can organize public works and pay people for their services," recalled one Croatian official. "In-kind help," by which he meant food commodities, "is less useful in terms of stimulating economic activity." Providing an economic stimulus was critical to the challenges faced by Croatian authorities. These included addressing the effects of the mass influx on health and education systems, generating more employment, and resolving the budgetary difficulties created by the war.

Moreover, the humanitarian agenda of the outside world, mediated through its international representatives on the scene, tended to focus on distinct groups of people whose plight provided the original point of entry for many donors into the war in the Balkans. These included youngsters orphaned by the conflict or otherwise unaccompanied minors, scrawny men imprisoned in detention centers reminiscent of World War II concentration camps, and victims of mass rapes.

In each instance, the well-intentional outside response created problems for insiders. International campaigns to establish orphanages ran counter to the Croatian preference for placing unaccompanied children within families. Well-publicized efforts to resettle former detainees in their countries progressed largely in isolation from needs of the more numerous internally displaced refugees. Fact-finding and rape counseling teams often arrived unaware of the special sensitivity of the issue among Muslim women, their families, and communities. It was some time before the initial emphasis shifted to enhancing the capacities of indigenous institutions, strengthening resident social service agencies, and enabling community leaders to cope more adequately with the needs.

As a result, the burdens assumed by the Croatian government and individual families became onerous—to the point of creating political pressure against continued hospitality. International aid, structured according to the needs of specific groups of people who were dispersed throughout a population that was also severely affected by the war, missed the mark.

By mid-1993, the initial hospitality was showing signs of strain. Croatian host families were having difficulty meeting their own needs, let alone those of their guests. The government, anxious to stimulate economic activity, evicted some refugees and displaced persons from resort hotels along the Dalmatian coast to make room for traditional customers able to pay with hard currency. Hospitality across ethnic lines, undercut by inadequate support from the international community, gave way to responses reflecting more fully the tensions of the war.

In the Federal Republic of Yugoslavia, the pattern was similar, although the particulars differed. Of the 570,000 refugees in April 1993 who had sought shelter in Serbia and Montenegro, over 96 percent also had found shelter with individual families. The others were housed in barracks, school buildings, and hostels. Again, the noninstitutional nature of the local response, clearly more humane from the standpoint of the refugees, created problems for the international humanitarian machinery. As in Croatia, the needs of refugees in Serbia and Montenegro were interwoven with those of their hosts—maddeningly, in the view of outsiders unprepared to be solicitous of the Serbs.

A political overlay thus complicated the international response. The Serb authorities, who reacted to the influx for the most part sympathetically, were also part of the same government that had wreaked destruction upon Dubrovnik and Vukovar, had supplied the Bosnian Serbs with arms, and in other ways was implicated in the suffering of civilians throughout the region. Moreover, Serbs were the target of an international economic embargo designed to apply pressure on Belgrade by fomenting discontent among its civilians.

Local animosity, however, began to be directed not at the Milosevic regime but at the United Nations for having imposed the embargo. Refugees who were a daily reminder of the war were also targeted. The world, which expected the Serbs to provide care for those displaced by the war, was simultaneously reducing the goods at their disposal. As the noose tightened further, some in Serbia directed their discontent not at their own political leaders but at UN refugee programs. Manipulating external aid became a conscious act of defiance, even of patriotism.

Exemplary though the humanitarian response may have been, the governments of Croatia and the Federal Republic of Yugoslavia also were implicated in systematic abuses of human rights and crimes against humanity. Even their hospitality was not totally beyond criticism. Some Bosnian Croats entering Croatia for the first time received Croatian citizenship, while Bosnian Muslims were denied it. Muslim refugees in Serbia and Montenegro and humanitarian organizations seeking to assist them were harassed.

Such practices are reminders that in civil wars host governments are also belligerents. That reality imposes limitations on how much they, as part of the problem, can also be part of the solution. In fact, probably the most humanitarian contribution that many belligerents can make, almost irrespective of the legitimacy of their cause, is to stop their war. All other actions, however compassionate, pale by comparison.

Beyond the resources provided by individual host governments, some recent conflicts have seen an impressive mobilization of regional responses. One such example is the political initiative by the Central American presidents in the 1980s to halt the region's civil wars. A less positive example is the effort by governments in West Africa to end the conflict in Liberia.

As noted earlier, the Central American case involved a series of meetings convened by the presidents of the region and undergirded by the Contadora support group. The process was noteworthy in asserting regional responsibility in the face of initially heavy contrary pressure from Washington. In fact, the dynamic that emerged reverses the conventional wisdom that only outside actors can bring along, or override, retrograde forces inside conflict areas.

In the case of Liberia's civil war, the Economic Community of West African States formed and fielded a regional peacekeeping force, the Economic Community of West African States Monitoring Group (ECOMOG). Actively involved since July 1990, the main mover was Nigeria, which also has committed the lion's share of troops and has borne virtually all of the financial costs. Its foreign policy preferences also have determined the shape and timing of the action. ECOMOG initially moderated the fighting among first two and then three factions and eased the delivery of humanitarian assistance.

More recently, however, ECOMOG forces have become identified with one side in the conflict and on occasion have actively obstructed the provision of aid by the UN and private relief groups. Although the assertion of regional leadership has drawn widespread praise, the results have left much to be desired. The UN has failed to provide consistent diplomatic support to enhance the chances of success.

Even when host governments are favorably inclined, the international humanitarian machinery can be offputting. In Jordan, an energetic and creative Ministry of the Interior official was assigned to coordinate the response to the influx of refugees from Iraq and Kuwait. Orchestrating day-to-day decisions from the situation room in the ministry's basement, he benefited little from his colleagues in the ministries of nutrition, health, agriculture, and labor who were familiar with the often arcane workings of institutions such as UNICEF, WHO, FAO, WFP, and ILO (International Labour Organisation).

Even to the initiated, the workings of many of the outside institutions are anything but user-friendly. Individual UN organizations have their own procedures, timetables, and representatives. Only a few have delegated the authority in the field to advance even limited funds to respond to an emergency. The Central Emergency Revolving Fund (CERF), set up in 1992 and administered by the UN's Department of Humanitarian Affairs, provides some additional flexibility, but rigidities remain in individual organizations and in the system as a whole. The need for agencies to reimburse funds advanced by the CERF remains a disincentive to their use.

The difficulties experienced by host governments in gaining access to resources from apparently impenetrable agencies are confirmed by the Nordic UN Project, an extensive review in 1990 and 1991 by four northern European governments.[19] "You need to hire an expert just to figure out where to start," said a high-level Swedish diplomat commenting on the difficulty of comprehending accessing international resources.

Directed at UN development activities, the Nordic study nevertheless found the UN's apparatus for dealing with emergencies also wanting. Similar criticisms often are directed at the confusing world of bilateral and nongovernmental organizations. Clearly host governments would benefit from greater simplicity in procedures and transparency in the operations of outside humanitarian agencies.

What are the respective strengths and weaknesses of host governments as inside actors? On the positive side, they have a direct stake in the issues and may be in a position to respond quickly. Sooner or later their cooperation will become recognized as a central ingredient in any well-functioning response to a given crisis. Outside actors may gain access to distressed populations without a government's consent, but sustaining effective action without a host government's cooperation, or at least acquiescence, has generally proved difficult.

On the negative side, host government attitudes and policies also can be an obstacle to effective humanitarian action. Reflecting the prevailing conflict, such regimes frequently view civilian populations in political and military rather than humanitarian terms. Resources available for civilian needs may also be limited, whether because war efforts have been given higher priority or because the economy as a whole has been affected by the conflict. Although their consent is normally indispensable to effective humanitarian action, they may view their own survival as jeopardized by effective humanitarian programs, moderating their cooperativeness accordingly.

## Armed Opposition Movements

Insurgencies that challenge governments exercise many of the same responsibilities in the areas they control as do governments. Providing for the welfare of civilian populations represents one of the ways available to them for establishing and reinforcing their claim to legitimacy.

Some insurgencies are well organized to deliver services to civilian populations. The Eritrean People's Liberation Front provided space and encouragement for its offshoot, the Eritrean Relief Association, to function. In addition, the EPLF developed over a period of years shadow ministries comparable to those of recognized governments. Once victorious over the Ethiopian army in 1991, the same insurgents assumed responsibilities for ministries in the provisional government of Eritrea and, after independence, will play similar roles in the new state. Likewise, training for soldiers in international humanitarian law and human rights is useful in wartime and equally valuable when they are demobilized or integrated into a new national army.

In stark contrast to the EPLF, many armed opposition movements have paid less attention, or none at all, to the needs of civilians and to organizing the necessary administrative apparatus to address them systematically. RENAMO, the Mozambique National Resistance, has lacked an articulated political program and has done little to win and retain the loyalty of people within the areas it controls. In Peru, the Shining Path guerrillas are a political movement without a humanitarian agenda, commitment, or infrastructure. In Nicaragua, the Contras served as a channel for assistance from the U.S. government and private groups but developed no organized social service apparatus accountable to outside providers.

Insurgencies articulate grievances against seated governments and rally people to their causes, many of them stated in strong and appealing moral terms. Legitimate or not, however, their firm ideological stances tend to sweep other considerations aside. "When a man has placed his own life on the line and is prepared to kill or die for a cause," remarked Francis Deng, a distinguished Sudanese diplomat and intellectual who for years has agonized about the impact of civil war in his native land, "it is difficult for him to be overly concerned about the humanitarian needs of those who have remained behind the enemy

Khmer Rouge soldiers in a zone in Cambodia controlled by the Khmer Rouge in 1992. (UN Photo 159497/J. Bleibtreu)

lines, especially if that would compromise the cause for which he has chosen to make the ultimate sacrifice."

One of the dynamics common to internal armed conflicts, particularly as they grind on inexorably, year after year, is that each side minimizes or denies the humanity of civilians on the other. A given cause is invoked to legitimate acts of brutality that, divorced from the motivating and rationalizing context of the war, would be abhorrent and unthinkable. Humanitarian obligations are often sidestepped when a political cause is made the transcendent good or people in enemy territory are portrayed as devoid of human rights or humanity.

On his annual visits to cultivate support in the United States, Commander John Garang of the SPLA has heard pleas from NGOs and government officials for the well-being of civilians in the southern Sudan who are bearing the brunt of the grueling civil war. On each occasion, Garang has acknowledged their suffering but pointed to the higher political objectives of his movement as well as the likely benefits to civilians when his cause prevails. Whatever the toll on civilian victims, winning the war has become the overriding goal for Garang no less than for his adversaries in Khartoum. In recent years, NGOs have suggested in increasingly strong terms that however noble the objectives of Garang's movement, the inhumanities and indignities that have resulted for civilians are unconscionable.

The annual colloquies with Garang are notable in another respect. They underscore how much insurgent movements seeking international respectability can be pressured to abide by international humanitarian law in their treatment of civilian populations. On one occasion, Garang conceded to a group of NGOs that the SPLA probably didn't have a copy of the Geneva Conventions in its field library. At the same time, he expressed his intention that the SPLA respect international law and offered to provide his men for ICRC instruction if the training could take place on SPLA ground.

If host governments have trouble dealing with the opaqueness of outside agencies, armed opposition groups often experience even greater difficulty. This reflects in part the structural bias of the UN system toward its member governments, which inhibits evenhanded dealings with insurgents. Bilateral government agencies also deal less easily with rebels in the bush than with constituted governments in national capitals. Interactions with governments are covered by the well-accepted traditions of government-to-government diplomatic rules; interactions with insurgents have few precedents and involve more terra incognita.

What are the strengths and weaknesses of armed opposition groups as humanitarian actors in civil wars? On the plus side, they bring a strong commitment to a cause that is their primary reason for being. In their cultivation of international support for their cause, they may benefit from facilitating humanitarian access to populations as part of their own strategy to win the hearts and minds of the people. This inclination should be capitalized upon to foster their greater devotion to purely humanitarian issues. On the minus side, their commitment to their particular cause may be so strong that humanitarian values are sacrificed and space for humanitarian action is reduced. In this respect, they are little different from the governments with whom they are vying for power. There also may be limits on the extent to which insurgents are prepared to provide sectoral interlocutors for donor agencies.

### Local NGOs

Many humanitarian crises take place in settings where there is an abundance of local talent and capacity. The example from the 1991 cyclone in Bangladesh suggests how conventional wisdom and press coverage can contribute to ignoring the reality of local resources and resourcefulness.

Western policy circles and publics focused their attention on the external components of Operation Sea Angel. There was, indeed, much to capture their attention. In dramatic fashion, U.S. military aircraft, returning to the Philippines from the Gulf War, where they also had played a dramatic role, successfully ferried essential supplies to many among the 5 million persons affected.

Once again, however, the humanitarian landscape looked different from the inside. Of major importance was not that 130,000 persons perished but that protective steps activated in 1991 had prevented an estimated 20 percent greater loss of life. A generation of progress on the development front—the health, telecommunications, and transport sectors had made particular strides—made Bangladesh better able to withstand and respond to the disaster. Even the "slow but important efforts to strengthen the economic base of the rural poor" were credited with having improved the "capacity of individual households to cope with natural disasters."

Such was the historical and social context within which "People from all walks of life ... became united at the time of national emergency and gave overwhelming and enthusiastic support to an energetic and effective national relief effort," which began under government and NGO direction on the morning after the cyclone. In this larger context, the contribution of the U.S. military was relatively modest, although indeed welcome.[20]

Local NGOs have played a major role in many of the examples of humanitarian action described earlier. In the former Yugoslavia, Croatian and Serbian national Red Cross societies began work during the early phases of the conflict in 1991, as did Muslim groups such as the Bosnian Red Crescent Society and Merhamet, a Muslim agency. In each instance, the organizations reached out to one extent or another across national, ethnic, and other dividing lines.

A particularly compelling example of indigenous NGO-led action comes from Croatia, where the Center for Peace, Nonviolence, and Human Rights, an offshoot of the Croatian Anti-War Campaign, has undertaken a five-year reconstruction and reconciliation project in Pakrac. Located in the UN Protected Area (UNPA) west of Croatia, the town is divided into Serbian- and Croatian-controlled areas. Largely destroyed by interethnic fighting in the first two years of the war, the town now hosts a work camp in which a small number of carefully trained international volunteers are living with local families and assisting local people to clean up after the fighting and begin rebuilding.

After a year of activity on the Croatian side, the project in January 1994 expanded to include homes formerly occupied by Serbs. Funds for building materials and other project costs are raised locally and among private groups abroad. The UNDP's Social Reconstruction Programme facilitates travel documents for project volunteers and provides other limited support. "The large international organizations are very important when it comes to organizing mass support," explains Zoran Ostric of the Anti-War Campaign. "But for reconciliation you must work with individuals and on the local level. This the United Nations cannot really organize."

Occasionally, local initiative comes not from organized humanitarian organizations but from more informal leaders, communities, and committees. An illuminating example was the first planned repatriation to Guatemala in January 1993. This initiative was orchestrated by Guatemalan Indian leadership in refugee camps in Mexico, where many people had lived for a decade. It illustrated the ability of local leaders to take charge of their own destiny and to make and execute carefully considered decisions to return and restart their lives in Guatemala, where conflict continued between insurgent groups and the government. The repatriation required successful negotiations by refugee leaders with Guatemalan authorities to assure readmission to the country, safe passage to rural destinations, and access to land and other rudiments of a new start. While the civilian presidency was persuaded initially to allow about 3,000 people back into the country, the nation's armed forces were uneasy about the entire affair.

As things turned out, the repatriation was a solid success. The refugees traveled from rural Mexico back to their homes in northeast Guatemala, taking an intentionally circuitous and highly visible route through Guatemala City. They were welcomed there by the nation's president and pictured on local television and made a strong political statement that they were not subversives but full-fledged Guatemalans exercising their legitimate rights as citizens. The more direct route would have been less taxing and less expensive but also would have had less political impact.

While the repatriation was decided, planned, and executed by inside actors, outside NGOs assisted in eliciting the government's consent and mobilizing international presence and concern. UN organizations also used their good offices and program funds to support the effort. It was clear, however, that outside assistance was supporting the local initiative rather than setting the priorities.

In one sense, however, the return of the refugees could have been even more all-embracing. Local organizers and their outside supporters may have lost an opportunity to engage more actively the cooperation of Guatemalan political and military authorities. Although the Guatemalan armed forces offered to help by providing transport and clearing mud slides, the returnees, after decades of repression by the military, rejected such overtures. Soldiers did apparently lend some assistance, but dressed as civilians.

One longtime observer of the region thus gave a carefully balanced assessment of the initiative in a confidential report to his headquarters. "The return was an enormous success," he wrote, that "paved the

Guatemalans display the names of missing family members. (Photo by Rob Brower reproduced by permission)

way for future returnees. I greatly admire the determination, patience, persistence, risk-taking, and collective organization and mobilization of the refugees/returnees."

At the same time, he expressed a certain foreboding for the future, noting, "The overall attitude of the military is still one of distrust and insinuation that the returnees will support the efforts of the armed opposition."

Sooner or later durable solutions require not only the acquiescence but the active cooperation of belligerents. This is yet another reason why a major goal should be to enlist their involvement in humanitarian action along the way. As of early 1994, another 150,000 Guatemalan refugees remained in Mexico, most of them intent on returning. Even in the remote areas of Guatemala where they will resettle, they will interact with local political authorities. Although the preference of returning indigenous peoples to keep their distance from political and military authorities is understandable, future opportunities to build bridges may materialize.

Unlike the vibrant participatory ethos in Central America, there are some settings where local nongovernmental organizations and their leadership are no longer robust or even in existence. This was true in

Cambodia, where a lengthy and brutal civil war took its toll on local leadership and civil society. Local leadership disappeared, and with the leaders went the NGOs. The damage became apparent when, after a decade of Khmer Rouge rule and foreign occupation, the international community turned its attention to the challenges of repatriation, reconciliation, and development.

Taking stock of the situation in 1989, a UNDP survey found only 360 Khmer with managerial skills, the result of years in which trained Cambodian professionals had been the specific target of the Pol Pot regime. In 1990 a UN team counted as few as 3,000 Khmer with postsecondary educations, none of them experienced in the kind of macroeconomic planning needed to rebuild the country. As a result, the interaction between the international community and Cambodia was fundamentally different from what took place in other regions.

In Cambodia, some effects of war that were less apparent to outsiders were visible to international NGOs, which, unlike governments and UN organizations, had managed to maintain a presence during most of the civil war and international economic embargo. "The basic units of Khmer society have been the family and the village," observed an NGO workshop in 1991, "both of which are in need of repair along with roads and bridges." In Cambodia there was very little at both local and national levels upon which to build.[21]

The experience in Cambodia cautions against taking for granted the capacities of inside actors. A vignette from Bosnia, however, contains a different reminder. Even where local capacity exists, it may be unwise to force it into the customary humanitarian mold.

Many Muslim communities in eastern Bosnia in late 1992 and throughout 1993 faced desperate shortages of essential food, medicines, clothing, and fuel. Road convoys of UN and international NGO supplies were being held up; airdrops helped fill the gap but were still inadequate. Through secret convoys into places like Goradze, villagers organized systems to move relief supplies on the backs of pack animals. Many communities dispatched their own trucks to pick up supplies from outside UN and NGO warehouses, somehow threading their way back. Local drivers knew the byways and even some of the soldiers manning the roadblocks.

The advantages of employing local drivers proved a liability, however, in June 1993, when a privately organized "Convoy of Peace" proceeded from the Dalmatian coast to central and eastern Bosnia. Many of the 170 trucks were halted by Bosnian Croat forces at roadblocks, their Muslim drivers forcibly removed from their cabs. Eight were shot dead; others were injured. The incident underscored the value of the UN practice of using expatriate drivers, many of them supplied by British, Swedish, and Danish bilateral aid agencies. "Due to ethnic tensions," WFP reported in November 1993, "it is not possible to employ locally recruited drivers to drive into Bosnia, thus international recruited drivers are used."[22] The higher cost of expatriates seemed justified in this case by the greater safety involved. Even they, however, were hardly secure. On October 25, 1993, a Danish driver and seven Dutch team members were killed when two convoys in central Bosnia came under fire.

The limitations of local NGOs, some of them more difficult to offset than others, lend urgency to efforts to help nurture inside institutions and leadership during major humanitarian emergencies but also for the longer haul as well. Many outside NGOs and their professional associations affirm a commitment to build local capacities as the only sensible way to strengthen the prospects for democratization and civil society.

One drawback of trying to build capacity through the interactions between insiders and outsiders in civil wars is that outsiders may impose inappropriate or politicized ideas of management and accountability. In late 1992 the U.S. Congress requested the U.S. General Accounting Office to review the role of NGOs in the postwar reconstruction in El Salvador. The congressional watchdog set out to establish "what experience NGOs working in El Salvador have had, especially as it relates to administering and accounting for program funds in line with U.S. standards." Of special concern was "the extent to which NGOs, particularly the five primary ones affiliated with the [FMLN] are participating in the reconstruction efforts."[23]

This badly misrepresented the situation. The foremost issue for inside nongovernmental organizations, even in the polarized atmosphere of the 1980s in Central America, was not Whose side are you on? but How can you help people in need? Representatives of the five NGOs mentioned in the GAO report conceded that their concern with helping people in need had moved them closer to the political cause of the FMLN. However, framing the issue in such stark terms represented a disservice to the organizations and the issues. Moreover, the assumption that U.S. assistance would continue to fight the war as the nation turned to the tasks of reconstruction ignored how much these funds and NGOs might play a helpful role in reconstruction.

Again, the diversity and complexity of civil war circumstances demand caution in reaching generalizations about the availability or authenticity of the structures of civil society. Local NGOs are no more assured of being right than are local customs. Fidelity to the guiding principle of appropriateness requires that outside humanitarian institutions also reach their own assessments about what is appropriate.

What are the strengths and weaknesses of local NGOs? Such groups are directly connected to indigenous populations and often are created specifically to address peoples' needs. They frequently produce or draw on local leadership with ties to the communities and with a vision of the future well grounded in local realities. It is their country and their people; they and not their outside counterparts will be the primary sustainers and guarantors of reconstruction, development, and peace. The sooner and more thoroughly they are involved, the better the chance for remediation of suffering and the rebirth of civil society.

On the negative side, these groups and their leaders may take a parochial or political approach to their tasks. They may lack familiarity with outside resources, with the means of projecting their needs onto the international stage, and with normal accountability expectations. They may come from societies with customs that from an international perspective may be questionable.

## Conclusion

Several conclusions emerge from this review of the interactions among humanitarian actors from outside and inside war zones about their respective strengths and weaknesses.

First, the array of resources represented by outside and inside actors is stunning. The existence of so many potential assets suggests a humanitarian creation of great vitality and diversity. This energy is dynamic and renewable. It deserves harnessing rather than hindering.

Second, as with the British police, the French cook, and the German mechanic, placing this array of resources at the service of distressed populations requires encouraging each actor to do what it does best. There is no point in expecting the United Nations to be the one-size-fits-all humanitarian agent, or in excluding the military automatically from all humanitarian involvement. There is room and work enough for all who are committed to the relief of life-threatening suffering.

Third, there have been, and probably always will be, temptations to bypass insiders. In the rush to save lives, outside organizations tend to assume that inside institutions will complicate their efforts. Outsiders also tend to define the problem in ways that require their direct involvement. New forms of mutuality are urgently required, both in understanding war-induced humanitarian crises and in tackling them effectively and together.

The presence of local actors (as in the insurgencies in Angola, Mozambique, and Nicaragua) or their absence (as in Cambodia) can deter expeditious action. However, there are also situations in which involvement can be hazardous for the local actors. At the end of the day, however, inside actors should not be consigned to the roles of "hewers of wood and drawers of water." Recent experience demonstrates that they can be pivotal and indispensable resources in charting their own future. In many situations, outside actors could and should take their cues.

For the global humanitarian community of the future, the challenge is to produce greater synergy among the major components of the world's humanitarian machinery. Outside resources include the universality of the United Nations system, the particularity of donor governments interests, the driving energy of NGOs, the ICRC's fidelity to principle, and the logistic and other capacities of military establishments. Inside assets include the long-term self-interest of host governments and insurgents in the welfare of civilians and the personal and institutional resources of civil society. Together, these inside assets represent the world's first line of defense in large and small emergencies.

Resources from these eight actors require more creative orchestration. Several generalizations have emerged about the necessary orchestration of energies. First, achieving rapid response in some settings will require that internal and external NGOs play a pivotal role in communities where they have been long involved at the grass-roots level.

Second, actors are required who can function on the front lines as bullets fly. In this respect, the ICRC seems to have the edge, although other agencies, properly trained, staffed, and insured, also may contribute. The military also has a significant role to play when the UN Security Council decides to insist upon access by force and when humanitarian organizations require counsel and support. Ensuring appropriate international accountability for such operations is crucial.

Third, an improved humanitarian system will require additional resources. In getting more productivity from current assets and in mobilizing new levels of resources, the UN's Department of Humanitarian Affairs should play a pivotal role. It should work to achieve fuller coordination of field activities and fund-raising and should provide intellectual leadership to the wider international community.

Finally, a comprehensive vision of humanitarian action needs to be developed—"An Agenda for Humanitarian Action." It requires length to move from emergencies to development, breadth to cut across many sectors, and depth to sustain efforts until durable changes have taken root. Whatever the competence and specialization of any one set of actors, all have a stake in the improved performance of the system as a whole. All actors share a common responsibility and face common constraints. All stand to benefit from improvements suggested in Chapter 5.

# 5
# The Future

The structure for future humanitarian action requires substantial reform. First, changes are needed to make activities in complex emergencies more effective. Second, a greater emphasis on preventing crises is required. Third, intervention in extraordinary circumstances may be necessary to support humane values. Finally, the institutions and individuals involved must demonstrate greater accountability.

In the final analysis, the most serious deterrent to developing a more effective global humanitarian community is triage, the process of separating those who can and must be helped from those who require no help and those who cannot be helped. The major unfinished business is creating a more effective global humanitarian system faithful to the principle of responding to need wherever it exists.

## The Current System: Making It Work Better

Given the range and complexity of the challenge to preserving a sense of humanity in times of war, the global humanitarian community needs greater creativity in orchestrating its various components. This will require increased attention to the tasks to be performed, a conductor who gets the best out of the musicians, and a new sense of commitment to the whole by all of the parts. The seven basic aspects of humanitarian action need revisiting with an eye to maximizing the contributions of the violin, the tuba, and the kettle drums.

In assessing the problem, the United Nations emerges as the preferred vehicle, acting fully in concert with others. One encouraging development has been the emergence of joint assessment missions, generally led by the UN Department of Humanitarian Affairs and including the full range of participants. Local NGOs, which frequently have the greatest familiarity with the suffering on the ground, should be increasingly enlisted in this process.

When it comes to the negotiation of access and the protection of humanitarian space, experience suggests that any one of several institutions can play this role, alone or in concert. The UN's international standing confers a comparative advantage in some settings. However, that edge may be squandered if special representatives of the secretary-general are chosen without clear terms of reference, as in the Persian Gulf crisis, without political clout with their own governments, as in the former Yugoslavia, or without the strong backing of other major actors, as in Somalia.

There may also be circumstances in which the United Nations lacks credibility and where other actors—bilateral governments, a single NGO, a group of NGOs, or the ICRC—are better placed. In any event, whoever undertakes the task of negotiating and maintaining access should keep the entire humanitarian community fully in the picture.

In resource mobilization, there is a clear role for the United Nations on behalf of the global humanitarian community. There is already movement in this direction, with the UN Department of Humanitarian Affairs increasingly framing consolidated appeals on behalf of the entire system, which are then circulated throughout the global humanitarian community. To date, however, they have not often elicited much greater donor response.

Concerning the physical delivery of relief and the provision of protection, inside and outside NGOs emerge as the preferred channels. Their strengths include familiarity with grass-roots needs and capacities, their community-level networks, their dedication, their risk-taking ethos, and their less expensive operations. There may be exceptional circumstances in which the transport and delivery capacities of outside military forces may be required. Although the increased involvement in recent years of UN organizations and donor governments had identified them with a positive response to the crises, they should by and large work with NGOs rather than undertake operations themselves.

In providing protection, all actors play useful roles. For those who qualify as refugees, UNHCR's protection efforts should be strengthened and probably expanded to include internally displaced persons.[1] Outside human rights organizations also play a pivotal role, complementing the critical but vulnerable work of inside private

A demobilized soldier of the Cambodian People's Armed Forces plows during an agricultural leave.(UN Photo 186070/P. S. Sudhakaran)

groups, which are well placed to sound the alarm but poorly placed to exert pressure.

Outside NGOs also have a clear comparative advantage in education and advocacy. If past is prologue, the necessary changes in the policies of donor governments and intergovernmental organizations may require a more energetic conceptual and lobbying nudge from activist NGOs.

NGOs are adept at alerting the media to crises and providing them with essential information. Educational activities by international nongovernmental organizations also are essential to direct attention toward preventing crises rather than waiting for them to erupt. In recent years, inside NGOs have encouraged outside NGOs to aim their education and advocacy work toward outside governments and publics, leaving the primary responsibility for dealing with governments in crisis areas to local organizations. Local NGO institution building would help exploit these comparative advantages within the NGO community.

Regarding the task of looking ahead to anticipate the negative effects of humanitarian activities and to identify longer-term priorities such as reconciliation and development, all actors seem equally disadvantaged. All are attracted by the greater availability of resources for immediate emergencies and all wish to be identified publicly with the dramatic delivery of relief. All are caught up in the dominant humanitarian ethos, approached more as a series of fifty-yard dashes than as a marathon run. All should take a more comprehensive and reflective view.

This brief review of six challenges and the best-positioned actors to handle each has saved until last what is perhaps the most arduous task, that of coordination. This challenge merits special attention since better orchestration is needed to assure improved results from each of the actors and from the system as a whole.

Who should conduct the humanitarian orchestra? Often there is little unanimity of views among the players. Although most do not question the desirability of playing from the same score or adopting a common tempo, many have serious reservations about who should be entrusted with the baton and what music should be selected.

Some of their hesitations are self-serving, others are legitimate. Some involve institutional turf protection, others reflect structural policies and politics that are more difficult to dismiss or to resolve. Coordination at its best can harmonize and energize activities, replace centripetal with centrifugal action, and enhance individual contributions. Coordination at its worst can require costly investments of time and money, frustrate action, centralize functions that are better left decentralized, and politicize humanitarian action.

Contrary to the proverbial wisdom, more coordination does not necessarily mean greater effectiveness. "The appearance of improved coordination at the center," says James C. Ingram, "does not necessarily lead to more effective and timely interventions in the field."[2] In civil wars, where insistence on coordination by the political authorities can be used to frustrate access, numerous independently moving parts may enhance the chances that at least some of the efforts may succeed.

Who is best suited to conduct the humanitarian orchestra? There is simply no single best maestro for all seasons. The United Nations, even with its new humanitarian coordinator, is not able to play that role at all times and in all places. Perhaps the UN should function instead as a principal guest conductor, with the emphasis on "guest." However, some major performances will require guest conductors from outside the UN if satisfactory results are to be produced. In any event, conductors will be effective because of respect they earn with each new crisis, not because of the title they carry.

In the interest of achieving a humanitarian system in which the basic tasks are performed by the actors best suited to tackle them, a number of basic changes in its policies and procedures are in order.

For the intergovernmental organizations of the United Nations, the primary challenge is to function more effectively as a system rather than as a loose amalgam of feudal entities, each with separate mandates, fund-raising, and programs. Achieving greater effectiveness and coherence represents a special challenge for the UN's Department of Humanitarian Affairs. After two years of start-up efforts, this new unit must now become the focal point for humanitarian interests in the United Nations and beyond. The UN system as a whole should also face squarely the gaps between its political-military and its humanitarian personas. In particular, there is an urgent need to explore the possibility of creating a new UN entity to provide assistance and protection in active war zones when Chapter 7 economic or military sanctions are in effect.

The central problem for bilateral organizations is to see themselves as agents for humanitarian goals rather than for their governments' short-term interests. National economic interests (for example, using relief activities to benefit the donor nation's producers, manufacturers, and balance of payments) are an obvious intrusion into genuine needs-based programming, as are short-term political considerations.

A second problem revolves around the lack of consistency of governments in funding humanitarian activities through various channels: UN, bilateral, NGO, and the ICRC. Parliaments and national publics cannot simultaneously insist on better use of scarce resources and still make their contributions available in fits and starts, with highly circumscribed ground rules for their use.

For outside NGOs, two major changes are in order. The first concerns a greater commitment in resource allocations, constituency education, and in philosophy to nurturing the development of indigenous institutions and leadership. This is particularly necessary for the mainly Western and Judeo-Christian institutions that are now increasingly active among the three-quarters of the world's refugees who are Muslim.[3]

A second change involves expanding the scale of NGO activities while preserving the traditional commitment by these organizations to responsiveness and independence. Ways should be found to scale up NGO activities, preserving at the same time their special heterogeneity and autonomy. Closer cooperation with intergovernmental and bilateral organizations and even with the military may be possible without undermining their distinctive focus on individuals at risk.

For the International Committee of the Red Cross, the need to maintain the exclusively Swiss character of the organization has eased, as the ICRC itself acknowledges in broadening the nationalities of its overseas delegates. Its traditional insistence on working on all sides of conflicts also may require reexamination. Already thrust into great prominence by the proliferation of interstate and civil wars that are its special preserve and area of competence, the ICRC should become even more energetic in seeking to promote respect for international humanitarian principles and in sharing its own experience with less-seasoned practitioners.

For outside military forces, the challenge of tailoring responses to new humanitarian missions requires significant remodeling. Greater familiarity with and sensitivity to international humanitarian law and the institutional values of other actors is essential. The rigidly hierarchical approach to decisionmaking that is the hallmark of the military may not be possible or desirable in the humanitarian crises where their help is needed. Rather than seeking to carve out for itself an entire spectrum of roles, the military should identify specific tasks at which it has a comparative advantage. If the level of military involvement increases, clearly demarcated command and control authority and multilateral accountability are of the essence.

At the same time, however, some tasks that the military might take on may be better pursued by specialized humanitarian organizations. Greater involvement in humanitarian emergencies should be undertaken to capitalize on military expertise, not to defuse public pressures to cut post–Cold War military expenditures. Since humanitarian activities have proved difficult for traditional civilian aid organizations to carry out in active wars when UN peace enforcement operations are under way, the UN should explore the idea of creating a new unit on the security side to assist when bullets are flying and a more unified approach is needed.

In addition to more careful attention to the comparative advantages of the major actors in tackling humanitarian action, the humanitarian enterprise needs a rekindled sense of collegiality and commitment and a new understanding of accountability.

In the present humanitarian system, each organization has a primary commitment to the success of its own undertaking. Substantial efforts for the larger good—for example, in joint programming, shared staff, common press releases, and coordination meetings—are the exception rather than the rule. Most agencies and individual practitioners are committed first and foremost, if not exclusively, to their own programs. Seeing the humanitarian forest is particularly necessary in civil wars because belligerents mark individual trees for felling and have no abiding love for the human preserve itself.

Although investments in coordination or information sharing may be a step in the right direction, complaints often arise about their limited return. NGOs are more often invited to UN gatherings than they are treated as equals at these gatherings. But many international NGOs are themselves hardly models of collegiality. For example, one international NGO official who had been denied permission to remain in Baghdad after June 1992 announced that upon returning home he would launch a media blitz against the Iraqi government. The impact on Iraqi nationals employed by his own organization and on the humanitarian staff was of no apparent concern to him.

Organizations working within the United Nations system under its blue flag share common ground. However, in many situations their offices are located in different buildings, their field staffs are stationed in distinct areas, and they report separately to their own headquarters. The designation of the UN Development Program's country representative as the UN's resident coordinator for emergencies has encouraged UN staff communications in countries at war, with variable results from crisis to crisis. Even wider gaps exist between UN humanitarian staff and peacekeeping personnel. The quality of professional relationships also varies widely among UN officials, NGOs, and the ICRC.

Many NGOs energetically pursue their own work, largely in a vacuum from UN organizations and sometimes even from other NGOs. Many also take a very narrow approach to their own activities. In Nairobi in 1990, one respected international NGO declined to make a modest contribution to defray the cost of an informal gathering bringing together representatives of the Sudan's warring factions. Its representative argued without apology that with extensive nutritional and agricultural responsibilities, he had no funds for activities unrelated to his own humanitarian agenda, and certainly not for reconciliation efforts.

There is frequently little consultation, even of an informal nature, between humanitarian assistance organizations and groups working on issues of human rights, freedom of the press, or democratization. Although there are institutional and political reasons for maintaining distinctions between these types of activities, future humanitarian action requires an animating spirit that approaches tasks comprehensively and unbureaucratically.

Rigid separation of agencies and compartmentalization of tasks reduces opportunities for synergism. Every humanitarian program requires a careful assessment of need, but not every agency should carry out its own assessment. All actors require space to operate, but not all should negotiate that space themselves. All actors require a well-informed public to maintain presence and programs in intractable emergencies, but not all are required to mount sophisticated public education efforts.

At present, few organizations invest significantly in the welfare of the humanitarian community as a whole, even though all have a stake in how well it functions. Unprofessional action by one organization can undercut confidence in others, just as cynicism at the global level can take its toll on agencies irrespective of their individual merits. Although the public often decries the "tribalism" that fuels civil wars, the same word often also characterizes jockeying for visibility and resources within the so-called humanitarian community.

In fairness, there is currently more collegiality today than there was a decade or two ago, partly because of the formidable obstacles confronting all actors in complex emergencies. Some organizations also are making heavy investments of personnel and resources in a better functioning system. Some individuals pursue interests larger than their own agency's. Yet the system does not encourage or reward such behavior.

Engendering greater collegiality among humanitarian professionals and a new sense of commitment to the humanitarian enterprise deserves high priority. It will require a more understanding public and greater incentives in individual organizations. But the benefits in terms of improved programs will be substantial.

### Accountability: Making It Real

Also essential is a new and broader sense of accountability. Humanitarian organizations have been more intent on action than on reflection, on doing than on assessing. This is a statement of fact, not a formal indictment. Yet it is time to cease viewing good intentions as a substitute for solid results, and warmheartedness as an alternative to tough-mindedness. The tasks of delivering aid and protection are too impor-

tant not to be held to the highest standards of performance and accountability. Given considerable differences of opinion about how this task should be approached, further debate about how to proceed represents a major element on the global agenda for humanitarian action of the future.[4]

In this context, David Forsythe has said, "As a political scientist rather than a lawyer, it is my inclination to suggest that we have far too many textual analyses of the Geneva Conventions of 1949 and the Additional protocols of 1977 [and] far too few inquiries about whether and to what extent the Geneva tradition of law makes any difference to the victims of armed conflict."[5] International law has been too much the exclusive preserve of international lawyers and too little the concern of humanitarian organizations. Humanitarian professionals need to be more savvy about the strategies that have proved most effective in holding political authorities to their would-be binding legal commitments.

Some observers believe that a new and more binding code of conduct is necessary to hold practitioners to higher standards of performance. Humanitarian action, they argue, is no different from law, medicine, social work, or education. Professionalism requires a clear commitment to assistance and protection, sound judgment in the implementation of programs, respect for the identity and confidentiality of those served, limits on the percentage of funds spent on promotion, and so on. Those who do not meet the minimum standards do not deserve the public trust.

Those pressing for more rigorous accountability point out that the recent performance by organizations in war theaters has been increasingly taken to task. As noted earlier, in the wake of the escalating famine and warfare in Somalia, Africa Watch called for a public inquiry into the misfeasance or malfeasance of the United Nations. Responding to the conduct of its troops in Somalia, a Canadian court-martial has found one of its soldiers guilty of killing Somali civilians. Decisions by individual officials to press ahead with humanitarian activities (e.g., an individual convoy) that have resulted in injuries or loss of life to staff have been, and should be, seriously questioned.

Some therefore make a strong case for tighter standards of accountability, but others are less enthusiastic about achieving higher performance by humanitarian personnel. They note past difficulty in winning community-wide agreement on, much less implementation of, a code of conduct. Given the diversity among the major actors—each representing different constituencies with their own cultures, performance expectations, and accountabilities—they see little possibility of hammering out common standards.

Still others find changes in the present structure not only unrealistic but also undesirable. Previous efforts to devise codes have failed, they recall, and highly divergent viewpoints on issues of principle and practice still exist. Moreover, the issues are so sensitive and public trust so fragile that the effort necessary to achieve consensus could be counterproductive. Taking steps to cashier those responsible for humanitarian programs that run amok might discourage future initiatives. It is preferable, some say, to concentrate energies on practical areas where meaningful cooperation and better programming are feasible.

Given the diversity among actors, the most practical approach would be for similar organizations to develop individual codes of conduct instead of trying to devise an all-purpose code. Thus, like-minded international NGOs—for instance, the various Oxfams and their cooperating partners, or the members of consortiums like the International Council of Voluntary Agencies and InterAction—should accelerate efforts to refine their own codes, which could, in turn, become the basis for discussions among other NGOs and eventually between NGOs and other organizations.

An incremental approach also would allow for fuller discussion of the multidimensional nature of accountability by like-minded organizations. Recent experience demonstrates that accountability involves not only responsible stewardship of resources but also the articulation of principles and their application. What should be the ground rules in civil wars for initiating programs, or for suspending them? Should an organization respect the law at all times, even when doing so constrains its ability to relieve life-threatening suffering? What are its responsibilities to provide for the security of local and expatriate personnel?

Do agencies entrusted with mounting programs in civil wars also have the authority and even the obligation to terminate them? Should Sadako Ogata, who suspended UNHCR activities in eastern Bosnia in February 1993, be charged with dereliction of humanitarian duty or applauded for defending humanitarian principle? The same question applies to UN Envoy Ambassador Mohamed Sahnoun, who resigned after unsuccessfully proposing in late 1992 a moratorium on aid operations in Mogadishu, since only a fraction of supplies were reaching their destination. In each case, greater clarity about what the UN would tolerate might have resulted in less confusion within the global humanitarian community and less abuse by belligerents.

The greater the sense of solidarity within the community, the greater the critical mass and momentum. Wider agreement on principle, even if practices diverge, would foster a common sense of purpose and have tangible payoffs. A common front among humanitarians in their dealings with governments and insurgents might make it more difficult for political authorities to play some agencies against others, as they did in Baghdad in 1992 and in Mogadishu in 1993.

In some respects, upgrading the professionalism of UN and bilateral aid practitioners may be at least as difficult as making similar strides among NGOs. A 1993 article in *The Economist,* "Heart of Gold, Limbs of Clay," observed that the United Nations is caught in a dilemma. "With peacemaking largely uncharted, rules have to be made, and lessons learnt, on the job." Writing a rule book requires a higher degree of agreement about procedures and principles. The article concludes, probably somewhat prematurely, "The UN is feeling its way towards greater professionalism. ... Gifted amateurishness is already on the way out."[6] The observation recalls the comment several years ago by a senior UN humanitarian official that the UN represented the "last bastion" of unprofessionalism.

Inspired and necessary on some occasions, amateurism and improvisation have been disastrous on others. "It's very hard to run a humanitarian operation according to a book that hasn't been written," observed a senior UN humanitarian official in 1993. In the humanitarian enterprise today, there is no alternative to greater professionalism, and no way of getting there apart from clearer objectives, methods, and accountability. At the same time, it is apparent that functioning effectively may require different skills of those who negotiate international access to the port of Massawa and those who help communities in the Krajuia overcome the legacies of "ethnic cleansing."

In the process of encouraging more effective performance by the international humanitarian system, the media may function as both an ally and an adversary of humanitarian action. Powerful images of widespread human suffering can spur governments to act. The media also can increase the accountability of aid organizations, for whom poor or scandalous performances represent a major liability with donors. Yet the media can also promote quick fixes, underestimate long-term realities, and ignore crises in which editors find no compelling copy or footage.[7]

Greater accountability could be advanced by a new humanitarian watchdog. Modeled on the success of organizations such as Human Rights Watch, such an institution should have both a human rights and a humanitarian assistance portfolio and include all humanitarian organizations within its purview. Private funding would be necessary to facilitate independent activities and assessments. A proposal for an International Crisis Group with some of these functions is currently being initiated by the Carnegie Endowment for International Peace in Washington, D.C.

A watchdog could conduct systematic investigations of efforts to reduce suffering in a country (for example, the former Yugoslavia) or a region (for example, the Horn of Africa). It could also evaluate sectoral activities (for example, refugees or food logistics) by all institutions (for example, Department of Humanitarian Affairs, AID, and Oxfam), challenging the performance of individual agencies or officials where necessary. Once this new entity became a recognized actor, individual organizations would be obliged to cooperate, and constituencies, administrative governing boards, and citizens would have to take its findings seriously.

### Prevention: Avoiding Major Emergencies

Improvements along these lines by the global community in its humanitarian system must be accompanied by greater efforts to prevent major human cataclysms. The reasons for doing so are self-evident.

The human need resulting from civil wars is staggering. Until the end of the Cold War, internal armed conflicts generally were considered to be a Third World monopoly. That has now changed. There are at least a million refugees from the former Yugoslavia and probably three times that many displaced within its boundaries. There are also significant numbers of refugees and internally displaced persons in the republics of the former Soviet Union, including 1 million from a clash between only two of them, Armenia and Azerbaijan, and another million in Tajikistan.

There are some 20 million refugees worldwide and more than that number of internally displaced persons. Even though the media connect faces with these statistics, a greater leap of imagination is required to conceive of the total costs in ruined economies and forgone development prospects, to say nothing of remedial action, whether peacekeeping or humanitarian. Would it not be more economical, not to say more humane, to head off such crises before they turn violent and expensive? Given how overextended the world's treasury and its humanitarian instruments are now, should preemptive action not be mounted before current flash points erupt and new crises materialize?[8]

The horrors of conflicts, the suffering of civilians in war zones, the testimony of practitioners, and the wisdom of diplomats erase any doubt that the most reasonable long-term solutions lie in the area of prevention. What is desperately needed is a broader understanding of the humanitarian enterprise that links it more integrally to conflict management, human rights protection, and development. Australian Foreign Minister Gareth Evans argues that prevention is the most effective way to tackle global problems; but all such measures are politically feasible only after conflict is more or less certain or has erupted.[9] A dramatic example of the need for a more comprehensive approach is provided by international responses in the former Yugoslavia. The fundamental humanitarian challenge there was not the large number of orphaned children, former detention camp occupants, and rape victims. It was rather the continuing war itself and the conduct of the belligerents.

To be sure, descriptions of five-year-old Irma, wounded by shrapnel and unable to get lifesaving treatment in Sarajevo, made a war come alive for the outside world after it had already dragged on for more than a year. Yet the central problem was not arranging a medical evacuation to a country with functioning surgical facilities but rather supplying Bosnian hospitals with the necessary water, medicines, and diesel fuel for their generators. Resources for emergency activities that benefit specific individuals were welcome, but the more fundamental challenge involved getting the Bosnian health system back to its prewar levels of excellence, which necessitated stopping the war that riddled its hospitals with bullets and inundated them with Irmas.

A key principle of humanitarian action examined earlier involves discerning the context. Rather than catering only to individuals, humanitarian initiatives should be framed in their larger perspective and should encourage links between these efforts and the underlying problems of poverty, powerlessness, injustice, and inequity. The new lenses

Destruction in Croatia. (UNHCR Photo by S. Foa/07.1992)

through which violence is viewed must be focused on preventive peace building rather than "simply" stanching the wounds of conflicts already under way.

Promulgating a new vision of the prevention imperative is not easy, nor is it easy to put it into practice. Human experience provides abundant confirmation of how difficult it is to initiate preventive measures and of missed opportunities to act on data from newly improved "early warning" mechanisms. It is natural to react more quickly to urgent and obvious emergencies than to long-simmering and less visible crises. But the eventual bills for deferred maintenance are demonstrably higher than for timely action. Here the proverbial wisdom may indeed be instructive. An ounce of prevention may be worth a pound of cure, but it is the squeaky wheel that gets the grease. A newspaper article reviewing the difficulties of generating the necessary political and institutional support for conflict prevention was entitled, "No One Cares Until It's War."[10]

There are encouraging signs that new thinking and strategies are taking shape. At their summit in January 1992, members of the UN Security Council recognized the frustrations and failures of the early post–Cold War era and requested that the newly elected UN secretary-general give fresh attention to the mission of the United Nations in a fundamentally changed world. Boutros Boutros-Ghali's report, *An Agenda for Peace,* covers much ground and offers many new ideas, among them the concept of conflict prevention. There is considerable ferment on such matters in policy, academic, and practitioner circles as well.

Governments have begun to take preventive actions such as the symbolic deployment of UN soldiers to Macedonia and Kosovo and to make expanded use of fact-finding teams, human rights monitors, and early warning systems. Confronted by a widening vortex of violence, governments are reexamining its root causes in poverty, the unjust distribution of resources, and the legacy of colonial boundaries in multiethnic societies. Longer-term economic and social development, reforms to distribute the benefits of future growth more equitably, and restructured global financial and trading systems assume new urgency. Governments seem more prepared to invest in effective prevention through the deployment of well-armed troops with contingency plans and reserve firepower.

Ultimately, the alternatives to better prevention strategies are hardly sensible. On the one hand, there is the proliferation of chaos, in the Balkans and elsewhere, requiring action later if not sooner to contain the spillover. On the other hand, more effective military intervention than has taken place to date might be needed. Neither course of action is a bargain. Neither is assured of success. Neither is without moral consequences.

It is long overdue for the global humanitarian community to think of prevention in radical terms. The hundreds of thousands of persons dead and the millions of persons displaced in conflicts are a clear demonstration of the necessity to nip problems in the bud before they blossom into full-fledged violence. Disasters waiting to happen in much of the former Soviet Union and in the Zaires of the Third World should provide an additional stimulus to greater investments in prevention.

### Intervention: Doing It Right

Improvements in the global humanitarian system and greater attention to prevention are indispensable. However, there will continue to be exceptional circumstances in which egregious suffering and human rights abuses require outsiders to interfere, using military force in certain instances. Here, too, though, significant conceptual and operational issues require attention.

First, there is the question of whether to intervene, whether to use force if necessary to create space for humanitarian activities and to protect human rights of civilians. Conventional wisdom, which seeks a quick fix or urges incremental pressure to bring belligerents to their senses, presents too narrow an array of options. Recent experiences—particulaly in Somalia and the former Yugoslavia—suggest the inadequacy of both the quick fix and ad hoc action without a strategic vision. Both approaches oversimplify complex situations and lead to quagmires. Such actions can be counterproductive and lead to a loss of credibility.

The U.S. intervention in Somalia in December 1992 represented the quintessential quick fix, with all the attendant strengths and weaknesses. The United States wanted to get out almost before it got in. In fact, the Bush administration promised that troops would be home before President Clinton's inauguration, less than two months away at the time. The narrowly circumscribed effort that the time frame dictated—excluding disarmament, help in reconstituting civil society, and assistance for reconstruction—could never restore peace or provide the minimal conditions for UNOSOM II to succeed. The subsequent heavy casualties among aid workers and UN soldiers, as well as the return of U.S. Cobra gunships and elite U.S. army commandos to retaliate on Mogadishu, illustrated just how ill conceived and unrealistic the original objectives and timetable were. Subsequent casualties and well-publicized photos of a U.S. soldier's corpse being dragged through the streets led to the Clinton administration's decision to withdraw by the end of March 1994.

A lack of realism also characterized international efforts in Angola and Cambodia. Ambitious by historical standards, these major UN initiatives were originally deployed using best-case scenarios, without contingency plans for the likelihood that things would go wrong. Although the emphasis on national elections in each country was understandable, the franchise addressed only one among many accumulated grievances in countries armed to the teeth after decades of bitter internecine wars.

It should therefore have come as no surprise that anarchy returned to Angola after the elections of December 1992, without effective resistance from the meager contingent of UN peacekeepers. When civil war reignited, claiming an average 1,000 deaths weekly in 1993, UN soldiers abandoned most of their positions altogether. The UN was similarly unprepared when, prior to Cambodian elections in May 1993, the Khmer Rouge attacked civilian populations and peacekeepers with impunity. The UN enabled a battered nation to chart its course through a secret ballot. But the low levels of violence during the elections and afterward depended at least as much upon luck as upon UNTAC. UN peacekeepers left the country soon after the elections. The United Nations also will be powerless to react should civil war return if one of the parties challenges King Norodom Sihanouk's approach to the transition to a new Cambodian government.

The quintessential example of ad hoc behavior was the piecemeal action that came about as a result of European and American dithering about the breakup of the former Yugoslavia. The initial deployment early in 1992 of 14,000 UN troops as a buffer in newly independent Croatia was accompanied by a token presence in nearby Sarajevo. But such symbols had little value in staving off "ethnic cleansing" and other atrocities in Bosnia and Herzegovina. Subsequent temporizing in 1992 and 1993 included posting first 1,500 UN soldiers and then 6,500 NATO forces to the area, creating no-fly zones, undertaking vast humanitarian efforts, passing countless Security Council resolutions, and holding endless negotiating sessions and cease-fires.

Such half-measures paradoxically fostered Serbian war aims. UN soldiers did not deter the Serbs, but they did deter more assertive international intervention because of their vulnerability to reprisals. Moreover, assistance to refugees not only saved lives, it also helped move populations the Serbs wished to disperse. Inadequate military and humanitarian action combined with half-hearted sanctions and a negotiating charade impeded more vigorous diplomatic and military pressure.

UN intervention did not work in Somalia or Bosnia. In UNOSOM II, the UN's association with a "shoot first" policy is implicated in the continued escalation of the violence in mid-1994, which the UN had originally sought to quell. But the world organization had inadequate military means and even less political support from troop contributors to act assertively enough to be successful. In Bosnia, the UN's association with what amounted to a "never shoot" policy emboldened the onslaught against civilians and aid workers. In spite of the authorization to use "all measures necessary," UN troops have not fought a single battle with any of the numerous factions that attack convoys. A carefully framed, widely vetted, and broadly understood "shoot sometimes" policy would have a better chance of success in each theater.

Early post–Cold War initiatives that failed to strike the proper balance between persuasion and coercion suggest a major lesson: The global humanitarian community should intervene effectively or not at all. The powerful urge to do something or, more likely, to be seen doing something should be resisted—unless the measures taken have a reasonable chance of achieving their objectives. This is particularly important at the present international political moment, when governments are overwhelmed by the new world disorder but not yet prepared to cede significant decisionmaking authority to the United Nations. As John Steinbruner has noted, these governments are "particularly prone to crisis induced reactions chosen for their symbolic value and ease of execution rather than their decisive effect."[11]

Hollow gestures, however, can be worse than no action at all. The UN should not allow itself to be abused by governments that wish to appear to be doing something while doing nothing at all. Interventions need to be approached with a longer-term and more comprehensive view of what is required to put war-torn societies back on their feet. Governments need to accept a new level of responsibility for the consequences of actions taken on their behalf. If the requisite support is unlikely to be forthcoming, realistically speaking, intervention in a given instance should be avoided.

Intervening effectively also means addressing the schizophrenia within the UN system. In each of the recent major interventions, the work of the UN's humanitarian organizations has suffered from association with punitive actions taken by the Security Council. UN economic sanctions and military force have created suffering among civilians, which has undermined the work and complicated the task of UN organizations such as UNHCR, UNICEF, and WFP. Efforts by UN aid officials to distinguish themselves as members of the "good UN" from the "bad UN" fail to address the structural issue.

The global humanitarian community is at something of a fork in the road regarding how it will resolve the prevailing schizophrenia. Those who believe that humanitarian action represents an important element in the secretary-general's *Agenda for Peace* recommend that such action be fully integrated into the political and military rubric of the

United Nations. UNICEF, WFP, UNHCR, and their sister organizations would then function within the political context provided by the Security Council, which would continue to specify where, when, and what humanitarian activities are to take place.

Others believe that incorporating humanitarian activities into that ultimately political rubric compromises their integrity irreparably. To prevent the violation of cardinal principles such as independence and nonpartisanship, the UN should not be entrusted with humanitarian activities in complex emergencies in which the Security Council has imposed economic or military measures over the objections of the authorities in charge. Where UN humanitarian activities will lose their impartiality by virtue of partiality shown by the Security Council, the ICRC and NGOs should be the primary actors.

Still others take more of a middle ground. That is, rather than either allowing the UN's behavior to continue at cross-purposes or exorcising its humanitarian stirrings altogether, the UN's schizophrenia should be treated. The dual persona of the United Nations—humanitarian and political—should be acknowledged, but with the former insulated as tightly as possible from the latter.

Thus, the same world organization that legitimized military action against the Iraqi regime and the Bosnian Serbs would carry out relief programs in those theaters, but with its humanitarian activities divorced from its political ones. Or again, the same UN system whose economic sanctions had undone the health systems of Serbia and Montenegro would be expected to provide emergency medical assistance to those most seriously affected by the war.

Procedures would be put into place so that actions with harmful humanitarian consequences taken by the Security Council would require prior consultation with the UN's own humanitarian agencies and would involve a commitment by governments to ease the impact of those actions on civilian populations. Once the Security Council decided upon coercion, it would commit the UN system to respond fully to the coercion's consequences. The unwieldy process of granting humanitarian exemptions by the Sanctions Committee would be streamlined, rather than rethinking the viability of economic sanctions themselves. In short, the organization's self-destructive behavior would be minimized.

At the moment, no consensus has emerged among either diplomats or humanitarians about which fork in the road to take. The issue, however, figures prominently in the global agenda for future humanitarian action. The decision ultimately reached will have major implications for the division of labor among actors and for the quality of humanitarian action well into the next century.[12]

## Triage: The Ultimate Humanitarian Nightmare

The four actions recommended above—reforming humanitarian operations, providing greater accountability, preventing the need for major emergency undertakings, and improving interventions mounted in the exceptional circumstances in which they are required—are all investments in an improved global humanitarian system. However, swift and concerted action on all four fronts still might fail to keep pace with the need for timely, more effective, and comprehensive humanitarian action.

The recent spate of high-visibility humanitarian hyperactivity has led to an uneasy sense of the growing inevitability of triage. The French term refers to "the process of sorting victims, as of a battle or disaster to determine priority."[13] Selecting among those in need of assistance challenges the integrity and applicability of fundamental humanitarian principles. Particularly at risk are the notions of relieving life-threatening suffering and proportionality. Triage represents a direct assault on the conviction that since life is equally precious everywhere on the planet, humanitarian action should correspond to the severity of the suffering involved.

In reality, the world has never treated all life as equal. The earlier discussion of the Cold War confirmed the extent to which ideological considerations had infiltrated the global response to human need. The valuation of human life was a function of the political system of the regime under which a person lived. As for the period predating the Cold War, the sense of global community was even more limited and international response to serious incidence of human need even more fragmentary.

Today, too, the international community selects those crises to which it will respond and calibrates its responses according to many variables, some more appropriate than others. "It is not always clear," pointed out an editorial in an Oxfam-UK publication, how far resource allocations "are purely historical and ad hoc, how much they are driven by donors, and how much they are determined by the political

Kurdish refugee. (ICRC Photo/IRAK 91-7/3/Ph. Dutoit)

views of NGO staff. Why were so many more agencies operating with refugees in Thailand than inside Cambodia? Why were agencies willing to work under the controls imposed by the since-overthrown Ethiopia regime, but not those of a similar regime in Burma?"[14] Other organizations face similar difficulties in identifying criteria for resource allocations and applying them consistently. Moreover, there is no "invisible hand" assuring that the allocations of all humanitarian actors will do justice to the total global need.

As it rethinks its commitments and reevaluates its capacities, the global humanitarian community faces many tough and unavoidable decisions. Is it desirable to channel limited resources to a selected population, or should such resources be distributed with less discrimination among as many suffering souls as possible? Rather than seeking to spare from gunfire those who will remain vulnerable to later shellings, should priority be given to providing succor in settings whose belligerents have already agreed to cease-fires? Should resources lavished on airlifting supplies to civilians trapped in war zones be redirected toward those dying undramatic deaths from preventable malnutrition and disease? Coming to terms with these and other equally troubling dilemmas represents crucial unfinished business for the international community and an unfortunate part of the present policy landscape.

Triage is the skeleton in the humanitarian closet. Rarely discussed by politicians or conceded by practitioners, not simply a cloud on some distant horizon, triage is a reality, the product of the workings of current arrangements. Today's humanitarian system does not apportion resources according to need. Resources can always be found for needs deemed compelling but are rarely provided to populations without patrons or publicity. Current humanitarian action embodies triage by default rather than by design.

Those who justify the need for certain selectivity because of a shortage of global resources overstate the constraint. Resources are not as limited as some suggest. Yet the growing demand for assistance in troubled spots around the world confronts budgetary pressures in many countries that have traditionally supported humanitarian undertakings. "The time has come," UN High Commissioner for Refugees Sadako Ogata has stated, "for a major dialogue on the hard choices that will have to be made in the face of finite humanitarian resources and almost infinite humanitarian demands."[15]

That dialogue and the institutional changes that flow from it constitute the central issue on the future agenda for humanitarian action. For the moment, the critical constraints are a paucity of vision, solidarity, and political will rather than a dearth of available resources in the face of an excess of humanitarian demand. That reality was confirmed by a recent survey of U.S. elite and public opinion. Four years after the official end of the Cold War, Americans were asked to identify the most urgent foreign policy priority. Most named a domestic issue, particularly the need to restart the U.S. economy.[16] Although the proliferation of conflicts large and small promises to heighten the demand for succor over present supply, the underlying questions are likely to remain moral rather than financial. If triage remains a moral failure rather than an economic necessity, the attendant embarrassment will be compounded.

Triage is also a threat to principled humanitarianism because of the cynicism on which it is based and to which it contributes. It undercuts the support on which the humanitarian enterprise depends and strikes at the fundamental optimism animating these efforts. Humanitarianism and hopefulness are cut from the same cloth. Both are affirmations that the most destructive instincts of peoples can be tamed and that the most fundamental needs and rights of humanity can be met and protected. Both humanitarianism and hopefulness seek to marshal the forces of decency, solidarity, and restraint against the onslaught of lawlessness, rapacity, and self-aggrandizement. Both see suffering in war zones as a threat not only to those in pain but also to the wider humanitarian family. Far more than a charitable reflex, humanitarian action becomes an investment in the kind of world that people want for themselves and their children.

Conversely, an ill-fitting and ill-functioning humanitarian system confirms the pessimism of those who find the world too large and the needs of suffering people too great. Disarray in the globe's humanitarian system and a lack of professionalism and accountability among its practitioners appear to make triage the only reasonable solution.

In the final analysis, triage represents a counsel of despair. It is the easy way out before all other exits have been tried. It is like the swimmer who gives up because the water appears suddenly too choppy and the shore too distant. The global humanitarian community has the ingenuity and the means, the experience and the persistence, to create a more effective and comprehensive humanitarian system.

## Intervention: More Wrongs Do Not Make It Right

Since work was concluded on this book, new and continuing humanitarian challenges have thrust themselves onto the agenda—and the threat of such crises is sure to persist. For example, in June 1994, the United States pulled its remaining troops out of Somalia, and a number of other contributors to UNOSOM II eventually followed suit. Responding to the further deterioration of the security situation, the United States withdrew diplomatic personnel in September. In a replay of the situation in 1991–1992, before the advent of large numbers of international aid and military personnel, UN troops, property, and operations have been increasingly targeted for violence. Non-UN aid personnel have also been harassed. As a result, the debate about the appropriateness and utility of the massive if belated international response to the crisis in Somalia has intensified.

In the former Yugoslavia, the international strategy of economic and occasional military pressure described earlier in the book has brought about some changes. In an effort to ease the pressure of international sanctions that had disrupted the economy and brought widespread suffering to the civilian population, the Serbian government of Slobodan Milosevic has distanced itself somewhat from the Bosnian Serbs, whose policies it had earlier supported unequivocally. For closing its border to Bosnia-bound commerce (except for humanitarian items) and for helping to isolate the regime of Radovan Karadzic, the Milosevic government won for itself a partial but controversial easing of sanctions in September. Meanwhile, the international arms embargo against the Bosnian government remains in place.

A political settlement among the warring parties in Bosnia-Herzegovina remains elusive, with the Bosnian Serbs continuing to obstruct aid efforts and to defy the weapons exclusion zone. In recent months, the UN has shown willingness to call in NATO airstrikes—"pinpricks," in the view of military analysts—to challenge actions by the Bosnian Serbs. However, differences in viewpoint persist between the UN and NATO, and also among the permanent members of the Security Council, who have differing degrees of exposure on the ground and different relationships with the warring parties. The suffering and displacement of people throughout the region continues, with the summer months even witnessing a fresh upsurge in "ethnic cleansing" by the Bosnian Serbs. Thus, while the world stays the course in the former Yugoslavia, a political settlement and an effective humanitarian strategy are lacking.

Events in Somalia and the former Yugoslavia were upstaged in April with the eruption of a bloodbath in Rwanda. The shooting down of a plane with the presidents of Rwanda and Burundi aboard was the occasion for the rekindling of civil war, which had raged from October 1990 to August 1993. The interethnic violence began in Kigali and spread quickly throughout the country, leading to what was described as "the largest and swiftest mass exodus of people" ever witnessed by UN agencies.

Within two days at the end of April, an estimated 400,000 Rwandans, mostly Tutsis, had fled into Tanzania. Soon an even larger number of Hutus—probably a million—had fled into Zaire to escape the victorious approaching army of the Rwandan Patriotic Front. Estimates of fatalities on both sides range from half a million to a million, although a precise figure may never be known. Of a prestrife population of some 8 million persons, some 2 million were refugees and a larger number were displaced within Rwanda. The specific targeting of Tutsis is widely viewed as genocide.

The global humanitarian community was overwhelmed by the scale and apparent suddenness of the crisis. The violence initially forced most aid agencies—and even the small UN peacekeeping contingent—to evacuate their personnel. A contingent of French troops was dispatched in June to enforce a "safe zone" in southern Rwanda in what was called Opération Turquoise. As the situation worsened and international pressure built, U.S. troops were sent in July to assist with humanitarian activities in Zaire. Aid agencies themselves eventually regrouped as the security situation became more stable. Struggling to respond, they transferred aid workers from Somalia, the former Yugoslavia, and elsewhere to Rwanda, Zaire, and Tanzania to meet the onslaught.

The wholesale displacement and staggering loss of life confirmed the world's fundamental lack of preparedness to deal with major emergencies, either to interpret the early warning signs and to preempt crises or to respond quickly and effectively once disaster has struck. As time has passed since the spring, the premeditated and political nature of the violence has become better understood, as have its roots in colonial policies, ethnic tensions, and the maldistribution of resources and power. At this writing, only limited resettlement has taken place. Those who might return to their homeland from camps in Zaire are discouraged by Hutu forces there and by violence encountered by some who have made the journey home.

Developments in Somalia, the former Yugoslavia, and Rwanda were in turn upstaged recently by events in Haiti, where a combination of economic and military pressure by the United States and the United Nations on the military regime of General Raoul Cédras had wide-ranging effects. An economic embargo, which caused widespread civilian suffering and thousands of departures from the island by people on flimsy crafts seeking asylum in the United States, increased pressure on the regime during the summer. However, it was the threat of U.S.-led military action that finally wrested concessions regarding the reinstatement of elected President Jean-Bertrand Aristide. A last-minute deal was struck with the military by a delegation dispatched by President Clinton, consisting of former President Jimmy Carter, Colin

Powell, former chairman of the Joint Chiefs of Staff, and Senator Sam Nunn. This avoided forced entry by U.S. troops into Haiti.

At this writing, 20,000 U.S. and other troops have helped to restore the elected president, and the UN Observer Mission in Haiti is about to begin consolidating a tenuous peace. A number of the problems noted earlier in this volume have been illuminated, including the interconnections between "loud" emergencies and underlying problems of impoverishment, disenfranchisement, and human rights abuses.

Reactions to the deployment of U.S. troops have also highlighted current difficulties in achieving consensus regarding U.S. interests in becoming involved, the appropriate roles of the United Nations and the United States, and the proper balance of coercion and consent. Although many welcomed the last-minute consent by the Haitian authorities to the arrival of troops, some held that President Clinton's application of force, avoided in other theaters, would have been useful if applied in Haiti to send a louder message beyond.

Recent events have also included developments on the policy side. In May 1994, President Clinton approved in Presidential Decision Directive 25 a new set of ground rules for U.S. involvement in international interventions. It included an elaborate list of conditions that would have to be met before the United States would invest personnel or resources in future crises. Representing a retrenchment from the "aggressive multilateralism" promoted by candidate Clinton in the 1992 presidential campaign, the new ground rules reflected the view that U.S. involvement should be far more circumscribed. Having approved the new ground rules, the administration soon found itself fending off efforts by members of Congress to delimit the scope and duration of U.S. activities in Haiti, as specified by its own new policy.

Recent developments have not been uniformly negative. Promising strides to turn the corner on long animosities have been made in such places as the Occupied Territories, South Africa, and northern Ireland. "A peace deal today really is a bargain," observed Thomas J. Friedman in the *New York Times*, who was struck by the resulting shift in attention in such places from waging war to long-deferred economic and social reconstruction. Meanwhile, in Sri Lanka, an election in August brought to power a government that moved quickly to begin serious discussions with the armed opposition to end a long civil war. In September the military government of Myanmar met with Nobel Prize–

winning opposition leader Daw Aung San Suu Kyi for the first time in five years.

Discussions are also proceeding among departments of the UN Secretariat that could result in greater respect for humanitarian imperatives on the part of the political and military sides of the UN. Heads of operational UN organizations are grappling with the issues framed in this book. NGOs are carrying out reviews of policy and programs that examine such critical linkages as those between humanitarian action on the one hand and conflict prevention and conflict resolution on the other. Major evaluations of agency performance in places such as Somalia and elsewhere have shed new light on the underlying problems and the effectiveness of the strategies adopted.

There will, of course, be still further developments, negative and positive alike, by the time of the book's publication in the spring of 1995. Our ongoing Humanitarianism and War study will continue to monitor and analyze them in detail. We do not regard the central propositions of *Mercy Under Fire* as having been overtaken by events. Rather, we see the humanitarian challenges of wars and conflicts framed in this volume confirmed by events.

Our observation in the body of this volume that the current system is overextended and our call for new and more effective approaches are indeed borne out by these late-breaking events. We thus offer our analysis and our observations as a contribution to the evolution of a more effective global humanitarian community, the need for which grows more urgent with each passing month and year.

# Notes

## Introduction

1. See Anthony Lake, ed., *After the Wars* (Washington, D.C.: Overseas Development Council, 1990).

2. For a discussion of these challenges, see James Rosenau, *Turbulence in World Politics: A Theory of Change and Continuity* (Princeton: Princeton University Press, 1990); August Richard Norton, "The Security Legacy of the 1980s in the Third World," in Thomas G. Weiss and Meryl A. Kessler, eds., *Third World Security in the Post–Cold War Era* (Boulder: Lynne Rienner, 1991), pp. 19–34; Lawrence Freedman, "Order and Disorder in the New World," *Foreign Affairs,* Vol. 71, No. 1, 1991–1992, pp. 20–37; James N. Rosenau, "Normative Challenges in a Turbulent World," and Charles W. Kegley, Jr., "The New Global Order: The Power Principle in a Pluralistic World," *Ethics and International Affairs,* Vol. 6, 1992, pp. 1–40; Daniel Patrick Moynihan, *Pandaemonium: Ethnicity in International Politics* (New York: Oxford University Press, 1993); Joel Kotkin, *Tribes: How Race, Religion, and Identity Determine Success in the New Global Economy* (New York: Random House, 1993); Ted Robert Gurr, *Minorities at Risk: A Global View of Ethnopolitical Conflicts* (Washington, D.C.: United States Institute of Peace Press, 1993); Morton H. Halperin and David J. Scheffer, *Self-Determination in the New World Order* (Washington, D.C.: Carnegie Endowment for International Peace, 1992); "Ethnic Conflict and International Security," special issue of *Survival,* Vol. 35, No. 1, Spring 1993; and "Reconstructing Nations and States," special issue of *Daedalus,* Vol. 122, No. 3, Summer 1993.

3. Gerald B. Helman and Steven R. Ratner, "Saving Failed States," *Foreign Policy,* No. 89, Winter 1992–1993, pp. 3–20.

4. See Thomas G. Weiss, David P. Forsythe, and Roger A. Coate, *The United Nations and Changing World Politics* (Boulder: Westview, 1994).

5. See Robert W. Gregg, *About Face? The United States and the United Nations* (Boulder: Lynne Rienner, 1993).

6. For elaboration of the point, see Larry Minear, "The Forgotten Human Agenda," *Foreign Policy,* No. 73, Winter 1988–1989, pp. 76–93.

## Chapter 1

1. For a further discussion, see the essays in Thomas G. Weiss, ed., *Collective Security in a Changing World* (Boulder: Lynne Rienner, 1993); and John M. Lee,

Robert von Pagnhardt, and Timothy W. Stanley, *To Unite Our Strength: Enhancing the United Nations Peace and Security System* (Lanham, Md.: University Press of America, 1992).

2. Brian Urquhart, "Who Can Police the World?" *New York Review of Books*, Vol. 41, No. 9, May 12, 1994, p. 29.

3. Throughout the text, frequent reference is made to the peacekeeping and other military activities of the United Nations. For the history of peacekeeping, see Alan James, *Peacekeeping in International Politics* (New York: St. Martin's Press, 1990); and *The Blue Helmets* (New York: United Nations, 1990). For more analytical treatments, see Thomas G. Weiss and Jarat Chopra, *UN Peacekeeping: An ACUNs Teaching Text* (Hanover, N.H.: Academic Council on the United Nations System, 1992); William J. Durch, ed., *The Evolution of UN Peacekeeping: Case Studies and Comparative Analysis* (New York: St. Martin's Press, 1993); Adam Roberts, "The United Nations and International Security," *Survival*, Vol. 35, No. 2, Summer 1993, pp. 3–30; Paul Diehl, *International Peacekeeping* (Baltimore: Johns Hopkins University Press, 1993); Marrack Goulding, "The Evolution of United Nations Peacekeeping," *International Affairs*, Vol. 69, No. 3, 1993, pp. 451–464; and Mats R. Berdal, *Whither UN Peacekeeping?* Adelphi Paper 281 (London: International Institute for Strategic Studies, 1993). For a focus on the military, see John Mackinlay and Jarat Chopra, "Second Generation Multinational Operations," *The Washington Quarterly*, Vol. 15, No. 2, Spring 1992, pp. 113–131, and *A Draft Concept of Second Generation Multinational Operations 1993* (Providence: Watson Institute, 1993); William J. Durch, *The United Nations and Collective Security in the 21st Century* (Carlisle, Penn.: U.S. Army War College, 1993); and *The Professionalization of Peacekeeping: A Study Group Report* (Washington, D.C.: U.S. Institute of Peace, 1993); and Dennis J. Quinn, ed., *Peace Support Operations and the U.S. Military* (Washington, D.C.: National Defense University Press, 1994).

4. See Michael Edwards and David Hulme, eds., *Making a Difference: NGOs and Development in a Changing World* (London: Earthscan, 1992); and *The UN System and NGOs: New Relationships for a New Era?* Report of a Stanley Foundation Conference, February 18–20, 1994 (Muscatine, Ia.: Stanley Foundation, 1994).

5. Ruth Sivard, *World Military and Social Expenditures 1993*, 15th ed. (Washington, D.C.: World Priorities, 1993), p. 20.

6. These documents are found in *The Geneva Conventions of August 12, 1949*, and *Protocols Additional to the Geneva Conventions of August 12, 1949* (Geneva: International Committee of the Red Cross, 1989).

7. Conference on Conflict and Humanitarian Action, Princeton, October 22–23, 1993.

8. See Ephraim Isaac, "Humanitarian Action Across Religions and Cultures," in Thomas G. Weiss and Larry Minear, eds., *Humanitarianism Across Borders: Sustaining Civilians in Times of War* (Boulder: Lynne Rienner, 1993), pp. 13–22. For other discussions, see *International Dimensions of Humanitarian Law*

(Dordecht: Nijhoff, 1988); Marcel A. Boisard, *L'Humanisme de l'Islam* (Paris: Albin Michel, 1979); Jack Donnelly, *Universal Human Rights in Theory and Practice* (Ithaca: Cornell University Press, 1989); David P. Forsythe, *The Internationalization of Human Rights* (Lexington, Mass.: Lexington Books, 1991); Emmanuel Bello, *African Customary Humanitarian Law* (Geneva: ICRC, 1980); and T. O. Elias, *New Horizons in International Humanitarian Law* (Dobbs Ferry, N.Y.: Alphen aan den Rijn, 1979).

9. For a discussion of these developments, see Weiss and Kessler, eds., *Third World Security;* Thomas G. Weiss and James G. Blight, eds., *The Suffering Grass: Superpowers and Regional Conflict in Southern Africa and the Caribbean* (Boulder: Lynne Rienner, 1992); and Brian Job, ed., *The Insecurity Dilemma: National Security of Third World States* (Boulder: Lynne Rienner, 1992).

10. For a discussion of the magnitude of suffering in this region and elsewhere, see Sadako Ogata, *The State of the World's Refugees 1993: The Challenge of Protection* (New York: Oxford University Press, 1993).

11. See Larry Minear et al., *Humanitarianism Under Siege* (Trenton, N.J.: Red Sea Press, 1991); and Francis P. Deng and Larry Minear, *The Challenges of Famine Relief: Emergency Operations in the Sudan* (Washington, D.C.: Brookings Institution, 1992).

12. Mary B. Anderson, *Rising from the Ashes: Development Strategies at Times of Disaster* (Boulder: Westview, 1989). See also Mary Anderson, "Development and the Prevention of Humanitarian Emergencies," in Weiss and Minear, eds., *Humanitarianism Across Borders*, pp. 23–38.

13. See Larry Minear and Thomas G. Weiss, "Groping and Coping in the Gulf Crisis," *World Policy Journal*, Vol. 9, No. 4, Winter 1992, pp. 755–778; and Larry Minear, U.B.P. Chelliah, Jeff Crisp, John Mackinlay, and Thomas G. Weiss, *United Nations Coordination of the International Humanitarian Response to the Gulf Crisis 1990–1992*, Occasional Paper 13 (Providence: Watson Institute, 1992).

14. James P. Grant, *State of the World's Children 1992* (London: Oxford University Press, 1992).

15. For a recent discussion of these issues, see Hilaire McCoubrey and Nigel D. White, *International Law and Armed Conflict* (Aldershot, Hantz, England: Dartmouth Publishing Co., 1992).

16. Independent Commission on International Humanitarian Issues, *Winning the Human Race?* (London: Zed Books, 1988), pp. 71–72.

17. See David P. Forsythe, *The Internationalization of Human Rights* (Lexington, Mass.: Lexington Books for the Free Press, 1991); Jack Donnelly, *Universal Human Rights in Theory and Practice* (Ithaca: Cornell University Press, 1989); and Gil Loescher, *Beyond Charity* (New York: Oxford University Press, 1994).

18. See Francis P. Deng, *Protecting the Dispossessed: A Challenge for the International Community* (Washington, D.C.: Brookings Institution, 1993).

19. See Thomas G. Weiss and Kurt M. Campbell, "Military Humanitarianism," *Survival*, Vol. 33, No. 5, September–October, 1991, pp. 451–465; Thomas

G. Weiss, "Intervention: Whither the United Nations?" *Washington Quarterly,* Vol. 17, No. 1, Winter 1994, pp. 109–128; and Adam Roberts, "Humanitarian War: Military Intervention and Human Rights," *International Affairs,* Vol. 69, No. 3, 1993, pp. 429–449.

20. Boutros Boutros-Ghali, "Empowering the United Nations," *Foreign Affairs,* Vol. 71, No. 5, 1992–1993, pp. 98–99.

21. See Jarat Chopra and Thomas G. Weiss, "Sovereignty Is Not Sacrosanct: Codifying Humanitarian Intervention," *Ethics and International Affairs,* Vol. 6, 1992, pp. 95–117.

22. See Bernard Kouchner and Mario Bettati, *Le Devoir d'ingérence* (Paris: Denoël, 1987); and Bernard Kouchner, *Le Malheur des autres* (Paris: Odile Jacob, 1991).

23. See Barbara Hendrie, "Cross-Border Relief Operations in Eritrea and Tigray," *Disasters,* Vol. 13, No. 4, 1989, pp. 351–360.

24. Humanitarian intervention has become the subject of numerous symposia. See, for example, "Humanitarian Intervention," *Harvard International Review,* Vol. 16, No. 1, Fall 1993, pp. 8–32; Elizabeth G. Ferris, ed., *The Challenge to Intervene: A New Role for the United Nations?* (Uppsala: Life and Peace Institute, 1992); Laura W. Reed and Carl Kaysen, eds., *Emerging Norms of Justified Intervention* (Cambridge, Mass.: American Academy of Arts and Sciences, 1993); "On Intervention," *Boston Review,* Vol. 18, No. 6, December–January 1993–94; and David J. Scheffer, Richard N. Gardner, and Gerald B. Helman, *Three Views on the Issue of Humanitarian Intervention* (Washington, D.C.: U.S. Institute of Peace, 1992). The classic academic treatments of this issue are R. J. Vincent, *Non-intervention and International Order* (Princeton: Princeton University Press, 1974), and Richard B. Lillich, ed., *Humanitarian Intervention and the United Nations* (Charlottesville: University Press of Virginia, 1973). The first intervention in northern Iraq triggered an in-depth look at the subject of intervention in general, for example, Gene M. Lyons and Michael Mastanduno, eds., *Beyond Westphalia? State Sovereignty and International Intervention* (Baltimore: Johns Hopkins University Press, forthcoming).

25. See Thomas G. Weiss, "On the Brink of a New Era? Humanitarian Intervention, 1991–1994," in Don Daniel, ed., *Beyond Traditional Peacekeeping* (London: Macmillan, forthcoming).

26. The discussion here and later is based on work by the Humanitarianism and War Project in Central America that appears in Cristina Eguizábal, David Lewis, Larry Minear, Peter Sollis, and Thomas G. Weiss, *Humanitarian Challenges in Central America: Learning the Lessons of Recent Armed Conflicts,* Occasional Paper 14 (Providence: Watson Institute, 1993).

27. See Werner J. Feld and Robert S. Jordan, *International Organization: A Comparative Approach* (Westport, Conn.: Praeger, 1994), pp. 9–38, 217–250.

28. For a discussion of these issues, see Neil S. MacFarlane and Thomas G. Weiss, "Regional Organizations and Regional Security," *Security Studies,* Vol. 2, No. 3, Fall–Winter 1992–1993, pp. 6–37; and Neil S. MacFarlane and Thomas G. Weiss, "The United Nations, Regional Organizations and Human Security:

Building Theory in Central America," *Third World Quarterly,* Vol. 15, No. 2, April 1994, pp. 277–295.

## Chapter 2

1. The principles form the structure for chapter 1 in Larry Minear and Thomas G. Weiss, *Humanitarian Action in Times of War: A Handbook for Practitioners* (Boulder: Lynne Rienner, 1993), pp. 7–41. They also provide the structure for a training manual developed for the UNDP and DHA, Larry Minear and Thomas G. Weiss, *Humanitarian Principles and Operational Dilemmas in War Zones* (Madison, Wisc.: Disaster Management Training Programme, 1993).

2. Ruth L. Sivard, *World Military and Social Expenditures 1993* (Washington, D.C.: World Priorities, 1993).

3. For a discussion, see Francis P. Deng, *Protecting the Dispossessed* (Washington, D.C.: Brookings Institution, 1993), and Gil Loescher, *Beyond Charity* (New York: Oxford University Press, 1994).

4. Sadako Ogata, *The State of the World's Refugees: The Challenge of Protection* (New York: Oxford University Press, 1993).

5. United Nations Fund for Population Activities, *The State of World Population 1993* (New York: UNFPA, 1993), pp. 7, 15.

6. For a discussion of these numbers, see World Bank, *World Development Report 1993* (New York: Oxford University Press, 1993); for a calculation of their human consequences, see United Nations Development Programme, *Human Development Report 1993* (New York: Oxford University Press, 1993).

7. Quoted in Larry Minear, Jeffrey Clark, Roberta Cohen, Dennis Gallagher, Iain Guest, and Thomas G. Weiss, *Humanitarian Action in the Former Yugoslavia: The UN's Role 1991–1993,* Occasional Paper 18 (Providence: Watson Institute, 1994), p. 120.

8. For a discussion, see Paul Kennedy, *Preparing for the Twenty-first Century* (New York: Random House, 1993).

9. Anthony Lake, ed., "Overview," in *After the Wars: Reconstruction in Afghanistan, Indochina, Central America, Southern Africa, and the Horn of Africa* (Washington, D.C.: Overseas Development Council, 1990), pp. 4, 5.

10. Quoted in *Humanitarian Monitor,* No. 1, June 1993, p. 28.

11. See Andrew S. Natsios, "Food Through Force: Humanitarian Intervention and U.S. Policy," *Washington Quarterly,* Vol. 17, No. 1, Winter 1994, p. 129.

12. "Strengthening the Coordination of Humanitarian Emergency Assistance of the United Nations," Unpublished remarks to the General Assembly, November 4, 1991, p. 3.

13. For a discussion of these issues with particular reference to the military, see Gayle E. Smith, "Relief Operations and Military Strategy," in Thomas G. Weiss and Larry Minear, eds., *Humanitarianism Across Borders: Sustaining Civilians in Times of War* (Boulder: Lynne Rienner, 1993), pp. 97–116.

14. Catholic Relief Services, Statement of Policy, 1993.

15. For a detailed review of the issues and dynamics, see Mark Duffield and John Prendergast, *Without Troops and Tanks: Humanitarian Intervention in Ethiopia and Eritrea* (Trenton, N.J.: Red Sea Press, 1994).

16. Office of the United Nations Disaster Relief Coordinator, "Shelter after Disaster: Guidelines for Assistance," Geneva, 1982, p. 60.

17. U.S. Agency for International Development, *Displaced Persons in El Salvador: An Assessment* (Washington, D.C.: USAID, 1984), p. 16.

18. Kofi N. Awanoor, "The Concerns of Recipient Nations," in Kevin M. Cahill, ed., *A Framework for Survival: Health, Human Rights and Humanitarian Assistance in Conflicts and Disasters* (New York: Basic Books, 1993), pp. 71, 78, 79.

19. For further discussion, see Jeff Clark, "Debacle in Somalia," *Foreign Affairs*, Vol. 72, No. 1, 1992–1993, pp. 109–123; and Samuel Makinda, *Seeking Peace from Chaos: Humanitarian Intervention in Somalia* (Boulder: Lynne Rienner, 1993). See also Refugee Policy Group, *Humanitarian Aid in Somalia 1990–1994* (Washington, D.C.: Refugee Policy Group, 1994); and John Prendergast, *The Bones of Our Children Are Not Yet Buried: The Looming Spectre of Famine and Massive Human Rights Abuse in Somalia* (Washington, D.C.: Center of Concern, 1994).

20. For a more extended discussion, see Larry Minear, U.B.P. Chelliah, Jeff Crisp, John Mackinlay, and Thomas G. Weiss, *United Nations Coordination of the International Humanitarian Response to the Gulf Crisis 1990–92*, Occasional Paper 13 (Providence: Watson Institute, 1992).

21. The more extended discussion here and elsewhere about the former Yugoslavia draws upon Larry Minear, Jeffrey Clark, Roberta Cohen, Dennis Gallagher, Iain Guest, and Thomas G. Weiss, *Humanitarian Action in the Former Yugoslavia: The UN's Role 1991–1993*, Occasional Paper 18 (Providence: Watson Institute, 1994).

22. Office of the United Nations Disaster Relief Coordinator (UNDRO), "The Iraq/Kuwait Crisis: International Assistance to Displaced People Through Jordan, August–November 1990" (Geneva: United Nations, undated), pp. 6, 17.

23. *Human Rights Watch World Report 1994* (New York: Human Rights Watch, 1993), p. 378.

24. As quoted in Larry Minear, et al., *Humanitarianism Under Siege: A Critical Review of Operation Lifeline Sudan* (Trenton, N.J.: Red Sea Press, 1991), p. 125.

25. Ibid., p. 131.

26. For a discussion of these issues, see William Maley and Fazel Haq Saikal, *Political Order in Post-Communist Afghanistan* (Boulder: Lynne Rienner, 1992).

27. For an extended discussion, see Thomas G. Weiss, "UN Responses in the Former Yugoslavia: Moral and Operational Choices," *Ethics and International Affairs*, Vol. 8, 1994, pp. 1–22.

28. Quoted in Minear et al., *Humanitarian Action in the Former Yugoslavia*, p. 64.

29. Ibid., p. 67.

30. Ibid., pp. 66–67.

31. Ibid., p. 66.

32. For a discussion, see *The Lost Agenda: Human Rights and U.N. Field Operations* (New York: Human Rights Watch, 1993).

33. Minear and Weiss, *Humanitarian Action in Times of War*, p. 37.

34. Awanoor, "The Concerns of Recipient Nations," pp. 67, 69.

35. Independent Commission on International Humanitarian Issues, *Winning the Human Race?* (London: Zed Books, 1988), p. 9.

36. For an extended discussion, see Jarat Chopra and Thomas G. Weiss, "Sovereignty Is No Longer Sacrosanct: Codifying Humanitarian Intervention," *Ethics and International Affairs*, Vol. 6, 1992, pp. 95–118. See also Adam Roberts, "Humanitarian War: Military Intervention and Human Rights," *International Affairs*, Vol. 69, No. 3, 1993, p. 429.

37. See Bernard Kouchner and Mario Bettati, *Le Devoir d'ingérence* (Paris: Denoël, 1987).

38. See Aengus Finucane, "The Changing Roles of Voluntary Organizations," in Cahill, *A Framework for Survival*, p. 180.

39. For a discussion of the pluses and minuses, see Thomas G. Weiss "Humanitarian Intervention, 1991–1994: On the Brink of a New Era?" in Don Daniel, ed., *Beyond Traditional Peacekeeping* (London: Macmillan, forthcoming).

40. As quoted in Minear et al., *Humanitarianism Under Siege*, p. 99.

41. Ibid., p. 101.

42. Quoted in Minear et al., *Humanitarianism Under Siege*, pp. 103–104.

43. *ACUNS Informational Memorandum*, No. 19, October 1993, p. 4.

### Chapter 3

1. See Fazle H. Abed, "Coping with Disasters: From Diarrhea to Cyclones," in Kevin M. Cahill, ed., *A Framework for Survival: Health, Human Rights, and Humanitarian Assistance in Conflicts and Disasters* (New York: Basic Books, 1993), pp. 221–233.

2. Larry Minear et al., *Humanitarianism Under Siege: A Critical Review of Operation Lifeline Sudan* (Trenton, N.J.: Red Sea Press, 1991), p. 39.

3. Ibid., p. 48.

4. James Ingram, "The Future Architecture for International Humanitarian Assistance," in Thomas G. Weiss and Larry Minear, eds., *Humanitarianism Across Borders: Sustaining Civilians in Times of War* (Boulder: Lynne Rienner, 1993), p. 187.

5. Refugee Policy Group, *Humanitarian Aid in Somalia 1990–1994* (Washington, D.C.: Refugee Policy Group, 1994).

6. UN Department of Humanitarian Affairs, "Consolidated Inter-Agency Humanitarian Assistance Appeals: Summary of Requirements and Contributions," DHA Summary 4, Geneva, April 20, 1994.

7. InterAction, "Letter to General Brent Scowcroft," November 19, 1982, Washington, D.C., p. 1.

8. See Thomas G. Weiss, "Intervention: Whither the United Nations?" *Washington Quarterly,* Vol. 17, No. 1, Winter 1994, pp. 109–128.

9. See *America: Learning the Lessons of Recent Armed Conflicts* (Providence: Watson Institute, 1993). See also Mary Ann Larkin, Frederick C. Cuny, and Barry N. Stein, *Repatriation Under Conflict in Central America* (Dallas: INTERTECT, 1991). For a historical overview of the region, see James Dunkerly, *Power in the Isthmus: A Political History of Modern Central America* (London: Verso, 1988). For the region's initial efforts to shape its own destiny, see Bruce Bagley, *The Contadora Process* (Boulder: Westview, 1987); and Jack Child, ed., *Conflict in Central America* (London: Hurst, 1986). For treatments of the entire process, including recent UN efforts, see Jack Child, *The Central American Peace Process, 1983–1991* (Boulder: Lynne Rienner, 1992); Stephen Barranyi and Lisa North, *Stretching the Limits of the Possible: United Nations Peacekeeping in Central America,* Aurora Papers 15 (Ontario: Canadian Centre for Global Security, 1992); David Holiday and William Stanley, "Building the Peace: Preliminary Lessons from El Salvador, *Journal of International Affairs,* Vol. 46, No. 2, Winter 1993), pp. 415–438; and Human Rights Watch, "El Salvador," in *The Lost Agenda: Human Rights and U.N. Field Operations* (New York: Human Rights Watch, 1993), pp. 13–35.

10. See Adolpho Aguilar Zinzer, *CIREFCA: The Promises and Reality of the International Conference on Central American Refugees* (Washington, D.C.: CIPRA, 1991).

11. Unitarian Universalist Service Committee, "President Bush Urged to Condemn Harassment of Humanitarian Relief Work in El Salvador," Press release, December 6, 1989, p. 1.

12. InterAction, "International Humanitarian Agency Delegation Returns from El Salvador with Warnings," Press release, January 11, 1990, p. 1.

13. See Boutros Boutros-Ghali, *An Agenda for Peace: Preventive Deployment, Peacemaking, and Peace-keeping* (New York: United Nations, 1992). For further discussions by the secretary-general, see Boutros Boutros-Ghali, "Empowering the United Nations," *Foreign Affairs,* Vol. 71, No. 5, Winter 1992–1993, pp. 89–102; and "An Agenda for Peace: One Year Later," *Orbis,* Vol. 37, Summer 1993, p. 332. For a critical review, see Thomas G. Weiss, "New Challenges for UN Military Operations: Implementing an Agenda for Peace," *Washington Quarterly* 16, No. 1, 1993, pp. 51–66.

14. Alvaro de Soto and Graciana del Castillo, "Obstacles to Peacebuilding," *Foreign Policy,* No. 94, Spring 1994, p. 70.

15. Boutros-Ghali, *Agenda,* para. 16.

16. UN Development Programme, *Human Development Report 1991* (New York: UNDP, 1991), p. 71.

17. UNDP, *Launching New Protagonists in Salvadoran Agriculture: The Agricultural Training Programme for Ex-Combatants of the FMLN* (San Salvador: UNDP, 1993), p. 78.

## Chapter 4

1. For a discussion of the organizational complexity of the system in dealing with security, human rights, and sustainable development, see Thomas G. Weiss, David P. Forsythe, and Roger A. Coate, *The United Nations and Changing World Politics* (Boulder: Westview, 1994).

2. For further views from two long-time practitioners on this subject, see Frederick C. Cuny, "Humanitarian Assistance in the Post Cold War Era," and James Ingram, "The Future Architecture for International Humanitarian Assistance," in Thomas G. Weiss and Larry Minear, eds., *Humanitarianism Across Borders: Sustaining Civilians in Times of War* (Boulder: Lynne Rienner, 1993), pp. 151–193.

3. For recent comprehensive treatments of this issue, see Francis P. Deng, *Protecting the Dispossessed: A Challenge for the International Community* (Washington, D.C.: Brookings Institution, 1993); and Gil Loescher, *Beyond Charity* (New York: Oxford University Press, 1994). See also Roberta Cohen for insights on this issue in "Strengthening International Protection for Internally Displaced Persons," in Louis Henkin and John Lawrence Hargrove, eds., *Human Rights: An Agenda for the Next Century* (Washington, D.C.: The American Society of International Law, forthcoming). See also Charles H. Norchi, "Human Rights and Social Issues," and José E. Alvarez, "Legal Issues," in *A Global Agenda: Issues Before the 48th General Assembly* (Lanham, Md.: University Press of America, 1993), pp. 213–311.

4. For an extended discussion, see Thomas G. Weiss, "UN Responses in the Former Yugoslavia: Moral and Operational Choices," *Ethics and International Affairs*, Vol. 8, 1994, pp. 1–22.

5. Larry Minear, Jeffrey Clark, Roberta Cohen, Dennis Gallagher, Iain Guest, and Thomas G. Weiss, *Humanitarian Action in the Former Yugoslavia, The U.N.'s Role 1991–1993*, Occasional Paper 18 (Providence: Watson Institute, 1994), pp. 31–32.

6. Quoted in Larry Minear, U.B.P. Chelliah, Jeff Crisp, John Mackinlay, and Thomas G. Weiss, *United Nations Coordination of the International Humanitarian Response to the Gulf Crisis 1990–1992*, Occasional Paper 13 (Providence: Watson Institute, 1992), p. 22.

7. See Harvard Center for Population and Development Studies, *Sanctions in Haiti: Crisis in Humanitarian Action*, Program on Human Society Working Papers Series (Cambridge, Mass.: Harvard University, November 1993). For more general treatments of the issue, see Lori Fisler Damrosch, "The Civilian Impact of Economic Sanctions," in Fisler, ed., *Enforcing Restraint: Collective Intervention in Internal Conflicts* (New York: Council on Foreign Relations, 1993), pp. 274–315; and Patrick Clawson, "Sanctions as Punishment, Enforcement, and Prelude to Further Action," *Ethics and International Affairs*, No. 7, 1993, pp. 17–38.

8. See Larry Minear, Jeffrey Clark, Roberta Cohen, Dennis Gallagher, Iain Guest, and Thomas G. Weiss, *Humanitarian Action in the Former Yugoslavia*, Occasional Paper 18 (Providence: Watson Institute, 1994), passim.

9. See Neil S. MacFarlane and Thomas G. Weiss, "Regional Organizations and Regional Security," *Security Studies*, Vol. 2, No. 3, 1992–1993, pp. 6–37.

10. For a discussion of the universe of outside donors for development, see Stephen Browne, *Foreign Aid in Practice* (New York: New York University Press, 1990).

11. For discussions, see Anne Gordon Drabek, ed., *Development Alternatives: The Challenge for NGOs*, special issue of *World Development*, Vol. 15, August 1987; Michael Edwards and David Hulme, eds., *Making a Difference: NGOs and Development in a Changing World* (London: Earthscan, 1992); and *The UN System and NGOs: New Relationships for a New Era?* Report of a Stanley Foundation Conference, February 18–20, 1994 (Muscatine, Ia.: Stanley Foundation, 1994).

12. Larry Minear, et al., *Humanitarianism Under Siege: A Critical Review of Operation Lifeline Sudan* (Trenton, N.J.: Red Sea Press, 1991), pp. 111–112.

13. For a discussion, see Michel Veuthey, "Assessing Humanitarian Law," in Weiss and Minear, eds., *Humanitarianism Across Borders*, pp. 125–150.

14. David P. Forsythe, "Choices More Ethical Than Legal: The International Committee of the Red Cross and Human Rights," *Ethics and International Affairs*, Vol. 7, 1993, pp. 131–169.

15. See Thomas G. Weiss and Kurt M. Campbell, "Military Humanitarianism," *Survival*, Vol. 33, No. 5, September–October 1991, pp. 451–465; and Adam Roberts, "Humanitarian War: Military Intervention and Human Rights," *International Affairs*, Vol. 69, No. 3, 1993, pp. 429–449.

16. See, for example, Thomas G. Weiss, "Triage: Humanitarian Intervention in a New Era," *World Policy Journal*, Vol. 11, No. 1, Spring 1994, pp. 59–68. For a more military analysis, see John Mackinlay, "The Significance of Effectively Conducted UN Military Operations," in Thomas G. Weiss, ed., *The United Nations and Civil Wars* (Boulder: Lynne Rienner, forthcoming).

17. "U.N. Bosnian Commander Wants More Troops, Fewer Resolutions," *New York Times*, December 31, 1993, p. A3.

18. *Defining Purpose: The U.N. and the Health of Nations* (Washington, D.C.: U.S. Commission on Improving the Effectiveness of the United Nations, 1993).

19. The Nordic UN Project, *The United Nations in Development: Reform Issues in the Economic and Social Fields, A Nordic Perspective* (Stockholm: Almqvist & Wiksell, 1991).

20. For a more detailed account, see Fazle H. Abed, "Coping with Disasters: From Diarrhea to Cyclones," in Kevin M. Cahill, ed., *A Framework for Survival* (New York: Basic Books, 1993), pp. 221–233.

21. For a more extended discussion, see Jarat Chopra, *United Nations Authority in Cambodia*, Occasional Paper 15 (Providence: Watson Institute, 1994), pp. 55–58.

22. World Food Programme, "WFP in Former Yugoslavia," Situation Report No. 6, November 1993, p. 19.

23. U.S. General Accounting Office, "El Salvador: Role of Nongovernment Organizations in Postwar Reconstruction" (Washington, D.C.: GAO/NSIAD-93-2032, November 1992), p. 1.

## Chapter 5

1. For a series of suggestions, see Gil Loescher, *Beyond Charity* (New York: Oxford University Press, 1994).

2. James C. Ingram, "The Future Architecture for International Humanitarian Assistance," in Thomas G. Weiss and Larry Minear, eds., *Humanitarianism Across Borders* (Boulder: Lynne Rienner, 1993), p. 181.

3. These figures are the basis for the argument by Frederick C. Cuny in "Humanitarian Assistance in the Post–Cold War Era," in Weiss and Minear, eds., *Humanitarianism Across Borders*, pp. 151–169.

4. For an extended discussion, see Larry Minear and Thomas G. Weiss, *Humanitarian Action in Times of War: A Handbook for Practitioners* (Boulder: Lynne Rienner, 1993), pp. 83–91.

5. David P. Forsythe, "Choices More Ethical Than Legal: The International Committee of the Red Cross and Human Rights," *Ethics and International Affairs*, Vol. 7, 1993, p. 137.

6. "The United Nations: Heart of Gold, Limbs of Clay," *The Economist,* June 12, 1993, pp. 21–22.

7. Efforts to understand and enhance constructive impacts of the media on humanitarian action are in their infancy. A new Geneva-based monthly newsletter, *Crosslines,* launched in 1993, represents an important effort by journalists who cover humanitarian emergencies to reflect upon the problems associated with telling their stories. Its editor, Edward Giradet, reflected on these issues as well in "Public Opinion, the Media, and Humanitarianism," in Weiss and Minear, eds., *Humanitarianism Across Borders*, pp. 39–55.

8. For a discussion of the costs of current arrangements, see Dick Thornburgh, *Reform and Restructuring at the United Nations: A Progress Report* (Hanover, N.H.: Rockefeller Center, 1993). See also other cautionary notes by Charles William Maynes, "Containing Ethnic Conflict," *Foreign Policy*, No. 90, Winter 1993, pp. 3–21; and Stephen John Stedman, "The New Interventionists," *Foreign Affairs*, Vol. 72, No. 1, 1993, pp. 1–16.

9. See, for example, Evans's recent book, *Cooperating for Peace: The Global Agenda for the 1990s and Beyond* (London: Allen and Unwin, 1994).

10. Jonathan Eyal, "No One Cares Until It's War," *The Independent,* March 10, 1994.

11. John Steinbruner, "Memorandum: Civil Violence as an International Security Problem," reproduced as annex C in Francis M. Deng, *Protecting the Dispossessed* (Washington, D.C.: Brookings Institution, 1993), p. 155.

12. For a more extended discussion, see Larry Minear, "The Emerging Humanitarian Order," in Thomas G. Weiss, ed., *The United Nations and Civil Wars* (Boulder: Lynne Rienner, forthcoming).

13. *Webster's Encyclopedic Unabridged Dictionary of the English Language* (New York/Avenel, N.J.: Gramercy Books, Dilithium Press, 1989).

14. As quoted by Minear and Weiss, *Humanitarian Action in Times of War,* p. 87.

15. Sadako Ogata, "Statement to the Economic and Social Council on Coordination of Humanitarian Assistance: Emergency Relief and the Continuum to Rehabilitation and Development," Geneva, July 1, 1993, p. 4.

16. *America's Place in the World: An Investigation of the Attitudes of American Opinion Leaders and the American Public About International Affairs* (Washington, D.C.: Times Mirror Center, November 1993).

# For Further Reading

Notes, which appear at the end of the text, refer to a number of books, documents, and articles on humanitarian action. This section lists under four generic headings selected up-to-date and informative sources in the secondary literature as a guide to readers who wish to pursue further research.

## The Post–Cold War Environment

Allison, Graham, and Gregory F. Treverton (eds.), *Rethinking America's Security: Beyond Cold War to New World Order* (New York: Norton, 1992).

American Academy of Arts and Sciences, *Reconstructing Nations and States*, special issue of *Daedalus*, Vol. 122, No. 3 (1993).

Appleyard, Reginald, *International Migration: Challenges for the Nineties* (Geneva: International Organization for Migration, 1991).

Boutros-Ghali, Boutros, *An Agenda for Peace: Preventive Deployment, Peacemaking, and Peace-keeping* (New York: United Nations, 1992).

Bramwell, Anna (ed.), *Refugees in the Age of Total War* (London: Unwin Hyman, 1988).

Brown, Michael E. (ed.), *Ethnic Conflict and International Security* (Princeton: Princeton University Press, 1993).

Carnegie Endowment National Commission, *Changing Our Ways: America and the New World* (Washington, D.C.: Carnegie Endowment for International Peace, 1992).

Clark, Jeffrey, *The U.S. Government, Humanitarian Assistance, and the New World Order* (Washington, D.C.: U.S. Committee for Refugees, 1991).

Damrosch, Lori Fisler, and David J. Scheffer, *Law and Force in the New International Order* (Boulder: Westview, 1991).

Evans, Gareth, *Cooperating for Peace: The Global Agenda for the 1990s and Beyond* (London: Allen and Unwin, 1994).

Gottlieb, Gidon, *Nation Against State: New Approaches to Ethnic Conflicts and the Decline of Sovereignty* (New York: Council on Foreign Relations, 1993).

Gurr, Ted Robert, *Minorities at Risk: A Global View of Ethnopolitical Conflicts* (Washington, D.C.: United States Institute of Peace Press, 1993).

Halperin, Morton H., and David J. Scheffer, *Self-Determination in the New World Order* (Washington, D.C.: Carnegie Endowment for International Peace, 1992).

Hannum, Hurst, *Autonomy, Sovereignty, and Self-Determination* (Philadelphia: University of Pennsylvania Press, 1990).

Hoffman, Stanley, *Duties Beyond Borders: On the Limits and Possibilities of Ethnic International Politics* (Syracuse, N.Y.: Syracuse University Press, 1981).

Job, Brian (ed.), *The Insecurity Dilemma: National Security of Third World States* (Boulder: Lynne Rienner, 1992).

Kennedy, Paul, *Preparing for the Twenty-first Century* (New York: Random House, 1993).

Lyons, Gene M., and Michael Mastanduno (eds.), *Beyond Westphalia? State Sovereignty and International Intervention* (Baltimore: Johns Hopkins University Press, forthcoming).

Moynihan, Daniel Patrick, *Pandaemonium: Ethnicity in International Politics* (New York: Oxford University Press, 1993).

Reed, Laura W., and Carl Kaysen (eds.), *Emerging Norms of Justified Intervention* (Cambridge, Mass.: American Academy of Arts and Sciences, 1993).

Rosenau, James, *Turbulence in World Politics: A Theory of Change and Continuity* (Princeton: Princeton University Press, 1990).

Salomon, Kim, *Refugees in the Cold War: Toward a New International Refugee Regime in the Early Postwar Era* (Lund: Lund University Press, 1991).

Sivard, Ruth Leger, *World Military and Social Expenditures 1993* (Washington, D.C.: World Priorities, 1993).

Thornberry, Cedric, *Ethnic Minorities and International Law* (Oxford: Clarendon Press, 1990).

Weiss, Thomas G., and Meryl A. Kessler (eds.), *Third World Security in the Post-Cold War Era* (Boulder: Lynne Rienner, 1991).

Young, Crawford (ed.), *The Rising Tide of Cultural Pluralism: The Nation-State at Bay?* (Madison: University of Wisconsin Press, 1991).

## The Political-Military Arena and the United Nations

Baehr, Peter R., and Leon Gordenker, *The United Nations in the 1990s* (New York: St. Martin's Press, 1992).

Berdal, Mats R., *Whither UN Peacekeeping?* Adelphi Paper 281 (London: International Institute for Strategic Studies, 1993).

Coate, Roger A. (ed.), *U.S. Policy and the Future of the United Nations* (New York: Twentieth Century Fund Press, 1994).

Diehl, Paul, *International Peacekeeping* (Baltimore: Johns Hopkins University Press, 1993).

Durch, William J. (ed.), *The Evolution of UN Peacekeeping: Case Studies and Comparative Analysis* (New York: St. Martin's Press, 1993).

Feld, Werner J., and Robert S. Jordan, *International Organization: A Comparative Approach* (Westport, Conn.: Praeger, 1994).

Ferris, Elizabeth G. (ed.), *The Challenge to Intervene: A New Role for the United Nations?* (Uppsala: Life and Peace Institute, 1992).

Gordenker, Leon, and Thomas G. Weiss (eds.), *Soldiers, Peacekeepers and Disasters* (London: Macmillan, 1991).

Gregg, Robert W., *About Face? The United States and the United Nations* (Boulder: Lynne Rienner, 1993).

James, Alan, *Peacekeeping in International Politics* (New York: St. Martin's Press, 1990).

Lee, John M., Robert van Pagenhardt, and Timothy W. Stanley, *To Unite Our Strength: Enhancing the United Nations Peace and Security System* (Lanham, Md.: University Press of America, 1992).

Mackinlay, John, *The Peacekeepers* (London: Unwin Hyman, 1989).

Mackinlay, John, and Jarat Chopra, *A Draft Concept of Second Generation Multinational Operations 1993* (Providence: Watson Institute, 1993).

Martin, Lisa, *Coercive Cooperation: Explaining Multilateral Economic Sanctions* (Princeton: Princeton University Press, 1992).

Roberts, Adam, and Benedict Kingsbury (eds.), *United Nations, Divided World: The UN's Role in International Relations*, 2nd ed. (Oxford: Clarendon Press, 1994).

Rosenau, James, *The United Nations in a Turbulent World* (Boulder: Lynne Rienner, 1992).

Volker, Paul, and Shituro Ogata, et al., *Financing an Effective United Nations* (New York: Ford Foundation, 1993).

Weiss, Thomas G. (ed.), *Collective Security in a Changing World* (Boulder: Lynne Rienner, 1993).

Weiss, Thomas G., David P. Forsythe, and Roger A. Coate, *The United Nations and Changing World Politics* (Boulder: Westview, 1994).

## Humanitarian Action

Anderson, Mary B., *Rising from the Ashes: Development Strategies in Times of Disaster* (Boulder: Westview, 1989).

Bello, Emmanuel, *African Customary Humanitarian Law* (Geneva: International Committee of the Red Cross, 1980).

Cahill, Kevin M. (ed.), *A Framework for Survival: Health, Human Rights, and Humanitarian Assistance in Conflicts and Disasters* (New York: Basic Books, 1993).

Claude, Richard P., and Burns H. Weston (eds.), *Human Rights in the International Community*, rev. 2nd ed. (Philadelphia: University of Pennsylvania Press, 1992).

Daniel, Don (ed.), *Beyond Traditional Peacekeeping* (London: Macmillan, forthcoming).

Deng, Francis M., *Protecting the Dispossessed: A Challenge for the International Community* (Washington, D.C.: Brookings Institution, 1993).

Deng, Francis M., and Larry Minear, *The Challenges of Famine Relief: Emergency Operations in the Sudan* (Washington, D.C.: Brookings Institution, 1992).

Donnelly, Jack, *Human Rights and International Relations* (Boulder: Westview, 1993).

————, *International Human Rights* (Boulder: Westview, 1993).

_____, *Universal Human Rights in Theory and Practice* (Ithaca: Cornell University Press, 1989).

Eduards, Krister, Gunner Rosen, and Robert Rossborough, *Responding to Emergencies: The Role of the U.N. in Emergencies and Ad Hoc Operations* (Stockholm: Nordic U.N. Project, 1990).

Field, John Osgood (ed.), *The Challenge of Famine: Recent Experience, Lessons Learned* (West Hartford, Conn.: Kumarian Press, 1993).

Forsythe, David P., *Human Rights and Peace: International and National Dimensions* (Lincoln: University of Nebraska Press, 1991).

_____, *Human Rights and World Politics* (Lincoln: University of Nebraska Press, 1989).

_____, *The Internationalization of Human Rights* (Lexington, Mass.: Lexington Books for the Free Press, 1991).

Goodwin-Gill, Guy, *International Law and the Movement of Persons Between States* (Oxford: Clarendon Press, 1978).

Gordenker, Leon, *Refugees in International Politics* (London: Croom Helm, 1987).

Grant, James P., *The State of the World's Children 1993* (New York: Oxford University Press, 1993).

Human Rights Watch, *The Lost Agenda: Human Rights and U.N. Field Operations* (New York: Human Rights Watch, 1993).

Independent Commission on International Humanitarian Issues, *Modern Wars: The Humanitarian Challenge* (London: Zed Books, 1986).

_____, *Refugees: The Dynamics of Displacement* (London: Zed Books, 1986).

_____, *Winning the Human Race?* (London: Zed Books, 1988).

International Committee of the Red Cross, *The Geneva Conventions of August 12, 1949, and Protocols Additional to the Geneva Conventions of August 12, 1949* (Geneva: International Committee of the Red Cross, 1989).

Kent, Randolph, *Anatomy of Disaster Relief: The International Network in Action* (London: Puster, 1987).

Kouchner, Bernard, and Mario Bettati, *Le Devoir d'ingérence* (Paris: Denoël, 1987).

Kuper, Leo, *Genocide: Its Political Uses in the Twentieth Century* (New Haven, Conn.: Yale University Press, 1981).

Lillich, Richard, *International Human Rights* (Boston: Little, Brown, 1991).

Loescher, Gil, *Beyond Charity* (New York: Oxford University Press, 1994).

_____, *Refugee Movements and International Security*, Adelphi Paper 268 (London: International Institute for Strategic Studies, 1992).

Loescher, Gil, and Laila Monahan (eds.), *Refugees and International Relations* (Oxford: Clarendon Press, 1989).

MacAlister-Smith, Peter, *International Humanitarian Assistance: Disaster Relief Organizations in International Law and Organization* (Dordrecht: Nijhoff, 1985).

Minear, Larry, *Helping People in an Age of Conflict: Toward a New Professionalism in U.S. Voluntary Humanitarian Assistance* (Washington, D.C.: American Council for Voluntary International Action [InterAction], 1988).

Minear, Larry, and Thomas G. Weiss, *Humanitarian Action in Times of War: A Handbook for Practitioners* (Boulder: Lynne Rienner, 1993).

Nanda, Ved (ed.), *Refugee Law and Policy* (Westport, Conn.: Greenwood, 1989).

Newman, Frank, and David Weissbrodt, *International Human Rights* (Cincinnati: Anderson, 1990).

Ogata, Sadako, *The State of the World's Refugees 1993: The Challenge of Protection* (New York: Oxford University Press, 1993).

Prendergast, John, *Sudanese Rebels at a Crossroads: Opportunities for Building Peace in a Shattered Land* (Washington, D.C.: Center of Concern, 1994).

Ramcharan, B. G., *The International Law and Practice of Early Warning and Preventive Diplomacy: The Emerging Global Watch* (Dordrecht: Nijhoff, 1991).

Randel, Judith, and Tony German (eds.), *The Reality of Aid '94: An Independent Review of International Aid* (London: Actionaid, 1994).

Smillie, Ian, and Henny Helmich, *Non-Governmental Organisations and Governments: Stakeholders for Development* (Paris: Organization for Economic Cooperation and Development, 1994).

Tolley, Howard, Jr., *The U.N. Commission on Human Rights* (Boulder: Westview, 1987).

United Nations Educational, Scientific and Cultural Organization, *International Dimensions of Humanitarian Law* (Dordrecht: Nijhoff, 1988).

Weiss, Thomas G., and Larry Minear (eds.), *Humanitarianism Across Borders: Sustaining Civilians in Times of War* (Boulder: Lynne Rienner, 1993).

## Country and Regional Cases

Child, Jack, *The Central American Peace Process, 1983–1991* (Boulder: Lynne Rienner, 1992).

Chopra, Jarat, *United Nations Authority in Cambodia,* Occasional Paper 15 (Providence: Watson Institute, 1994).

Crisp, Jeff, and Nick Cater, *The Human Consequences of Conflict in the Horn of Africa: Refugees, Asylum and the Politics of Assistance* (London: International Institute for Strategic Studies, 1990).

Cuénod, Jacques, *Assistance to Regions with Large Numbers of Refugees* (Washington, D.C.: Refugee Policy Group, 1989).

Damrosch, Lori Fisler (ed.), *Enforcing Restraint: Collective Intervention in Internal Conflicts* (New York: Council on Foreign Relations, 1993).

Davis, Morris (ed.), *Civil Wars and the Politics of International Relief: Africa, South Asia, and the Caribbean* (New York: Praeger, 1975).

Duffield, Mark, and John Prendergast, *Without Troops and Tanks: Humanitarian Intervention in Ethiopia and Eritrea* (Trenton, N.J.: Red Sea Press, 1994).

Eguizábal, Cristina, David Lewis, Larry Minear, Peter Sollis, and Thomas G. Weiss, *Humanitarian Challenges in Central America: Learning the Lessons of Recent Armed Conflicts,* Occasional Paper 14 (Providence: Watson Institute, 1993).

Ferris, Elizabeth, *Central American Refugees and the Politics of Protection* (New York: Praeger, 1987).

Gorman, Robert F., *Coping with Africa's Refugee Burden: A Time for Solutions* (Dordrecht: Nijhoff, 1987).

Harvard Center for Population and Development Studies, *Sanctions in Haiti: Crisis in Humanitarian Action,* Program on Human Security Working Paper Series (Cambridge, Mass.: Harvard University, November 1993).

Johnstone, Ian, *Aftermath of the Gulf War: An Assessment of UN Action* (Boulder: Lynne Rienner, 1994).

Kaplan, Robert, *Surrender or Starve: The Wars Behind the Ethiopian Famine* (Boulder: Westview, 1988).

Lake, Anthony (ed.), *After the Wars: Reconstruction in Afghanistan, Indochina, Central America, Southern Africa, and the Horn of Africa* (Washington, D.C.: Overseas Development Council, 1990).

Makinda, Samuel, *Seeking Peace from Chaos: Humanitarian Intervention in Somalia* (Boulder: Lynne Rienner, 1993).

Maley, William, and Fazel Haq Saikal, *Political Order in Post-Communist Afghanistan* (Boulder: Lynne Rienner, 1992).

Minear, Larry, U.B.P. Chelliah, Jeff Crisp, John Mackinlay, and Thomas G. Weiss, *United Nations Coordination of the International Humanitarian Response to the Gulf Crisis 1990–1992,* Occasional Paper 13 (Providence: Watson Institute, 1992).

Minear, Larry, Jeffrey Clark, Roberta Cohen, Dennis Gallagher, Iain Guest, and Thomas G. Weiss, *Humanitarian Action in the Former Yugoslavia: The U.N.'s Role 1991–1993,* Occasional Paper 18 (Providence: Watson Institute, 1994).

Minear, Larry, et al., *Humanitarianism Under Siege: A Critical Review of Operation Lifeline Sudan* (Trenton, N.J.: Red Sea Press, 1991).

Refugee Policy Group, *Humanitarian Aid in Somalia 1990–1994* (Washington, D.C.: Refugee Policy Group, 1994).

Reynell, Josephine, *Political Pawns: Refugees on the Thai-Kampuchean Border* (Oxford: Refugee Studies Programme, 1989).

Shawcross, William, *The Quality of Mercy: Cambodia, the Holocaust and Modern Conscience* (New York: Simon and Schuster, 1984).

Shepherd, Jack, *The Politics of Starvation* (Washington, D.C.: Carnegie Endowment for International Peace, 1975).

Weiss, Thomas G. (ed.), *The United Nations and Civil Wars* (Boulder: Lynne Rienner, forthcoming).

Weiss, Thomas G., and James G. Blight (eds.), *The Suffering Grass: Superpowers and Regional Conflict in Southern Africa and the Caribbean* (Boulder: Lynne Rienner, 1992).

Zinzer, Adopho Aguilar, *CIREFCA: The Promises and Reality of the International Conference on Central American Refugees* (Washington, D.C.: CIPRA, 1991).

# About the Book and Authors

From Bosnia to Somalia, and most recently from Rwanda to Angola and the Sudan, humanitarian aid and international interventions have gone awry. Although the need for humanitarian assistance has not diminished in the wake of the Cold War, success stories will almost certainly be harder to come by. This book addresses that grim prospect. Based on scholarly research, practical experience, and in-depth interviews with over 1500 humanitarian, political, and military officials in active war zones, *Mercy Under Fire* articulates key principles of humanitarian action and shows what has to be done, in what way, and by whom in order to avert failure in future humanitarian interventions.

Undeterred by controversy, Larry Minear and Thomas G. Weiss critique current practices of UN organizations, private aid agencies, and governments, offering new guidelines to make humanitarian efforts more timely, comprehensive, adequately funded, and keyed to local resources. Filled with case studies, examples, and illustrations drawn from hot spots around the globe, *Mercy Under Fire* persuasively argues for greater efforts at conflict prevention and a more savvy approach to the politics and violence that complicate international efforts to provide a safety net for civilians caught in the throes of war.

**Larry Minear** has worked on humanitarian and development issues since 1972 on behalf of nongovernmental organizations and has served as a consultant to UN and U.S. government organizations. He is currently codirector and principal researcher of the Humanitarianism and War Project at Brown University's Thomas J. Watson Jr. Institute for International Studies. **Thomas G. Weiss** has written extensively about international security and organizations in addition to having held a number of UN posts as well as the executive directorship of the International Peace Academy. He is now associate director of Brown University's Watson Institute and executive director of the Academic Council on the UN System.

# About the Humanitarianism and War Project

The Humanitarianism and War Project is a policy research initiative based at the Thomas J. Watson Jr. Institute for International Studies of Brown University. From 1991 to 1993, it was also cosponsored by the Refugee Policy Group in Washington, D.C., which remains a significant partner. The project serves recent experience in providing protection and assistance to civilians in armed conflict, with an eye to the changes needed to contribute to a more effective international humanitarian regime for the post–Cold War era.

The initiative builds on the methodology of a 1990 case study of Operation Lifeline Sudan, but it encompasses a wider range of regional and country experience. Since its inception in 1991, the project has conducted field research in five regions: the Persian Gulf (Iraq and neighboring countries); the Horn of Africa (Ethiopia/Eritrea, the Sudan, and Somalia); Southeast Asia (Cambodia); Central America (Nicaragua, El Salvador, and Guatemala); and the Balkans. Conflicts in other areas also are being monitored. Two books, a number of scholarly articles, and pieces for the public have been written as a result of the project.

The project currently receives financial support from UN organizations (UNICEF, WFP, UNHCR, UNDP, DHA/UNDRO, UNSEPHA); four governments (the Netherlands, France, the United Kingdom, and the United States); eleven nongovernmental groups (Catholic Relief Services, Danish Refugee Council, International Centre for Human Rights and Democratic Development [Canada], International Federation of Red Cross and Red Crescent Societies, Lutheran World Federation, Lutheran World Relief, Mennonite Central Committee, Norwegian Refugee Council, Oxfam-UK, Save the Children Fund-UK, and World Vision International); and four foundations (Pew Charitable Trusts, Rockefeller Foundation, Arias Foundation, and United States Institute of Peace). In January 1994, the project began a second three-year phase, and it continues to add new sponsors.

# Index